RECONSIDERING
LAURA INGALLS WILDER

Children's Literature Association Series

RECONSIDERING LAURA INGALLS WILDER

Little House and Beyond

Edited by **MIRANDA A. GREEN-BARTEET** and **ANNE K. PHILLIPS**

University Press of Mississippi / Jackson

The University Press of Mississippi is the scholarly publishing agency of
the Mississippi Institutions of Higher Learning: Alcorn State University,
Delta State University, Jackson State University, Mississippi State University,
Mississippi University for Women, Mississippi Valley State University,
University of Mississippi, and University of Southern Mississippi.

www.upress.state.ms.us

The University Press of Mississippi is a member
of the Association of University Presses.

Copyright © 2019 by University Press of Mississippi
All rights reserved

First printing 2019
∞

Library of Congress Cataloging-in-Publication Data

Names: Green-Barteet, Miranda A., editor. | Phillips, Anne K., editor.
Title: Reconsidering Laura Ingalls Wilder : Little House and beyond / Edited
by Miranda A. Green-Barteet and Anne K. Phillips.
Description: Jackson : University Press of Mississippi, [2019] | Series:
Children's Literature Association series | "First printing 2019." |
Includes bibliographical references and index. |
Identifiers: LCCN 2018057425 (print) | LCCN 2018061543 (ebook) | ISBN
9781496823090 (epub single) | ISBN 9781496823106 (epub institutional) |
ISBN 9781496823113 (pdf single) | ISBN 9781496823120 (pdf institutional)
| ISBN 9781496823076 (hardcover : alk. paper) | ISBN 9781496823083 (pbk. :
alk. paper)
Subjects: LCSH: Wilder, Laura Ingalls, 1867–1957—Criticism and
interpretation. | Wilder, Laura Ingalls, 1867–1957. Little house books. |
Wilder, Laura Ingalls, 1867–1957—Political and social views. | Wilder,
Laura Ingalls, 1867–1957—Influence. | Authors, American—20th
century—Biography. | Women pioneers—United States—Biography.
Classification: LCC PS3545.I342 (ebook) | LCC PS3545.I342 Z826 2019 (print) |
DDC 813/.52—dc23
LC record available at https://lccn.loc.gov/2018057425

British Library Cataloging-in-Publication Data available

To all collaborators, recognized and unrecognized,

and

to all the scholars of earlier eras who deemed the
Little House series worthy of academic consideration:
we honor your work in this volume.

CONTENTS

Acknowledgments xi

List of Abbreviations xiii

Introduction xv
Miranda A. Green-Barteet and Anne K. Phillips

I. WILDER AND "TRUTH"

"Play It Again, Pa": Repetition in *Pioneer Girl: The Annotated Autobiography* and *Little: Novels* 3
Katharine Slater

"It All Depends on How You Look at It": Laura Ingalls Wilder, Rose Wilder Lane, Independence Day, and Family Economics 18
Dawn Sardella-Ayres

The Complicated Politics of Disability: Reading the Little House Books and Helen Keller 32
Keri Holt and Christine Cooper-Rompato

II. WILDER AND CONSTRUCTIONS OF GENDER

Naked Horses on the Prairie: Laura Ingalls Wilder's Imagined Anglo-Indian Womanhood 49
Vera R. Foley

Her Own Baby: Dolls and Family in "Indians Ride Away" 63
Jenna Brack

Laura's Lineage: The Matrilineal Legacy of Laura Ingalls Wilder's Little House Narratives 77
Sonya Sawyer Fritz

Laura's "Farmer Boy": Fictionalizing Almanzo Wilder in the Little House Series 91
Melanie J. Fishbane

III. WILDER, PLAINS STUDIES, AND THE AMERICAN LITERATURE CANON

Mobile Stickers and the Specter of Snugness: Pa's Place-Making in Dakota Territory 105
Lindsay R. Stephens

"More Than Grassy Hills": Land, Space, and Female Identity in the Works of Laura Ingalls Wilder and Willa Cather 119
Elif S. Armbruster

Breathing Literary Lives from the Prairie: Laura Ingalls Wilder and the Promises of Rural Women's Education in the Little House Series 133
Jericho Williams

The Undergraduate American Studies Classroom: Teaching American Myths and Memories with Laura Ingalls Wilder 148
Christiane E. Farnan

IV. CULTURAL AND INTERCULTURAL WILDER

The Wilder Mystique: Antimodernism, Tourism, and Authenticity in Laura Ingalls Wilder Country 165
Anna Thompson Hajdik

A Little Place in the Universe: An Ojibwe, Osage, and Dakota View of Laura Ingalls 181
Margaret Noodin

Kawaii Wilder: Little House in Japan 196
Emily Anderson and Shosuke Kinugawa

List of Contributors.. 211

Index... 215

ACKNOWLEDGMENTS

As with any project of this magnitude, many people were involved in ensuring that this collection made it to print. First and foremost, we thank our contributors, without whom this collection would not exist. We appreciate their dedication to this project, their attention to detail, and their willingness to respond to our countless queries. We are proud of the essays and look forward to seeing how they inspire new strands of the critical conversation on Laura Ingalls Wilder and her works. Any collection takes time to come together, and this was no exception. We also thank each of you for your patience.

We are grateful to our universities and departments. We are fortunate to work in welcoming environments with colleagues who recognize the need to highlight writers, genres, and topics that have been overlooked or understudied or that merit reconsideration. We appreciate the thoughtful input of the editing staff at University Press of Mississippi, Katie Keene in particular, as well as the guidance of the community of children's and young adult lit scholars, many of whom have given us advice or offered suggestions throughout this project. We also thank the organizing committee for the 2015 Triennial Conference for the Society for the Study of American Women Writers; this collection began as a roundtable for this conference. The panelists and audience members gave us a great deal to think about as we worked on this collection, and their input was invaluable.

Miranda thanks the Departments of English and Writing Studies and Women's Studies and Feminist Research at the University of Western Ontario. She especially thanks Helen Fielding and Kathleen Fraser for encouraging her to take on a project about a writer unfamiliar to many Canadians. She also thanks the librarians at Weldon Library, who purchased every book on Wilder she requested; Caroline Diezyn for her research assistance; the Dean's

Travel Fund for enabling her to attend the 2015 SSAWW Conference and the 2016 Children's Literature Association Conference; Meghan Gilbert-Hickey, Sara K. Day, and Sonya Sawyer Fritz for their suggestions and willingness to listen as this project came to fruition; and Katharine Slater for introducing her to Anne. To Sawyer, Owen, and Graeme, I thank you for reading along with me. Your thoughts, input, and questions have helped shape this project—and all that I do. To Cody, thank you for always believing in me. You're always my first sounding board, and I couldn't do any of this without you. Finally, I thank Anne, my wonderfully thoughtful coconspirator and partner on this journey. You've been the best coeditor and coauthor I could have asked for, and along the way, you've become a mentor and a friend.

Anne thanks the Department of English at Kansas State University and its head, Karin Westman, for financial and intellectual support during the gestation of this project. K-State's English Department is a remarkably stimulating, dynamic, and convivial place in which to produce scholarship. Thanks are due to Beverly Tabor, who first suggested to my mother that we should read the Little House books, and to Patricia Anne Phillips, who read the Wilder canon alongside me, traveled with me to De Smet and Mansfield, and demonstrates perpetually the pioneer woman ingenuity and ability to make do that would earn her the Caroline Ingalls Award if such a thing existed. I am deeply grateful to Dr. Sarah Riforgiate, across the table from whom I happily edited essays for this collection, for creating a productive, serene environment in which all things get done in a timely fashion. Finally, thank you, Miranda, for your invitation to join the SSAWW panel, for your invitation to coedit this volume, for your support and enthusiasm throughout the project, and for your friendship. I am honored to have been your coconspirator!

ABBREVIATIONS

The following abbreviations are used for Laura Ingalls Wilder's writings:

Banks	*On the Banks of Plum Creek*
Farmer	*Farmer Boy*
First	*The First Four Years*
Happy	*These Happy Golden Years*
Pioneer	*Pioneer Girl*
Prairie	*Little House on the Prairie*
Selected	*Selected Letters*
Shores	*By the Shores of Silver Lake*
Town	*Little Town on the Prairie*
Winter	*The Long Winter*
Woods	*Little House in the Big Woods*

INTRODUCTION

Miranda A. Green-Barteet and Anne K. Phillips

In 2015, five literary scholars gathered in Philadelphia to discuss Laura Ingalls Wilder. This roundtable, included on the program for the Society for the Study of American Women Writers Triennial Conference, was organized for several reasons. Most of the panelists grew up reading Wilder's Little House series. A number have also presented on, contributed articles and dissertation chapters to, reviewed, and otherwise followed Wilder scholarship. The panelists were focused on critically considering Wilder's current place in North American literary studies.

The panel was inspired by the publication of *Pioneer Girl: The Annotated Autobiography* (2014), Wilder's unpublished work from which she drew and adapted the content of her Little House series, annotated and introduced by Pamela Smith Hill and published by the South Dakota Historical Society Press. Miranda particularly was struck by the contrast between the autobiography's astonishing commercial success and the relative lack of critical attention paid to Wilder's writings, finding this juxtaposition emblematic of the way critics have historically dismissed many commercially successful women writers, a reality that especially affects women writing for children. Seeing the conference as a venue that would welcome conversations about Wilder's place in US literary scholarship and the ongoing recovery work surrounding overlooked women writers, Miranda organized the roundtable with the goal of participating in a sustained and cogent analysis of Wilder's work, particularly in light of *Pioneer Girl*'s publication.

The roundtable was held in the conference hotel's smallest meeting room, and the panelists didn't expect the room to fill. In fact, they were concerned that individuals interested only in celebrating Wilder's work would attend, thereby making it difficult to have a critical discussion. But the room did fill, and those who attended didn't come to celebrate Wilder. Most attendees were scholars working on other sometimes canonical but often historically overlooked American women writers, including Emily Dickinson, Maria Cummins, Sarah Winnemucca, and Maria Ruiz de Burton. These scholars asked, among many questions, why Wilder had not received the critical attention accorded many of her contemporaries. The resulting conversation convinced the panelists, Miranda and Anne especially, of the need to explore several issues.

Specifically, what is the current state of Wilder studies? How do Wilder's books engage in conversation with works of other writers of her era? How does Wilder's fiction influence readers' awareness of nineteenth-century gender roles? What is Wilder's impact on children from a variety of backgrounds who are reading her books, both inside and outside classrooms as well as on their own and with adults? The panelists and their audience raised more specific questions: What role does truth play in readers' views of Wilder? Are scholars hesitant to consider Wilder through critical frameworks because of the series' blending of fact and fiction? Does fans' seeming sense of ownership over Wilder's legacy discourage scholars from engaging critically with her novels? Will *Pioneer Girl*, previously only available at scholarly archives, inspire more specific comparisons between the autobiography and the fiction that ensued from it as well as critical analysis of Wilder's other autobiographical writings? Finally, how should the works' collaborative nature be acknowledged, especially given continuing developments in the scholarship concerning Rose Wilder Lane's role in writing the series?

While considering these questions, we also knew that we must acknowledge the central issue in scholarly consideration of Wilder's work in our era. Given problematic representations of Native peoples, *should* her work merit greater critical consideration? In 2018, the Association for Library Service to Children (ALSC), a division of the American Library Association (ALA), established a task force to consider removing Wilder's name from an award recognizing "substantial and lasting contribution to literature for children" (Lindsay). The award was created to honor Wilder in 1954, but in the six plus decades since, as Nina Lindsay put it, the ALSC board has come to recognize "that Wilder's legacy is complex and that her work is not universally embraced. It continues to be a focus of scholarship and literary analysis, which often brings to light anti-Native and anti-Black sentiments in her work. The ALSC Board recognizes that legacy may no longer be consistent with the intention of the award named for her." On 23 June 2018, the board voted to rename the Laura Ingalls Wilder Award the Children's Literature Legacy Award. The organization explained that changing the award's name did not represent "an attempt to censor, limit, or deter access to Wilder's books"; rather, it constituted an effort to have the award represent the ALSC's principles. According to the Legacy Award's new website, the decision reflects "the fact that Wilder's legacy, as represented by her body of work, includes expressions of stereotypical attitudes inconsistent with ALSC's core values of inclusiveness, integrity and respect, and responsiveness." As an ASLC member wrote to Lindsay, "the Wilder [Award] is a monument that says something about our profession's history, but every year it is given out it also says something about our present" (Lindsay). The sentiments expressed by Lindsay, the member she quotes, and the ALSC Board point to the ways Wilder privileged the white settler experience and validated, both explicitly and implicitly, the erasure of Native American peoples and culture through her stereotypical representations of them as primitive, violent, and ignorant.

These concerns resonate with many of our own. How could we argue for Wilder's inclusion in a more diverse canon of US women writers given her problematic and racist representations of peoples of color generally and Native Americans specifically? *Should* we argue for the series' inclusion, particularly since we have read and respect powerful, insightful assessments of Wilder's perspective and work produced by Native scholars such as Frances W. Kaye, Debbie Reese, and Waziyatawin Angela Cavender Wilson? These scholars, among many others, offer compelling critiques that need to be more widely read and acknowledged. Wilson, for example, writes with outrage and eloquence that "Wilder crafted a narrative that transformed the horror of white supremacist genocidal thinking and the stealing of Indigenous lands into something noble, virtuous, and absolutely beneficial to humanity" (67). Wilson and other scholars have articulated a context for the Little House books that cannot—and should not—be ignored.

Ultimately, we believe we must continue to engage in scholarly conversations about Wilder's life and work and her representations of US history. While engaging in that difficult but necessary work, we must continue to welcome and learn from all who wish to participate in such conversations. The answer is not simply to put away Wilder's work but to engage with it analytically. We can acknowledge its enduring appeal for many readers, but we also must interrogate it, delineate its limitations, enhance the conversations that scholars, teachers, and fans are having about it, and place it in context with other voices and works that can bring into focus the larger truths of our history. In doing so, we aspire to enrich the existing critical conversation, offer a forum accessible and pertinent to Wilder's fans, and generate perspectives and strategies that will enable teachers, librarians, and others to talk more effectively with child readers about Wilder's strengths and weaknesses and about how to read her works with context, awareness, and nuance.

Reconsidering Laura Ingalls Wilder: Little House and Beyond explicitly acknowledges and examines the series' representation of Native American and African American characters. Native and nonnative contributors work to chart the implications of these issues for contemporary audiences. For example, in her essay in this volume, Vera Foley concludes that although Wilder infuses her novels with motifs and imagery comparable to those used by Native authors such as Mourning Dove and Charles Alexander Eastman, she employs Native elements "not to establish a historical record" but to "signify aspects of her own emotional and psychological experience as a young girl caught between the influence of a genteel mother and an unstable frontier"—a perspective different from Bethany Schneider's suggestion that *Little House on the Prairie* has engaged in "both ontological and epistemological cannibalism" from Zitkála-Šá's autobiographical stories (67). In her essay discussing the spin-off novels, particularly the Caroline books of the 1990s–2000s, Sonya Sawyer Fritz acknowledges that while Native characters are included, "the texts always cast Indians as the primitive Other." Jenna Brack posits in her essay that Wilder's and Lane's references to the neighbor child's "scalping" of Charlotte, Laura's doll, in *On the Banks of Plum Creek* seemingly acknowledge Euro-American violence against indigenous peoples and criticizes the cruelty of white settlers. However, Brack argues, "even Laura's sympathy ultimately reflects an attitude of possession and furthers a white savior narrative. After Laura rescues the helpless doll, she brings Charlotte back into *her* home and *her* culture, where the doll is remade to more closely reflect an Ingalls family ideal." Asked whether she sees any separation between Laura's perspective and the attitudes articulated by others or any meaningful alignment of Laura with Native perspectives—arguments raised by scholars in response to Native critiques—Margaret Noodin explained privately, "I think Laura does occasionally view the land differently than some of her family and certainly some of her peers, but she does not connect with the land in the way that the native cultures do. She does question her parents, but this mostly shows she was intelligent, inquisitive and eager to learn. I don't think there is any indication that she connects her view of the land with the 'Indians' or that she views the wolves or the water or stars as equals to herself." The conclusions independently reached by these scholars, then, acknowledge, attend to, and validate perspectives that have addressed the explicit and implicit racism of Wilder's novels.

It is essential to address such issues even as we recognize that strikingly diverse audiences will read this collection. As the reaction to the renaming of the Children's Literature Legacy Award demonstrates, scholars and fans on all sides have intense, personal feelings about Wilder and her works. This passion demonstrates that the Little House series remains firmly embedded within North American culture. In part, it endures because of its publisher's active involvement in maintaining its relevance.[1] HarperCollins's publication of spin-off novels involving Laura's mother, grandmother, great-grandmother, and daughter ensures that Little House remains competitive with other historical fiction for child readers, including the Dear America and American Girl series. Additionally, picture book versions of Little House books, containing illustrations similar to Garth Williams's work for the 1953 uniform edition, invite young readers into the franchise. Other cultural artifacts cater to adults' nostalgia for the series, including cookbooks, songbooks, and recordings of the material Pa Ingalls played on his fiddle as well as occasional live performances of that music.[2] Diverse social media networks and postings keep Wilder's life and works at the forefront: in June 2018, for example, a recipe for Laura's wedding cake was shared across Facebook.[3] A "Laurapalooza" convention is held annually. Tourist sites from Wisconsin to South Dakota maintain Wilder-themed attractions that draw domestic and international visitors. Much traffic stems from the continued appeal of the NBC television series (1974–83), but other adaptations perpetuate interest, including plays, a musical, and a six-hour Disney miniseries (2005).[4] The novels have also inspired much Wilder-related nonfiction, such as Jeannine Atkins's *Borrowed Names: Poems about Laura Ingalls Wilder, Madam C. J. Walker, Marie Curie, and Their Daughters* (2010), Wendy McClure's *The Wilder Life: My Adventures in the Lost World of Little House on the Prairie* (2011), Kelly Kathleen Ferguson's *My Life as Laura: How I Searched for Laura Ingalls Wilder and Found Myself* (2011), Nancy McCabe's *From Little Houses to Little Women: Revisiting a Literary Childhood* (2014), Bich Minh Nguyen's *Pioneer Girl* (2014), Marie Tschopp's *Mary Ingalls—The College Years* (2017), Sarah Miller's *Caroline: Little House, Revisited* (2017), and other tributes too numerous to mention. This list doesn't account for Wilder's international popularity. Her books have been translated into numerous languages, inspiring multitudes of adaptations, including a Japanese anime series, *Laura, the Prairie Girl*.[5]

Simultaneously, the past few decades have seen a relative boom in scholarship dedicated to Wilder's life and works. Ann Romines's *Constructing the Little House: Gender, Culture, and Laura Ingalls Wilder* (1997) set a high standard for literary and cultural analysis of the series and remains an essential resource for Wilder scholars. Anita Clair Fellman's often-quoted study of how the Little

House series has been represented in classrooms and in popular/political discourse, *Little House, Long Shadow: Laura Ingalls Wilder's Impact on American Culture* (2008), is another scholarly touchstone. In 2012, the Library of America published a two-volume authoritative edition of the series prepared by Caroline Fraser. Wilder's *Selected Letters* (2016), edited by William Anderson, makes available resources previously accessible only at research sites such as the Herbert Hoover Presidential Library and Museum in West Branch, Iowa; the Detroit Public Library; and the Wilder Home and Museum in Mansfield, Missouri.

These resources and others promote new awareness of Wilder's works, but they also contribute essential evidence to the fierce debate regarding Rose Wilder Lane's role in writing the series. William Holtz's 1993 monograph, *The Ghost in the Little House: A Life of Rose Wilder Lane*, famously claimed that Lane was the series' primary author. Among other scholarly responses, John E. Miller's *Becoming Laura Ingalls Wilder: The Woman behind the Legend* (1998) provided archival evidence to challenge and qualify Holtz's conclusion, specifically tracing what each author contributed to the series. Recently, Christine Woodside's *Libertarians on the Prairie: Laura Ingalls Wilder, Rose Wilder Lane, and the Making of the Little House Books* (2016) expands Holtz's argument, offering specific textual evidence supporting claims that Lane played a central role in the series' creation, "transform[ing] the whole of her mother's life by removing many parts and changing details where necessary to suit an idealized version of the pioneer story" (xvi).[6]

Pioneer Girl's epic success has ensured that the South Dakota Historical Society Press's Pioneer Girl Project will complete other planned ventures "dedicated to exploring [Wilder's] life and works" (*Pioneer Girl Project*), including some focusing on the series' authorship. Edited by Nancy Tystad Koupal, *Pioneer Girl Perspectives* (2017), the second of four planned volumes, features new scholarship from respected North American Wilder scholars, including Elizabeth Jameson, Fraser, Miller, and Romines. Fraser's essay on Lane's training in yellow journalism is particularly useful when considering questions about authorship and collaboration, and *Pioneer Girl Perspectives* has already inspired new analysis of Wilder's and Lane's works. Finally, Fraser's comprehensive historical biography, *Prairie Fires: The American Dreams of Laura Ingalls Wilder* (2017), is receiving deserved acclaim, including a Pulitzer Prize, and assuredly will influence future Wilder studies.

With the majority of scholarship directed specifically at Wilder's life rather than her literary works, deciding to assemble a volume of essays focusing on her writings was relatively easy. Determining the collection's scope was not. While we acknowledge the role Wilder's fans have played in maintaining her relevance, we weren't interested in compiling essays that simply celebrated the author. Rather, we wanted to showcase innovative theoretical lenses and analytical approaches to offer scholars, teachers, students, and fans new ways to consider Wilder and the very specific view of US settler history that her books present. These essays demonstrate such approaches. Often, they highlight how Wilder's books normalize settler colonialism generally and specifically the experiences of white settlers, especially women and children, while eliding Native peoples, perspectives, and cultures. The contributors to this volume also examine Wilder's emphasis on women's agency and independence while recognizing that Wilder had a conflicted relationship with feminism and women's suffrage.

The essays are organized according to central themes that resonate with experienced and emerging scholars of Wilder's works. Part 1, "Wilder and Truth," considers how the series matches (and often challenges) the historical record and how the autobiography and the fiction convey distinct, almost contradictory, messages. Although Wilder and Lane attested that the series was true, scholarship has shown that the fiction omits or alters much factual information about the Ingalls family. In fact, Wilder's letters and other writings acknowledge that the fiction is not entirely "true." Following *Pioneer Girl*'s publication, for example, many readers were upset to learn that Jack, Laura's beloved pet, didn't die of old age shortly before the family left Minnesota. Rather, Wilder writes that as the family departed the Osage Diminished Reserve, "Jack wanted to stay with Pet and Patty as he always did [so] Pa gave him to the man who had them" (22).[7] Fraser succinctly acknowledges that Wilder's and Lane's concept of truth, both in their lives and writings, was "elastic," "reflect[ing] not objective reality but something closer to felt experience" (236).

The volume's first essay, Katharine Slater's "'Play It Again, Pa': Repetition in *Pioneer Girl: The Annotated Autobiography* and *Little: Novels*," addresses truth in the Little House series. Slater considers fans' and scholars' assertions that Wilder's books capture and preserve an authentic nineteenth-century settler experience, arguing that the series possesses no "core truth" but instead relies on "ceaseless acts of repetition that generate rhizomatic offshoots that engage with its settler colonial worldview. These acts of repetition—literary and cultural—are ultimately responsible for building the *semblance* of truth." Slater develops her argument by comparing *Pioneer Girl* to Emily Anderson's *Little: Novels* (2015), which reimagines and exhumes Wilder's Little House novels.

In "'It All Depends on How You Look at It': Laura Ingalls Wilder, Rose Wilder Lane, Independence Day, and Family Economics," Dawn Sardella-Ayres asserts that scholars have yet to fully "delineate the subtle differences between Wilder's and Lane's political ideologies or the ways they occur in the two women's shared and individual work." Focusing on a key phrase repeated throughout the series, *free and independent*, Sardella-Ayres argues that the words mean something different for each collaborator: "For Wilder, the notion is personal and/or familial, grounded in her family's physical situation on the open prairie land[, and] has economic connotations: to be as free from debt as possible. In contrast, Lane's idea of being *free and independent* is more individualistic and theoretical, conveying a psychological or spiritual independence." Sardella-Ayres fleshes out her analysis by comparing draft and final versions of the Fourth of July episodes from *Farmer Boy* and *Little Town on the Prairie*, including context from *Pioneer Girl* and *The First Four Years* along with Lane's single-authored works.

In "The Complicated Politics of Disability: Reading the Little House Books and Helen Keller," Keri Holt and Christine Cooper-Rompato contrast Wilder's representation of Mary's blindness in the *Pioneer Girl* manuscript and the fictional series, noting that in *Pioneer Girl*, "Wilder treats Mary's blindness as a factual event in her life, rather than a focus for extended attention [and] primarily represents her experiences in terms of loss and limitation." In the series, however, a very different Mary emerges, encapsulating Wilder's attitude toward "truth" in her fiction. Wilder "transforms Mary's disability into an experience that no longer separates her from society or limits her involvement within it." Aligning Wilder's depiction of disability with the work and activism of Helen Keller, these scholars delineate "a shared engagement with the politics of disability that offers a new lens for considering the cultural and political influence of Wilder's work [and] the complicated consequences of her representations."

Part 2, "Wilder and Constructions of Gender," addresses Elizabeth Jameson's call for "accurate Western stories, in which adult women play important roles, in which family settlement is not the end of the frontier adventure but the beginning of the important task of building human social relationships. We need to imagine stories in which our real mothers and grandmothers helped create the West we inherited. We need to hear their stories" (51). Wilder creates an alternate model of mature US femininity that negotiates the outdoor space and the indoor, more conventionally domestic space and that purposefully challenges the model of womanhood embodied by her mother.

Contributors Vera Foley and Jenna Brack are inspired by the same (notorious) passage from the end of *Little House on the Prairie* in which an uncharacteristically assertive Laura demands an Indian baby—the scene from the series that has perhaps evoked the most commentary by scholars. Moving in separate directions from that starting (and startling) point, Foley and Brack offer significant new observations. In "Naked Horses on the Prairie: Laura Ingalls Wilder's Imagined Anglo-Indian Womanhood," Foley asserts that the significant element in this scene is the unbridled "happy pony." She then extrapolates from the scene throughout the series' other books, arguing that "by constructing for herself an American legacy of freedom and partnership in the form of the naked Indian ponies of her childhood, Wilder models the process by which a girl on the frontier may reshape ideas about femininity and coming of age to honor the pursuit of liberty and happiness."

Brack, in contrast, focuses on the baby and its significance to Laura, interrogating in "*Her Own* Baby: Dolls and Family in 'Indians Ride Away'" "the racial subtexts of Laura's doll, Charlotte, and the racial, gendered, and familial dynamics of the Ingalls family." Brack demonstrates "that Laura's response to the Indian baby might be read as a desire for *her own* baby, in opposition to Ma's claim that the family has '*our* own baby' (*Prairie* 310; emphasis added)" and contends that the idea of the baby offers Laura compensation for displacement within her own family. Brack extends Robin Bernstein's influential research on racialized play to representations of Native Americans in children's literature and culture.

Part 2 also includes "Laura's Lineage: The Matrilineal Legacy of Laura Ingalls Wilder's Little House Narratives," a critical analysis of nearly two dozen spin-off novels about Laura's matrilineal descendants and ancestors published in the 1990s and early 2000s. The first scholar to explicitly focus on these supplements to Wilder's series, Sonya Sawyer Fritz draws on Sanne Parlevliet's definition of historical fiction as "a cultural practice that brings images of the past into circulation" (354), asking, "How then do the images of the past that [these spin-offs] circulate interact with Wilder's presentation of history to shape American collective memory and reinforce or revise Wilder's place in the story of America's origin?" Fritz concludes that while "the spin-off Little House books do share women's stories, and . . . recast a portion of American history that has traditionally been traced through men," they replicate the failures of Wilder's series by "ignor[ing] intersections of race and gender" and "privileging the views of Anglo-American mothers and daughters. In doing so, these new series relinquish one mythic version of history so that another can take its place; together, they amplify and crystallize the notion, latent in Wilder's fictionalized accounts of her own girlhood—that the history of America is comprised of the girlhoods of its white mothers."

In "Laura's 'Farmer Boy': Fictionalizing Almanzo Wilder in the Little House Series," Melanie J. Fishbane offers a gender studies analysis of Laura's husband, tracing the shifts in the representations of him offered throughout her career. Fishbane concludes that "Wilder carefully constructs each version to represent a man who wants an equal partnership with his wife," thus "encourag[ing] readers to redefine traditional notions of marriage."

Part 3, "Wilder, Plains Studies, and the American Literature Canon," places Wilder's novels in conversation with works by other canonical American authors, including Ole Rølvaag, Willa Cather, Wallace Stegner, and Hamlin Garland. Contributors offer innovative models for reconfiguring the canon of US literature to more fully include Wilder's works, simultaneously granting scholars greater context for thinking about, constructing scholarship on, and teaching such texts. In "Mobile Stickers and the Specter of Snugness: Pa's Place-Making in Dakota Territory," Lindsay R. Stephens draws from Stegner's foundational distinction between boomers and stickers, arguing that "Pa Ingalls, then, is not strictly a boomer but rather a place-making opportunist with boomer tendencies—in other words, what I conceive as a sticker in motion, seeking refuge for his family even as his area of influence expands to encompass the De Smet community." Drawing on Diane Quantic's scholarship on space and place in Plains literature, Stephens argues that "sticking and place-making are central concerns in the Dakota novels, with Pa's strategies of music, snugness, mobility, and community becoming markedly more complex."

In "'More Than Grassy Hills': Land, Space, and Female Identity in Laura Ingalls Wilder and Willa Cather," Elif S. Armbruster uses Edward Soja's concept of Thirdspace to consider space and place in Wilder's and Cather's work. Focusing on Wilder's *On the Banks of Plum Creek* and *By the Shores of Silver Lake* along with Cather's *O Pioneers!* and *My Ántonia*, Armbruster argues that in these novels, "girls and women who might have felt dwarfed by the vast landscape instead feel inspired and empowered by it." While Cather and Wilder focus on white female characters, eliding the experience of Native peoples, these novels nonetheless provide young women "with new ways of being in the world." Armbruster asserts, "Cather's women and Wilder's Laura sever themselves from the conventional, feminine, and domestic realms, which they experience as limited. As a result, like the space itself, they are 'always becoming'...: each moment out-of-doors presents them with a new experience in which they can actively participate." Rather than becoming more traditionally domesticated, like Cather's heroines, Wilder's Laura retains an essential, "spiritual" connection to the natural world throughout the series.

In "Breathing Literary Lives from the Prairie: Laura Ingalls Wilder and the Promises of Rural Women's Education in the Little House Series," Jericho Williams examines Laura's identity as both a schoolteacher and a newly married woman, focusing on *Little Town on the Prairie*, *These Happy Golden Years*, and *The First Four Years*. Williams highlights Wilder's depiction of education as empowering to girls living in rural areas, providing a representation that significantly contrasts with Garland's characterization of Rose Dutcher in *Rose of Dutcher's Coolly* (1895) and Cather's portrayal of Thea Kronborg in *The*

Song of the Lark (1915). Cather and Garland assert that rural life is confining for creative, intelligent women, and insist that these heroines can find fulfillment only in cities far from their rural hometowns. However, Wilder's books disrupt the belief that rural life created uneducated, uninformed women and redefine the purpose of rural women's education, offering an alternative view of womanhood that advocates the mastery of traditional and nontraditional literacies as a path to personal fulfillment.

In the final essay in part 3, "The Undergraduate American Studies Classroom: Teaching American Myths and Memories with Laura Ingalls Wilder," Christiane E. Farnan positions Wilder's works alongside the writings of Mary Rowlandson, Thomas Jefferson, and J. Hector St. John de Crèvecoeur and within theoretical frameworks created by Henry Nash Smith: "As the course examines the creation and perpetuation of models, memories, and myths of the American Dream through the cultural modification of America's changing landscape, the looming mythic/historic figure of the American farmer is central to our analysis." While acknowledging the perspectives of many Wilder critics that the Little House books are problematic in their exceptionalism and nostalgia, Farnan asserts that Wilder's representation of the American farmer, particularly in the series' early novels, "demonstrates a ... complicated, multifaceted stance in relation to the American Dream." Investigating the novels' depictions of and attitudes toward mechanical and technological innovation, Farnan then reads *Little House on the Prairie* through the lens of Rowlandson's captivity narrative, aligning "the terror of the unknown on the Kansas prairie" with "the terror of the unknown New England forest," highlighting Wilder's novel "as the narrative of a white woman and her children vulnerably dependent on an irresponsible, imprudent white man."

The essays in part 4, "Cultural and Intercultural Wilder," explore the ways the Little House series is imbricated within American tourism, Native relationships to and perspectives on the lands that serve as the series' settings, and Japanese adaptations and extensions of Wilder's writings and culture.

Focusing primarily on Wilder sites in Walnut Grove, Minnesota, and De Smet, South Dakota, Anna Thompson Hadjik writes in "The Wilder Mystique: Antimodernism, Tourism, and Authenticity in Laura Ingalls Wilder Country" that "the phenomenon of Laura Ingalls Wilder–related tourism [and] her enduring cultural currency [are] connected to the still salient role of frontier nostalgia in popular culture, involving conservative interpretations of American history, the complex relationship between heritage and tourism, and the search for authenticity on the American landscape." Hadjik examines the continuing appeal that these tourist sites hold for fans. Positioning the Wilder-related locales alongside comparable attractions including New

Salem, Illinois (home of young Abraham Lincoln), and Plimoth Plantation in Massachusetts, Hajdik considers how the Wilder sites distinctively configure authenticity and engender nostalgia. She concludes that "small tourism industries in Walnut Grove, De Smet, and other Wilder-related communities are also indicative of a postindustrial economy that prioritizes experience, recreation, and commodification over the industrial capitalism of an earlier age." Her essay particularly resonates because of the wealth of interviews she conducted with owners, employees, and neighbors of the sites as well as the tourists who continue to visit them.

While also attending to locations in which the Ingalls family sojourned, Margaret Noodin offers an alternate perspective on those places and the people who have populated them. Her essay, "A Little Place in the Universe: An Ojibwe, Osage, and Dakota View of Laura Ingalls," offers a model through which to "reread and review the series from the perspective of the cultures Wilder was shaped by yet never fully explored." Drawing on the cultural practices and perspectives of the diverse tribes that occupied the lands on which the Ingalls family homesteaded, Noodin highlights the omissions and limitations of Wilder's narration: "It is easy to associate Wilder with some of the ignorance and drive for Manifest Destiny of the times. It is more challenging to note instead the relevant history that surrounds her novels and imagine how Ojibwe, Osage, and Dakota beliefs might offer young readers a way to better understand the stories of the woods, the prairie, and the riverbanks that had been populated for thousands of years by a diverse range of complex, creative societies." Noodin writes eloquently about the colonization and appropriation infused throughout the Little House series, demonstrating the need to better analyze these works, particularly in classroom lesson plans, and to "contextualize and include more memories in what is classified as history."

Finally, in "Kawaii Wilder: Little House in Japan," Emily Anderson and Shosuke Kinugawa move beyond existing critical conversations about translations of Wilder's work for readers in post–World War II Japan. The authors examine the Little House series' influence on Japanese culture, including "neglected modes of reception, including dollhouses, homeware, interior design, and quilting practices." Elucidating the series' enduring appeal to Japanese readers, Anderson and Kinugawa suggest that Wilder's "novels are successful in Japan because they are congruent with the Japanese aesthetic category of *kawaii*, which roughly translates as 'cute,' 'endearing,' and 'adorable.'" The adaptations studied by Anderson and Kinugawa both "present readers with visual representations of miniature Little House homes and homeware" and "encourage readers to participate in its materialization." "In finding and adapting Wilder's *kawaisa*," the authors conclude, "Japanese

Little House fans draw Wilder and her national tradition into an aesthetic tradition that is both ancient and keenly relevant for contemporary global pop culture."

The essays in this volume not only engage in innovative research that is informed by a range of theoretical perspectives but also acknowledge, interrogate, and build on the most recent and significant developments in Wilder scholarship. Contributors to this volume offer some of the first substantive, sustained responses to *Pioneer Girl* and Hill's editorial choices therein, demonstrating how fiction is purposefully revised from the autobiography. In addition, while acknowledging Woodside's 2016 monograph, numerous contributors temper her conclusions, arguing compellingly that both Lane and Wilder made identifiable contributions, pursued individual agendas, and achieved different goals in the fiction. Moreover, Lane's and Wilder's aims evolved over time. Adapting *Pioneer Girl* in the Little House fiction and other writings for a range of artistic, sociological, philosophical, and political purposes, Wilder and Lane were purposefully creating, controlling, and tracking a range of messages. The contributors to this volume have based their analyses on their engagement with archival materials as well as the published autobiography, fiction, and journalism and thus anticipate the projected volumes of the Pioneer Girl Project, *Pioneer Girl: Revised Texts* and *Pioneer Girl: The Path into Fiction*, which will continue to unveil and interrogate the nature of Wilder's and Lane's collaboration.

The essays in this collection do not and cannot answer all of the questions that arose from the roundtable that initiated our work or all of the concerns prompting reconsiderations of Laura Ingalls Wilder's life and work. They do, however, reconsider Wilder and her works to the best of their ability in the present moment. The essays validate the importance of continuing to read, interrogate, and generate scholarship about Wilder's writings, using traditional literary, historical, and cultural approaches as well as Native American studies, gender studies, spatial theory, and other theoretical lenses. Further, this volume provides teachers at all levels with new avenues for promoting insight and raising awareness about the author and her series. While there is no doubt that aspects of Wilder's works are deeply problematic, there is also little doubt that Wilder and her works continue to capture the imagination of readers of varied ages and backgrounds. Reconsidering Wilder can lead to greater understanding not only of the era in which the Little House series is set but also of the era in which the books were written and the eras in which they have continued to resonate. Fans and scholars alike will no doubt continue to ask hard questions and in formulating answers to those questions continue to expand and enrich the critical conversation.

NOTES

1. Springen notes the need for a "makeover" for the Little House books, including Ilene Cooper's acknowledgment that the HarperCollins editors "walk this fine line between trying to make [Wilder's novels] contemporary enough to appeal to today's audience but at the same time to have enough of a nostalgia factor to remind parents and grandparents they want to share these books with their families" (15).

2. For an extended feature on Dale Cockrell, director of the Center for Popular Music at Middle Tennessee State University, who has staged performances inspired by the music in the Little House series, see Beck.

3. The Facebook announcement was a recycling of a recipe originally published by Worthy.

4. For comparison and analysis of the 1974 television pilot film and the 2005 miniseries, see Lefebvre.

5. Twenty-six thirty-minute episodes were produced between 1975 and 1976 and were later dubbed into Italian and Spanish and broadcast in Latin America. For a detailed description of the show, see "Laura, the Prairie Girl." For more on the Japanese reception of Wilder's work, see Anderson and Kinugawa, this volume.

6. For a fictionalized depiction of Lane's central role in the writing of the Little House series, see Albert.

7. See, for example, Graham, and the lively conversation in the comments section as the general public encounters the content of *Pioneer Girl*. See also "Jack the Brindle Bulldog," which notes that "perhaps the most disconcerting piece of information is the fact that Jack the bulldog did not die peacefully shortly before the family set out for Silver Lake."

WORKS CITED

"About *The Pioneer Girl Project*." *The Pioneer Girl Project*. South Dakota Historical Society Press, 2010, https://pioneergirlproject.org/about/.

"ALA, ALSC Respond to Wilder Medal Name Change." *ALA News*, American Library Association, 25 June 2018. http://www.ala.org/news/press-releases/2018/06/ala-alsc-respond-wilder-medal-name-change.

Albert, Susan Wittig. *A Wilder Rose*. Lake Union, 2015.

Anderson, Emily. *Little: Novels*. BlazeVOX, 2015.

Atkins, Jeannine. *Borrowed Names: Poems about Laura Ingalls Wilder, Madam C. J. Walker, Marie Curie, and Their Daughters*. Henry Holt, 2010.

Beck, Ken. "Fiddling Father Gets His Due." *Murfreesboro Post*, 24 May 2012.

Bernstein, Robin. *Racial Innocence: Performing American Childhood from Slavery to Civil Rights*. New York University Press, 2011.

Children's Literature Legacy Award. Association for Library Service to Children, 2018. http://www.ala.org/alsc/awardsgrants/bookmedia/wildermedal.

Fellman, Anita Clair. *Little House, Long Shadow: Laura Ingalls Wilder's Impact on American Culture*. University of Missouri Press, 2008.

Ferguson, Kelly Kathleen. *My Life as Laura: How I Searched for Laura Ingalls Wilder and Found Myself*. Press 53, 2011.

Fraser, Caroline. *Prairie Fires: The American Dreams of Laura Ingalls Wilder*. Metropolitan/Henry Holt, 2017.
Graham, Ruth. "Those Happy Golden Years." *Slate Book Review*, 7 November 2014.
Holtz, William. *The Ghost in the Little House: A Life of Rose Wilder Lane*. University of Missouri Press, 1993.
"Jack the Brindle Bulldog." *America's Dog*, 4 April 2013. http://americasdog.blogspot.com/2013/04/jack-brindle-bulldog.html.
Jameson, Elizabeth. "In Search of the Great Ma." *Journal of the West* 37, no. 2 (1998): 42–52.
Kaye, Frances W. "Little Squatter on the Osage Diminished Reserve: Reading Laura Ingalls Wilder's Kansas Indians." *Great Plains Quarterly* 20, no. 2 (Spring 2000): 123–40.
Koupal, Nancy Tystad, ed. *Pioneer Girl Perspectives: Exploring Laura Ingalls Wilder*. South Dakota Historical Society Press, 2017.
"Laura, the Prairie Girl." Little House on the Prairie Wiki, 2008–18. http://littlehouse.wikia.com/wiki/Laura,_a_Little_Girl_on_the_Prairie.
Lefebvre, Benjamin. "Our Home on Native Land: Adapting and Readapting Laura Ingalls Wilder's *Little House on the Prairie*." In *Textual Transformations in Children's Literature: Adaptations, Translations, Reconsiderations*, edited by Benjamin Lefebvre, 175–96. Routledge, 2013.
Lindsay, Nina. "Action Update: The Laura Ingalls Wilder Award." *ALSC Blog*, 11 February 2018. http://www.alsc.ala.org/blog/2018/02/board-action-update-laura-ingalls-wilder-award/.
"Little Classroom on the Prairie: Upcoming Immersion Focuses on the Life and Times of Quintessential Prairie Girl Laura Ingalls Wilder." University of Minnesota College of Continuing Education, 20 January 2011. https://cce.umn.edu/news/little-classroom-on-the-prairie.
McCabe, Nancy. *From Little Houses to Little Women: Revisiting a Literary Childhood*. University of Missouri Press, 2014.
McClure, Wendy. *The Wilder Life: My Adventures in the Lost World of Little House on the Prairie*. Riverhead/Penguin, 2011.
Miller, John E. *Becoming Laura Ingalls Wilder: The Woman behind the Legend*. University of Missouri Press, 1998.
Miller, Sarah. *Caroline: Little House, Revisited*. William Morrow, 2017.
"MSU Offers Free Online Course on Laura Ingalls Wilder." *Springfield News-Leader*, 28 July 2014.
Noodin, Margaret. Correspondence, 22 October 2017.
Nguyen, Bich Minh. *Pioneer Girl*. Viking, 2014.
Reese, Debbie. "Indigenizing Children's Literature." *Journal of Language and Literacy Education* 4, no. 2 (2008): 59–72.
Romines, Ann. *Constructing the Little House: Gender, Culture, and Laura Ingalls Wilder*. University of Massachusetts Press, 1997.
Schneider, Bethany. "A Modest Proposal: Laura Ingalls Wilder Ate Zitkála-Šá." *GLQ: A Journal of Gay and Lesbian Studies* 21, no. 1 (2015): 65–93.
Springen, Karen. "A 'Little House' Makeover." *Newsweek*, 29 January 2007, 15.
Tschopp, Marie. *Mary Ingalls—The College Years*. CreateSpace, 2017.
Wilder, Laura Ingalls. *Laura Ingalls Wilder: The Little House Books*. Edited by Caroline Fraser. 2 vols. Library of America, 2012.

Wilder, Laura Ingalls. *Pioneer Girl: The Annotated Autobiography*. Edited by Pamela Smith Hill, South Dakota Historical Society Press, 2014.

Wilder, Laura Ingalls. *The Selected Letters of Laura Ingalls Wilder*. Edited by William Anderson. HarperCollins, 2016.

Wilson, Waziyatawin Angela Cavender. "Burning Down the House: Laura Ingalls Wilder and American Colonialism." In *Unlearning the Language of Conquest*, edited by Wahinkpe Topa AKA Don Trent Jacobs, 66–80. University of Texas Press, 2006.

Woodside, Christine. *Libertarians on the Prairie: Laura Ingalls Wilder, Rose Wilder Lane, and the Making of the Little House Books*. Arcade, 2016.

Worthy, Tatanisha. "Laura's Wedding Cake Recipe—Traditional and Blueberry Topping Variation." *Little House on the Prairie.com*, 2015. http://littlehouseontheprairie.com/lauras-wedding-cake-recipe-traditional-and-blueberry-topping-variation/.

Part 1

WILDER AND "TRUTH"

"PLAY IT AGAIN, PA"

Repetition in *Pioneer Girl: The Annotated Autobiography* and *Little: Novels*

Katharine Slater

The chimera of truth haunts the Little House on the Prairie series. Fans and scholars continually return to "truth" as a defining reason for the books' appeal, arguing that Laura Ingalls Wilder has captured and preserved a fundamental authenticity in her representations of nineteenth-century US settler life. In his biography of the professional partnership between Wilder and her daughter, Rose Wilder Lane, who edited and likely cowrote parts of the series, John E. Miller notes several factual differences between Wilder's writing and her lived experiences but nevertheless concludes that these differences "should not concern us overmuch, because once we understand that these stories ... are autobiographical fiction, we can read behind the words to discover the core truth that is situated there. Something solid remains" (39). For Miller, that "something solid" stems in part from Wilder's ability to balance the minutia of lived experience with "real appreciation" (40) for human life. What the "something solid" is, however, nonetheless evades the microscope of scrutiny.

The ontology of the series—the "something solid remain[ing]" that Miller perceives—indeed contributes to the sense of truth so many see as fundamental to the Little House books' allure. Departing from Miller, however, I argue that no "core truth" can be located within the Little House series, which relies on ceaseless acts of repetition that generate rhizomatic offshoots that engage with its settler colonial worldview. These acts of repetition—literary and cultural—are ultimately responsible for building the *semblance* of truth, acts for which there is no original, manufacturing Miller's "something solid." Serial repetition is, therefore, a process that also functions as a symptom, encouraging us through multiple iterations to look more carefully. The repetition that defines Wilder's legacy builds a convincing impression of a singular reality while simultaneously creating the conditions within which we might challenge that impression.

In exploring the relationship between repetition and the Little House series, I examine two recently published texts that reprint Wilder's writing with different aims and comparable effects: *Pioneer Girl: The Annotated Manuscript*, edited by Pamela Smith Hill, and Emily Anderson's *Little: Novels*. *Pioneer Girl*, released in 2014, is a comprehensively researched and footnoted edition of the unpublished first-person manuscript Wilder originally produced with her daughter before they revised and expanded it into seven book-length children's novels.[1] The 2015 book *Little: Novels* is erasure literature, removing language from Wilder's novels to encourage readers toward a new way of looking at the familiar. Although the popular scholarship of Hill's annotations and the creative erasure of Anderson's repackaging are formally dissimilar, both directly foreground for readers the extent to which Wilder's writing has always relied on the act of repetition to earn its cultural power. In Hill's annotations and Anderson's creative process, there is no definable original, despite the way Hill and Anderson's words seemingly gesture toward that certainty. Wilder's childhood experiences as sifted through layers of language are clearly mediated by the vagaries of perspective. By participating in literary and cultural acts of reprinting, reproducing, and repeated embodiment that mirror Wilder's own reiterative process, Hill's and Anderson's texts join in constructing the potency of this series' cultural position.

Literature retains its cultural and social command through "multiple acts of reiteration" that enable the work to endure through "a horizon of infinite iterability" (McGill 3). These reiterations not only define the Little House series and its related productions but ensure their cultural durability, in part by modeling a method of encouraged (re)interaction. Reflecting on her reading experiences as a child in the 1950s, Ann Romines suggests that "part of the allure of these books was the fact that they were multiple. After you had finished ... you could go back and begin again.... That serial ritual of repetition was the deepest, most addictive satisfaction. The same houses, the same things, the same family, again and again" (2). The stability that Romines invokes through her descriptions gestures toward that "something solid": a nourishing promise of certainty that both Romines and Miller believe the Little House series delivers and keeps. Yet here, as in Miller, Romines neglects the unwritten implications of her childhood satisfaction, declining to examine how repetition might not return a reader to "the same houses, the same things, the same family" but might instead constitute an act that inevitably "alters, contaminating parasitically what it identifies and enables to repeat 'itself'" (Derrida in Bearn 449). What about this serial ritual enables Romines to associate with total certainty the act of repetition with sameness? How does rereading Wilder encourage Romines and countless other readers toward a belief in a "core truth" of similar experience?

As a literary and theoretical device, repetition is a hybrid creature, ideally perceived through a critical multiplicity that can more effectively conceive of its complex effects than a single lens. Central to hybridity is the pervading belief among scholars that repetition is a critical act of meaning-making, whether manifested through "repetition as consolatory, repetition as confirmatory, repetition as unsettling, [or] repetition as a setting in motion" (Reimer et al. 11). I read repetition in and around Wilder as both unsettling and confirmatory, a dual act that resists visibility precisely because it refuses singularity. Repetition creates the semblance of truth, encouraging Wilder's readers to locate a fundamental authenticity in her narratives. Simultaneously, however, repetition indirectly enables Wilder's readers to acknowledge what is not present, compelling us to revisit and rethink the familiar. Thus, we can understand repetition as a complex and shifting ideological formation. The process through which repetition functions ideologically is perhaps most visible in Judith Butler's field-defining work on gender performativity, in which she argues that gender earns its power through reiteration: "The action of gender requires a performance that is *repeated*. This repetition . . . is the mundane and ritualized form of [gender's] legitimation" (191). It is in this repetition that Butler locates the power of gender to be perceived as true, as tied to the notion of "an essential sex": repetition is the act that consolidates common perceptions of the subject as a continuous or homogenous totality. Gender, then, has no original but is "a construction that regularly conceals its genesis; the tacit collective agreement to perform, produce, and sustain . . . is obscured by the credibility of those productions. . . . [T]he construction 'compels' our belief in its necessity and naturalness" (191–92). We view gender as innate because we typically perpetuate its performative iterations in a way that reinforces dominant social norms. Repeated performance, therefore, cannot be extricated from systems of belief.

As a ritualized act rather than an act of ontology—something it shares with gender—reading is a process that encourages the perception of truth through repetition. Many readers certainly have historically viewed these texts as "real" despite their categorization as historical fiction and despite the series' consistent reproduction of white supremacist ideologies. Wilder and Lane's prose carefully manufactures a sense of authenticity, frequently through language that interpellates its imagined child readers, encouraging them to repeatedly link the Ingalls family to readers' own lives (Slater 63–64). Other contexts for the series also reinforce its mythology of truth, including the numerous connections between names and events within Wilder's writing and factual people and occurrences. The publication of excerpts in numerous US history textbooks during the second half of the twentieth century also suggested the veracity of those excerpts to generations of schoolchildren (Fellman 125). Perhaps most significantly, during their lifetimes, Wilder and Lane unambiguously stressed the fundamental truth of their books, insisting publicly that the truth outweighed fictional aspects. "Every story," Wilder told a Detroit audience in 1937, "all the circumstances, each incident are true. All I have told is true" ("Notes" 104). Lane was equally adamant. William Anderson, who edited the *Selected Letters of Laura Ingalls Wilder*, notes that "there was a movement some years back, perhaps among librarians, to have the books shifted into the nonfiction category. Now that is preposterous, but Rose thought it was a good idea" (Fraser).

This series' insistence on truth is most visible through Wilder and Lane's statements, but these texts and related Wilderiana[2] inscribe the semblance of truth through the multiple iterations of Wilder's writing, confirming through repetition Wilder and Lane's subjective worldview as objectively authentic. In addition to the eight original novels and the posthumously published *The First Four Years*, Wilder's writing now both reproduces and constitutes empire, growing to comprise a conglomerate of Ingalls-related narratives. Perhaps the most famous of these is the 1970s television show starring Michael Landon, but there are countless Ingalls reiterations, including cookbooks, museums, scrapbooks, series-inspired decor, scholarship, and a recent spin-off book series that chronicles the lives of Laura's great-grandmother, grandmother, mother, and daughter—including the common ritual of rereading the Little House books that Romines describes. Each of these relies heavily on Wilder's narrative and language, reproducing again for readers the original series' emphasis on family, snugness, white supremacy, and self-reliance. The series and its offshoots ultimately gain their substantial cultural power through acts of reproduction defined not by ontology but by the "various acts which constitute [their] reality," creating an illusory coherence (Butler 136). In each text, we encounter some repetition of Pa's songs and stories, Ma's quiet severity, Mary's supercilious reserve, Laura's struggle to behave, an emphasis on self-reliance above all other values, and—perhaps most significantly—the family's construction of a snug home space defined through othering contrast with indigenous people. "Each iteration ... extends the identification with the earlier ones," constructing the semblance of truth through the familiarity of these components (Robinson 62).

However, stylized acts of repetition construct the semblance of a coherent truth, not actual truth, so these repetitions often fail or rupture, exposing their performative qualities. This failure can be viewed as productive. It also reifies coherence, as repetition uncovers the lie of homogeneity, creating conditions within which we can acknowledge difference. This function brings into focus the psychoanalytic resonance of repetition: Karen Coats observes that reiteration is a legible symptom, calling on readers "to pay attention to something we cannot see, or have forgotten or denied . . . things that through repetitive action show us that there is something we cannot tell or even know about ourselves" (198). Rather than allow readers to reacquaint themselves with the familiar, repeated acts of reading create a paradox in which meaning-making reinforces the presence of what is silent, what is invisible, or what cannot be articulated. In Wilder's writing, those silences are manifold. Through the act of reiterating Wilder, both Hill and Emily Anderson enable us to see what readers have "forgotten or denied" when engaging with Wilder, what Wilder and Lane themselves denied when writing: the series' "truth" is a construct that upholds white supremacist worldviews. In reencountering Wilder's texts, readers participate in the cocreation of a space in which we might acknowledge what is not explicitly said regardless of the extent to which the reiterating actor reproduces or destabilizes the mythology of truth surrounding Wilder. The "again and again" of her texts and their serial offshoots ultimately forces us into a subject position that makes seeing more possible. In short, repetition does not return readers to "the same houses, the same things, the same family" but instead constitutes a process that inevitably summons alterity. The act of reiterating, then, can be both confirmatory and unsettling, encouraging us toward an experience that seems like authenticity while opening a gap in which we might see that perception as subjective.

The publication of *Pioneer Girl*, Wilder's 1930 first-person manuscript intended for adult readers, garnered nearly universal acclaim and astonishing sales. Hill's edition reproduces the draft that Wilder and Lane reworked into the Little House series, adding lengthy and meticulously researched annotations. These annotations, which are factual, editorial, and interpretive, provide readers with substantial information about the Ingalls family, their experiences, the people with whom their lives intersected, the sociocultural and natural context in which they existed, and Wilder and Lane's collaborative writing process. In *Pioneer Girl*'s introduction and afterword, Hill acknowledges the instability of truth that partially defines the series: "For Wilder, the 'truth' in [her] entire series centered on her vision of historical truth. . . . Her work is not a history but a true story founded on historical fact" (326–28). The book jacket is less meticulous, with the publisher promising readers that *Pioneer Girl* "reveals the true stories of [Wilder's] pioneering life; the real Laura Ingalls and her family. . . . [D]iscover that truth is as remarkable as fiction." While the annotations are distinct from the book jacket, accurately labeling the Little House series as historical fiction, they also aim at locating something essentialized. This constructed authenticity relies in part on the presence and encouragement of Hill's editorial voice but also emerges through the reification of Wilder's authorial voice through repetitive acts: narrative, formal, and editorial. Despite this reinforcement, however, elisions remain, drawing readers' attention to the silences and traumas that haunt Wilderiana.

Reprinting Wilder's manuscript, first and foremost, legitimizes this draft as literature, aligning *Pioneer Girl* with earlier publications. In theorizing the role of reprinted texts through a lens she terms "echocriticism," Meredith L. McGill contends that "imperfect repetition, and the editorial and critical will to overcome it, has structured the literary field.... [W]hat counts as literature is constituted through the circulation and recirculation of texts" (2, 20). As Hill acknowledges, Wilder's draft manuscript was never meant for publication. However, the simple act of reprinting it, even with a significant amount of variation, codifies the manuscript as a work of literature. This codification is reinforced through the symbiotic relationship between Wilder's autobiographical memories and factual matters often referenced in the annotations. Hill's annotations primarily substantiate an event, person, or place description in Wilder's manuscript and/or Wilder's fiction or clarify a discrepancy between what is written and what is verifiable. While the annotations that affirm Wilder's story are certainly an explicit part of the process through which Wilder and Hill's book[3] reinforces the perceptual relationship between Wilder and truth, the annotations that point out discrepancies are also participants. For example, when Hill points out that Wilder "had actually turned four in February 1871," a fact at odds with Wilder's statement that she was a "little girl not quite four years old," we encounter a lexical ouroboros, a repeating articulation that feeds on itself for survival (29). Hill repeats a fact that predates Wilder's manuscript— Wilder turned four in 1871; Wilder wrote the manuscript in 1930—but this act is also an implicit repetition of Wilder's incomplete statement to defend the fact's presence in the margins. In other words, Hill and Wilder are not creating isolated iterations but are instead repeating one another without end: I/ Wilder was not four years old, but I/Wilder was four years old, but I/Wilder was not four years old, and so forth. "Real repetition," Gordon C. F. Bearn writes, "would require not just resemblances and analogies but two different things whose identity was so complete that they shared the identical conceptual representation.... Two, which repeat, must be two, so they must be different, but they must repeat, so they must be conceptually identical" (444). If repetition structures and legitimizes literary culture, then in *Pioneer Girl*, Hill, Wilder, and Lane are working across temporal gaps to coauthor and legitimize the textual construct that is Laura Ingalls Wilder: a formation that seems homogeneous but that ultimately cannot be disentangled from a complex amalgam of inventions, lived experiences, and subjectivities.

One of *Pioneer Girl*'s most significant repetitive acts occurs through a concluding appendix, "The Benders of Kansas," a fictional anecdote presented as fact that reifies Wilder's authorial voice. Hill reprints an excerpt from the Brandt Revised[4] version of Wilder's manuscript detailing the supposed intersections between the Ingalls family and the Bender family, notorious serial killers operating in the early 1870s near the Ingallses' Kansas homestead. We learn that Kate Bender once invited Pa to stay at the Benders' inn, presumably in an attempt to add him to their list of victims. Several years later, after authorities raid the Benders' inn, Pa relays their findings in gruesome detail to his family: "Already twenty or more, in the cellar.... They found [the body of] a little girl, no bigger than Laura. They'd thrown her in ... and tramped the ground down on [her], while the little girl was still alive" (353–54). Wilder and Lane emphasize the child Laura's deep terror, her identification with the little girl, and the silences that grow within their family over the next twenty-four hours. Pa, they write, rides out that evening with his gun and returns the next day at sundown, informing Ma, "Yes, Caroline. Kate Bender with the rest. She deserved it just as much as they did" (354). The Benders are never discovered, and the strong implication, underscored by similarly vague comments Pa makes years later, is that Pa was one of the vigilantes who murdered the Bender family.

This is a deeply unnerving story, but it is not factual. Much of the Bender section of this story is historically verifiable: that family existed, murdered a number of guests at their inn, and disappeared before the bodies were found, never to be seen again. However, as Hill points out in her annotations, no evidence exists for Charles Ingalls's involvement, and the data in fact suggests that it would have been nearly impossible for him to have participated in a search for them. Because "the Benders' place was ... about thirty miles northeast of the Ingalls cabin," Charles is extremely unlikely to have passed by on his way to Independence; even more damning, the Benders' crimes were not discovered until 1873, more than two years after the Ingalls family departed Kansas for Wisconsin (353–54). Despite these discrepancies, the story still appears in the Brandt Revised manuscript as autobiographical, and Wilder repeated the tale for a Detroit audience in 1937, emphasizing its accuracy: "All I have told [in my books] is true, but it is not the whole truth. There were some stories I wanted to tell but would not be responsible for putting in a book for children.... There was the story of the Bender family that belonged in" *Little House on the Prairie* ("Notes" 104). Without any substantiation other than memory, Wilder and Lane present their family's intersection with the notorious Benders as provable history.

Although Hill's annotations state that Wilder and Lane's version of events is nearly impossible, the presence of "The Benders of Kansas" accompanying editorial equivocations repeats a narrative connecting Wilderiana and truth. The anecdote may be much darker in tone than most of the Little House series, but the story reinforces familiar ideological themes. The character of Charles Ingalls is defined by a list of traits that constitute Wilder and Lane's Libertarian ideal: independence, ingenuity, hard work, refusal to rely on institutions for support, and "the mutual, voluntary helpfulness of good (if distant) neighbors" (Fellman 86). The man who does not wait for law enforcement to bring murderers to justice is also the man who does not wait for the government to tell him whether he can settle on Osage land, a characterization that survives Wilder's manuscript and emerges in her writing for children. While the salacious emphasis on violence grabs our attention, "The Benders of Kansas" constructs Charles Ingalls as possessing what both Lane and Wilder believed was the uniquely American trait of individual resourcefulness. "I have often thought," the chapter concludes, "of that wagon with the Benders in it, driven fast across the empty prairie, overtaken at last and stopped by those men on horseback" (Wilder, *Pioneer* 355). The final image focuses not on the Benders but on the vigilantes—presumably including Pa—who ensure justice through an act that relies on superiority, strength, and skill.

The inclusion of "The Benders of Kansas" in *Pioneer Girl* may be the first time this particular chapter has been made available to the public, but its printing is nevertheless an act of reiteration that reifies Wilder and Lane's ideology: repetition as confirmation. In her annotations, Hill reinforces this affirmative practice, relying on supposition to create a narrative that affirms the dominant Wilder narrative. The language here is equivocating, yet it suggests possibilities that elide the possibility of intentional falsehood. Wilder "could have easily confused the circumstances that created the memory," Hill writes: "Given the fact that both Wilder and Lane were confused throughout *Pioneer Girl* about the chronology of Wilder's life, they may not have been aware that the vigilante activity actually took place after the Ingallses had left Kansas. Perhaps Wilder grew up on those stories.... What harm could there be, [they] may have concluded, in embellishing this connection?" (355). In positing various explanations for why Wilder and Lane presented a fictional story as fact, Hill participates in and extends the Wilderiana mythology, upholding Wilder in particular as fundamentally truthful. Neglecting to acknowledge the possibility that Wilder and Lane may have knowingly lied—a possibility that certainly cannot be eliminated—the language here seeks, without clear evidence, to explain their subterfuge. The *may nots* and *perhapses* and *may haves* that define Hill's guesswork may lead readers to accept explanations without wholly extinguishing a long-held belief in Wilder's authenticity. The repetition of *may not, perhaps,* and *may have* allows us to see the presence of these phrases, Hill's language foregrounding its objectives through restated rhetoric. Again, Hill, Wilder, and Lane participate in coiteration without clear origin, a lexical ouroboros that reproduces the single Wilder story, albeit with gaps that invite scrutiny. Hill cannot credibly defend Wilder and Lane without the preexisting dominant narrative that aligns Wilder with authenticity. Wilder and Lane's story needs Hill's annotations to reinforce the dominant narrative to achieve bare credibility. This is coconstructing, as Hill's language ultimately makes clear: "What is billed as a 'true' story," she concludes, "seems to resonate more deeply with readers than a fictional one" (356). This statement, intended as commentary on Wilder and Lane, might equally apply to *Pioneer Girl* and its annotations. In its efforts to authenticate Wilder, *Pioneer Girl* does not depart from the Wilderiana tradition but instead replicates it, both reinforcing the holistic Wilder narrative of truth and paradoxically creating an opening within which we might challenge that narrative.

Perhaps the aspect of *Pioneer Girl* that most effectively demonstrates the extent to which repetition occurs and fails, exposing the lie of homogeneity, is in the way readers are encouraged to interact with the text. As an annotated book, *Pioneer Girl* must create space on the page for marginal comments. These notes frequently take up more space than the original manuscript, sometimes occupying three-quarters of a page. *Pioneer Girl*'s annotations are not marginalia as we traditionally understand it. Instead, they constitute a significant majority of the full page, displacing the manuscript. Given the considerable length of Hill's annotations, readers intent on reading a given footnote must frequently turn the page to read it and turn the page back again to continue with Wilder's manuscript, repeating the process. The replication that defines *Pioneer Girl* and its place in the larger canon of Wilderiana is embodied through this encouraged interaction. To read *Pioneer Girl* as suggested, the reader must participate in and extend a reiterative tradition. Reading becomes an act of repetition that recalls the intoxicating "serial ritual" Romines describes defining her childhood relationship with the Little House series. Despite the way embodied acts of repetition replicate familiar Wilder reading experiences, this process of engaging with *Pioneer Girl* disrupts any notion of homogeneity that shadows repetition. "The same things . . . again and again" become fundamentally dissimilar through a forced disruption.

Most readers are accustomed to a linear reading process, creating a sense of forward momentum. *Pioneer Girl* disrupts that process with its antilinear construct. A number of reviews on the website *Goodreads* note frustration with this obligation:

> Because you keep going back and forth between the memoir and the annotations there was never a flow that felt good. (Harris)
>
> The annotations really threw off the flow of the book.... I found it difficult to go back and forth between the story and the annotations. (Duggan)
>
> Unfortunately, the annotations ruined it for me. They took up all the margins and continued on extra pages. It made the reading experience disjointed. (Hoerner)

While for these reviewers, a "disjointed" reading experience "ruin[s]" the other pleasures *Pioneer Girl* offers, these discontinuities can be understood to be ultimately productive. They formally replicate a construct that resembles Butler's concept of selfhood: "repeated acts that seek to approximate [a cohesive] ideal, but which, in their occasional discontinuity, reveal the temporal and contingent groundlessness of this 'ground'" (141). If *Pioneer Girl*'s annotations typically reiterate and affirm the presence of a "core truth" or deep-seated authenticity within the Wilder mythology, then the form of the book itself is the rupture that creates a space for resistance to a singular reality. Despite the book jacket's explicit promises and the annotations' implicit ones, no fundamental truth exists at the heart of Wilderiana, even with the semblance that repetition creates. The absence of a linear "flow" from the reading experience is thus encouraging because it formally points us toward the sociocultural absence of a linear "flow" within the multiplicity and subjectivity of human beings' lived experiences. If reading is an act that uses reiteration to construct a shaky facade of continuity, then repetition can also constitute the antithesis of homogeneity, showing its seams, forcing us away from "a flow that [feels] good." *Pioneer Girl: The Annotated Autobiography* may rely primarily on a narrative of authenticity, but the experience of engaging with it calls us to acknowledge the discursive fragments that fail to achieve wholeness.

Published shortly after *Pioneer Girl*, *Little: Novels* departs from Hill's research-based text, suggesting a fundamental disparity that obscures a shared affect: repetition that both extends Wilder's cultural power and disrupts hegemonic perceptions of it. The book itself reinforces a distinction on first glance, occupying a tiny 6" by 4" to *Pioneer Girl*'s substantial 11" by 9.5", and this size difference reflects a different approach. Anderson stresses absence, a rhetorical and critical move that contrasts with *Pioneer Girl*'s consistent emphasis on scholarly and historical sources. A work of erasure literature that removes paragraphs, sentences, words, and letters, *Little: Novels* reprints all nine of Wilder's Little House books in fewer than 150 small pages, enabling

Anderson to appropriate Wilder's language "to reshape a landscape," similar to the way Wilder's characters appropriate the Native-owned lands and resources they encounter (Anderson n.p.). Despite their formal and generic differences, Hill and Anderson undertake similar efforts through this act of reprinting. Throughout *Little: Novels*, Anderson repeats Wilder both literally and thematically, using Wilder's language, taking up and extending the Little House novels' consistent emphasis on consumption. This practice is, in many ways, the same practice Hill perpetuates, extending Wilder's power and mythology through reiteration. Although *Pioneer Girl* creates a space through repetition within which readers might challenge the supposed homogeneity of the dominant Wilder narrative, *Little: Novels* uses erasure to literally create space, pointing readers toward alternative ways of seeing. As Anderson's preface implies, this practice of appropriating language repeats the acts of Wilder's characters, mirroring settler occupation. Through erasure and reiteration, then, *Little: Novels* participates in the Wilderiana culture of repetition in simultaneously confirmatory and unsettling ways.

Although Anderson underscores consumption as a major theme throughout *Little: Novels*, the second chapter, "Farm," which erases *Farmer Boy*, is the most explicit way this book acknowledges the rapaciousness that hums beneath the surface of Wilder's work. The 1933 novel, which chronicles a year in her husband's childhood, famously focuses on cooking and eating. Nine-year-old Almanzo is endlessly hungry, and descriptions of decadent-sounding concoctions abound. In Anderson's "Farm," these descriptions become explicitly cannibalistic through removing very few words:

> There on the table was Mother, cooked in brown gravy and crab-apple jelly.
> "It takes a great deal to feed a growing boy," Mother said. Almanzo took up his spoon and ate every bite. (27)

Each plot point in "Farm" depicts Mother's cheerful self-sacrifice for the purposes of feeding her family, shocking in its implicit violence but—in its depiction of maternal martyrdom—not significantly different from Wilder's novels. Mother is endlessly self-regenerating, her body providing constant sustenance for her family: "Mother, rolling, rolling into the big copper kettle, came popping up to float and slowly swell, her pale golden back going into the fat" (27). What unnerves here is arguably not difference but similarity, as Anderson's reiteration retains the visceral imagery of Wilder's text—language that despite the shift in object, encourages us toward hunger. By entirely collapsing the divide between Mother's body and her primary purpose in *Farmer Boy*—cooking—*Little: Novels* constructs an overtly gendered critique that considers how the

Ingalls and Wilder families use and consume the bodies of Ma and Mother, how Ma and Mother must cheerfully give of themselves repeatedly. Anderson acknowledges other systemic consumptions, too. Throughout "Farm," the act of going in accompanies Almanzo's relentless hunger: he goes "in to dinner," he heads "into the kitchen," Mother climbs "into the big pail of yellow custard" (31). This constant and subtle emphasis on *in* becomes an explicit critique in the following chapter, "Our Air," where Anderson notes that she has erased the last four letters from the word *Indian*. This cutting makes a multiplicity of meanings, reiterating both the series' emphasis on interior spaces and, through transparent absence, the consistent erasure of Native people and perspectives from Wilder's books; it also inevitably reproduces acts of narrative disappearance that have historically eliminated Native textual presences. Retrospectively, then, "Our Air" invites us to acknowledge what hums beneath the surface of "Farm," the repeated *in* that gains significance on looking back. The relentless hunger that gnaws at Almanzo in "Farm" not only consumes his mother but transcends his chapter, standing in for the appetites of white settlers who consume the land, resources, and property of Native people. Wilder's writing consistently dehumanizes those who have historically owned the lands her characters occupy; she "insists on not just the inevitability but the desirability of native dispossession and erasure as a means to facilitate frontier settlement" (Smulders 200). By erasing Wilder's language to create a cannibalistic narrative, *Little: Novels* repeats the thematics of Wilder's writing; here, absence has the potential to gesture readers toward presence.

White settler violence against Natives emerges again in "Long," a chapter erasing *The Long Winter*, where Wilder's language becomes almost entirely removed from realism. Throughout, Anderson erases the first letter of the name of the youngest Ingalls sibling, *Grace*, juxtaposing that deletion with a description that, in Wilder's novel, is tethered to snow: "Mary's eyes opened and saw white. Race slept, her white breath a flannel nightgown. Mary settled down to read. She could see white" (105). The surreal imagery here is entirely commensurate with the Little House series: race personified as a vulnerable white girl, a figure who constitutes, reinforces, and legitimizes white supremacy. Just as "Farm" acknowledges settlers' choices as consumption, "Long" forces us to recognize how the Little House books rely on a consistent narrative of racial superiority that encourages Laura "to embrace whiteness (whether in women, sugar, or flour) as a sign of refinement" (Smulders 195). Snow functions effectively as a metaphor for the series' continual deployment of whiteness: omnipresent, controlling, dominant, unquestioned. In "Long," Wilder's characters can see "nothing but whiteness, a confusion of whiteness, a blinding" that not only evokes Mary's literal inability to see but also speaks to the Ingalls family's inability to recognize perspectives or experiences not part of their purview (104). Mary is blind, but Wilder and Lane are sightless, unable to acknowledge the moral atrocities of their reproduction of white supremacy.

While *Little: Novels* reiterates Wilder, this repetition departs from *Pioneer Girl* in that much of *Pioneer Girl*'s repetition indirectly reaffirms the ideologies that structure Wilder and Lane's worldview. *Little: Novels* is a deliberate failure of representation, repeating to unsettle. Just as it reifies hegemonic cultural practices, repetition also functions as a countercultural act that "can subvert dominant culture through parody and insubordination," stressing the irreconcilable over a manufactured wholeness (Reimer et al. 19). In bringing Wilder and Lane's ideological beliefs to the forefront, *Little: Novels* asks readers to acknowledge the extent to which these beliefs assume white supremacy, crafting imagery that challenges the ostensibly comforting tone of the series. What distinguishes *Little: Novels* is the pervading sense of the uncanny in each chapter, the construction of a literary tableau that is both deeply familiar and horrifyingly strange. The use of unnerving language and imagery, then, asks us, through repetition, to acknowledge the silences, absences, and erasures that structure Wilder and Lane's writing. This explicit departure, however, still relies on previous iterations—and its participation in the chain of iterations, as Wilderiana—to achieve its impact. In a blurb on the back cover of *Little: Novels*, humorist Daniel Mallory Ortberg labels the book "playful, and frightening, and truer, somehow, than the original," a description that challenges Miller's "true core" of authenticity to locate a form of truth in Anderson's critical perspective rather than in Wilder and Lane's. However, Ortberg's comment also pursues the same rhetoric that has always defined the Little House series, locating in the book a fundamental and singular truth rather than in the multiplicity that structures literary texts. Like *Pioneer Girl*, which ostensibly tells the "true stories" of Wilder's early years, *Little: Novels* is marketed as "truer" than Wilder's novels, with both texts affirming their place in the corpus of Wilderiana by returning to this supposition of a discernibly authentic experience. The repetitive disruption *Little: Novels* creates is thus repurposed as constructing truth, a practice not dissimilar to the historical perception of Wilder's work. It unsettles our perceptions but simultaneously confirms the long-held notion that a "core truth" exists somewhere within Wilder's legacy.

Implicit in Karen Coats's reading of repetition as an indicator of something unarticulated or lost is a question that demands our attention: What is the broader thing to which Wilder and her reiterations call our attention? What symptom are we called to acknowledge? *Pioneer Girl: The Annotated Autobiography* and *Little: Novels* answer these questions by demonstrating that "truth" in Wilderiana is not singular, stable, or universal. The insistence on truth, again and again, ultimately reveals the lack of it. In pursuing legitimacy and objectivity, Hill's annotations occasionally reinforce the idea of a core truth, neglecting or glossing over the possibility of other narratives that might equally be perceived as "true." Making transparent the process of elision, however, paradoxically enables us to acknowledge the existence of these gaps. Anderson is more insistent than Hill on creating explicit alternatives to Wilder lore. Anderson's acts of erasure intentionally open space for the visibility Coats identifies. Despite their fundamentally different approaches to Wilder, Hill and Anderson are linked by the fact that they make their processes explicit: research and creativity that requires them to think critically about the repetition of Wilder's words, Wilder's stories, Wilder's mythology and that often slips to make room for an alternative way of seeing. Here, in this process, readers can acknowledge how repetition proves both confirmatory and unsettling in Wilderiana, creating the powerful semblance of truth while simultaneously disrupting that semblance.

NOTES

1. *Pioneer Girl* does not include the events chronicled in *Farmer Boy* or *The First Four Years*.
2. Hastings uses *Wilderiana* to refer to the vast number of "scholarly and semi-scholarly" publications about Wilder's life and writing (95). I use the term here as shorthand for all printed, filmed, or curated texts that centrally engage with Wilder and/or the Little House books.
3. While *Pioneer Girl* emphasizes Wilder's original manuscripts, I credit both Hill and Wilder with authoring the book. Hill's annotations, present on every page, encourage readers toward a particular way of engaging with Wilder's language and narrative. The omnipresence of her editorial voice is ultimately impossible to separate from Wilder's authorial voice.
4. Hill refers to the third draft of Wilder's original manuscript, which was heavily edited by Lane, as "Brandt Revised." In recognition of Lane's significant role in crafting this section of the autobiography, I credit Wilder and Lane with coauthorship of "The Benders of Kansas."

WORKS CITED

Anderson, Emily. *Little: Novels*. BlazeVOX, 2015.
Bearn, Gordon C. F. "Differentiating Derrida and Deleuze." *Continental Philosophy Review* 33 (2000): 441–65.
Butler, Judith. *Gender Trouble*. Routledge, 1990.
Coats, Karen. "The Mysteries of Postmodern Epistemology: Stratemeyer, Stein, and Contemporary Mystery for Children." In *Mystery in Children's Literature: From the Rational to the Supernatural*, edited by Adrienne E. Gavin and Christopher Routledge, 184–201. Palgrave Macmillan, 2001.
Duggan, Lindsay. Review of *Pioneer Girl: The Annotated Autobiography*. Goodreads, 26 June 2015.

Fellman, Anita Clair. *Little House, Long Shadow: Laura Ingalls Wilder's Impact on American Culture*. University of Missouri Press, 2008.

Fraser, Caroline. "The Wilder Women." *Slate*, 7 March 2016.

Gach, Mary Victoria. "Laura Ingalls Wilder: Art versus Reality." Master's thesis, Iowa State University, 1980.

Harris, Gina. Review of *Pioneer Girl: The Annotated Autobiography*. Goodreads, 25 July 2015.

Hastings, A. Waller. Review of *Pioneer Girl: The Annotated Autobiography*. *Children's Literature Association Quarterly* 41, no. 1 (2016): 95–97.

Hoerner, Kristina. Review of *Pioneer Girl: The Annotated Autobiography*. Goodreads, 24 December 2014.

McGill, Meredith L. "Echocriticism: Repetition and the Order of Texts." *American Literature* 88, no. 1 (March 2016): 1–29.

Miller, John E. *Laura Ingalls Wilder and Rose Wilder Lane*. University of Missouri Press, 2008.

"Notes from the Real Little House on the Prairie." *Saturday Evening Post*, September 1978, 104.

Reimer, Mavis, Nyala Ali, Deanna England, and Melanie Dennis Unrau, eds. *Seriality and Texts for Young People: The Compulsion to Repeat*. Springer, 2014.

Robinson, Laura. "'Anne Repeated': Taking Anne Out of Order." In Reimer et al., 57–73.

Romines, Ann. *Constructing the Little House: Gender, Culture, and Laura Ingalls Wilder*. University of Massachusetts Press, 1997.

Slater, Katharine. "'Now We're All Snug!': The Regionalism of *Little House on the Prairie*." *Genre* 47, no. 1 (2014): 55–77.

Smulders, Sharon. "'The Only Good Indian': History, Race, and Representation in Laura Ingalls Wilder's *Little House on the Prairie*." *Children's Literature Association Quarterly* 27, no. 4 (2002): 191–202.

Wilder, Laura Ingalls. *Pioneer Girl: The Annotated Autobiography*. Edited by Pamela Smith Hill. South Dakota Historical Society Press, 2014.

Wilder, Laura Ingalls. *The Selected Letters of Laura Ingalls Wilder*. Edited by William Anderson. HarperCollins, 2016.

"IT ALL DEPENDS ON HOW YOU LOOK AT IT"

Laura Ingalls Wilder, Rose Wilder Lane, Independence Day, and Family Economics

Dawn Sardella-Ayres

It is almost impossible to separate the sentimentalized, nearly mythical figure of Laura Ingalls Wilder from the books published under her name. It also has been difficult to distinguish the authorial voice of Laura Ingalls Wilder from that of her daughter, Rose Wilder Lane, ever since Rosa Ann Moore and others first demonstrated that the series was actually a collaborative effort (see Moore, "Laura"; Moore, "Little"; Anderson, *Story*; Holtz, *Ghost*; Woodside). Lane's influence on her mother's Little House books, both as an editor and an emerging Libertarian, has been the subject of much debate: scholars including John E. Miller, Pamela Smith Hill, and Christine Woodside have undertaken detailed explorations of Lane's involvement in Wilder's writing. The authors' differences often overshadowed their similarities. As Miller explains, "One was devout, the other a skeptic.... One was ruled by convention, the other ridiculed it. One enjoyed rural ways, the other escaped to the city as soon as she could. One settled down and lived with a man for two-thirds of a century, the other found it impossible to accommodate herself to any other person for any length of time" (253). Nonetheless, similarities are evident and have complicated our understanding of the authors' collaboration. For more than sixty years, these women often shared living space and political ideals. Both were strong-willed, opinionated, critical, perfectionist, and ambitious. Both were nontraditional, challenging conventional female roles to different extents. But they did not believe exactly the same things, and the complex and covert nature of their collaboration complicates efforts to delineate the subtle differences between Wilder's and Lane's political ideologies and the ways they occur in the two women's shared and individual written work.

One key phrase that is repeated throughout the Little House series, *free and independent* becomes a useful lens through which to examine the collaborators' principles. For Wilder, the notion is personal and/or familial, grounded in her family's physical situation on the open prairie land. *Free* has economic connotations: to be as free from debt as possible. In contrast, Lane's idea of being *free and independent* is more individualistic and theoretical, conveying a psychological or spiritual independence. These distinctions become more apparent in examinations of Wilder's posthumously published *The First Four Years* and Lane's mediated Independence Day episodes from *Farmer Boy* and *Little Town on the Prairie*, particularly when Wilder's original handwritten manuscripts and the now-published autobiography, *Pioneer Girl*, are brought into consideration.

Mother and daughter aligned on many political issues. Although Wilder was a longtime Democrat and ran for tax collector in 1925, she and her daughter came to share a "mutual antipathy toward increased government intervention in people's lives" as well as the "common opinion that President Roosevelt and the New Deal had been disastrous for the country" (Miller 233). Both women believed that reliance on government assistance compromised the individual's freedom, a concept rooted in the ideology of American exceptionalism. Both questioned their political affiliations and saw their political ideals shift while writing the Little House books. However, to a far greater degree, Lane "continued to play with ideas and test them against her own experience and knowledge and against the opinions of people" (Miller 178) until "the leftist critique of American values and mores that she had formulated during the early 1920s now gave way to celebration of them" (203). By the time she was editing *Little Town on the Prairie* (1941), Lane had begun writing a newspaper column and a series of pamphlets showcasing her conservative philosophy, analyzing ideas about the role of government and the place of the individual in modern society. And, according to Anderson, when their collaborative work on the Little House books concluded, Lane "was finished with fiction" and "committed to write what Wilder called 'American propaganda,' referring to Lane's passion for a return to small government, absolute individual freedom, and a life free of interference by politicians in office" (*Selected* 256–57). While Wilder expressed criticism of the New Deal and its Public Works Administration in letters (*Selected* 193–94), Lane's political philosophy regarding American individuals and their role in the nation flavored the fictionalized story of her mother's childhood to a far greater degree. By 1939, Lane was already identifying herself as "a revolutionary" during US Senate committee testimony in favor of the Ludlow Amendment, which asserted that ordinary citizens should have a direct vote in America's military conflicts. Within ten years, Lane had focused her writing almost entirely on correspondence and editorials, and, as Woodside notes, Lane "molded the theme of independence" (149) hinted at in the Little House books into more comprehensive arguments for policy change. Zealously exploring economics and politics, and advocating individual free will, Lane argued "that the leaders of the country had lost sight of their root principles" (149). "I am becoming a professional fanatic," Lane wrote to retired Du Pont executive Jasper Crane in the 1940s (150).

Both Wilder and Lane often use the phrase *free and independent* in their individual works to indicate a certain all-American philosophy, but the context in which each uses it indicates different nuances of liberation and obligation, different ideological truths. Wilder's definition of what it means to be *free and independent* is personal, practical, and spatial. The sensation of freedom is found in the pioneer homesteader-farmer's solitude: a family unit struggling to survive, separate from neighbors and community. This is clear in the posthumously published *The First Four Years* (1971), the only Little House book published without Lane's emendations. Freedom, according to Wilder's ideology, is pragmatic and individualistic and tied to familial self-sufficiency.

The First Four Years explicitly focuses on the family's economic reality. When Almanzo proposes, Laura says she does not want to be married to a farmer because "a farm is such a hard place for a woman" (4).[1] They agree to try farming for three years, and the book is structured around Almanzo's attempts to prove to Laura that they will be more successful—and more independent— than merchants. Laura objects to Almanzo's farming because "a farmer never has any money. He can never make any because the people in towns tell him what they will pay for what he has to sell and then charge him what they please for what he has to buy. It's not fair" (4). But Almanzo, or Manly, as Laura called him here, insists, "Farmers are the only ones who are independent. How long would a merchant last if farmers didn't trade with him?" (5). He ties this idea to a man's work ethic, telling Laura that someone who "is willing to work and give attention to his farm . . . can make more money than the men in town and all the time be his own boss" (5). This contention will be proven wrong multiple times in the text, as natural disasters ruin Manly's hard work on the farm. However, Laura consents to farming because she "liked the horses and enjoyed the freedom and spaciousness of the wide prairie land" and thinks it "would be much more fun living on the land than on the town street with neighbors so close on each side" (6–7), thus defining *freedom* as open space and distance from other people. In this context, *freedom* means being free from social scrutiny.

For Wilder, who often described herself as shy and private and is characterized as such in the Little House books, social interaction was never as important as space and place. Throughout the series, Laura's family is company enough for her. For example, during the isolation of *The Long Winter*, Laura does not mourn the loss of social activities and friends as much as she does her schooling. When Laura participates in social activities, she is depicted taking long walks with Ida Brown or going on forty-mile buggy rides with Almanzo. Laura's preferred activities always emphasize her awareness of the open landscape and her feelings of peace and seclusion in such an environment. The Wilders' first little houses provide them with independence and freedom, reflected in their unconventional "play" as they race their horses across the prairie. More than sixty years later, Wilder still manifested this preference, writing to a friend about a driving trip she and Almanzo were taking, "If we are by ourselves we will be independent" (qtd. in Miller 228). In *The First Four Years*, to be free is to be alone. It also means to be as free as possible from debt.

The First Four Years is infused with numbers and prices and commerce—accountings of the cost of a plow to break a certain number of acres to plant wheat or oats that will be worth a certain price; references to small luxuries chosen from the Montgomery Ward catalog. Laura often mentally adds up the notes, debt, and interest until she "must stop counting it or she would have her head queer" (58). The farming struggle in *The First Four Years* lacks the grand, sweeping vision of similar story arcs in *On the Banks of Plum Creek* and *Little Town on the Prairie*, which, with Lane's editorial input, emphasized a mythological human-against-nature tale, an expansive nationalistic vision. In *The First Four Years*, newlyweds Laura and Almanzo are pitted not only against nature but also subtly against each other as they battle to make a financial success of their three years of farming (which Almanzo maneuvers into four). The novel depicts Laura's pragmatic resignation in light of Almanzo's sometimes foolish-sounding optimism that "everything evens up." The Wilders begin marriage already in debt, and Laura is conscious of not wanting to "be an expense to Manly right at the beginning" (17). When Laura fails to contribute to the household by selling eggs and butter to stores in town, she tells herself, "Why worry? Manly didn't" (28). However, when Laura discovers additional debt after they lose their crops in a hailstorm, her anger is apparent: "Five hundred dollars debt on the house! Oh, I didn't know that!" Manly responds with, "I didn't think there was any need to bother you about that" (57). When he buys an expensive new coal heater, he rationalizes the expense with a breakdown of longer-term potential savings in coal costs. Laura still "felt that they couldn't afford the beautiful new stove, but that was Manly's business. She need not bother about it" (85). The text repeatedly indicates that Laura must learn to manage her husband's financial missteps by resigning herself to them. The undercurrent of helpless anger continues as Almanzo buys more farm equipment on credit and ruins his health by ignoring doctors' orders to rest after contracting diphtheria: a bout of temporary paralysis leaves him physically unable to work the farm without hired help for the rest of his life. Each new bill shows a young wife frustrated not only by her lack of economic solvency but also by her inability as a woman and wife to do anything about their situation. Neighbors and family help the Wilders during illnesses and after a house fire and a tornado, demonstrating just how necessary a community is in times of crisis. Almanzo's promise that they will be "free and independent" on their farm is revealed to be a failed philosophy, even on the most practical levels. Raising crops and livestock, living off the land, is not "free"; moreover, if one is part of a community, one can never be entirely free and independent. Laura ekes out what economic autonomy she can under her circumstances.

For Wilder, freedom also means escaping social mores or restrictions. On their farm, Laura is happiest when she and her husband are partnered in activities, "two people thoroughly in sympathy" (31), whether it is haying or taking long horseback rides, things she would not be able to do freely living in town, under others' close scrutiny. Laura also covertly establishes her economic importance in the Wilder family when she uses her last paycheck from teaching to buy a colt as an investment.[2] She later sells the colt to buy sheep, one of the only profitable ventures in the book. The only truly successful farming ventures are the ones for which Laura has had not only financial say but financial control.

In *The First Four Years*, becoming completely free and independent proves impossible, particularly in an economic sense, which may reflect Wilder's adult experiences in Dakota, Florida, and Missouri. Contrasting with descriptions of the Ingalls family's resilience and unity in the face of hardship in earlier books, which are to varying extents saturated with Lane's economic and political theories, *The First Four Years* shows the Wilders unable to survive without help from their extended families and neighbors. In the end, despite debts, illness, death, and countless disasters, Almanzo insists that farming can be considered successful because "it all depends on how you look at it" (132), including his repeated philosophy that "everything evens up" because "the rich have their ice in the summer, but the poor get their ice in the winter" (49). While Laura at first laughs with him over this, she later grimly "mutters" it to herself when a summer hailstorm destroys "three thousand dollars worth of wheat" (56); she repeats it again at the end of the book regarding the "incurable optimism of the farmer" despite the fact that a fire has destroyed their house and everything in it, and they are "making a fresh start with nothing" (133). This is the darker side of Pa Ingalls's boundless vision, a bleak reality that the earlier Little House books covered up or turned into American mythology. The ideology of solitary free and independent survival simply does not exist in the reality of American economic structures, where things rarely even up the way Manly suggests.

In 1932, while working with Wilder on *Farmer Boy*, Lane was also writing a serialized novel, *Let the Hurricane Roar*, republished in 1976 as *Young Pioneers*. The original version reflects Lane's continued reliance on material from her family's history; the main characters were originally named Charles and Caroline (later changed to David and Molly, the same names used in Lane's 1938 novel, *Free Land*). *Let the Hurricane Roar* was a direct "reply to pessimists," a reminder that, as Lane later wrote, "living is never easy, that all human history is a record of achievement in disaster (so that disaster is no cause for despair), and that our great asset is the valor of the American spirit—the undefeated spirit of millions of obscure men and women who are as valiant today as the pioneers were in the past" (qtd. in Holtz 235). Lane's definition of *pioneers*, rooted in American exceptionalist ideals of liberty and democracy, has an intellectual element, an ongoing exploration of human and national possibilities, not merely physical movement to a new place. In *Let the Hurricane Roar*, Lane presents her ideology of the American spirit through the story of a newly married pioneer couple homesteading amid disaster. When crops fail and David leaves to find work, seventeen-year-old Molly holds down their claim alone. Molly's encounter with a recently ruined immigrant farmer illustrates Lane's philosophy. When the farmer "attacked the whole country, the West, she was angry":

> "Ta tam country," he said. "No tam goot."
>
> "The country's all right, Mr. Svenson," Molly said. Suddenly she felt that he was a foreigner; no American would talk like that. She said sharply, "No country's going to feed you with a spoon."
>
> ... "Ta tam country, she feed nobody," Mr. Svenson said bitterly. "She iss devils, ta country."
>
> Molly was silent. In politeness she could not say, "It's men that make a country. What's the matter with you?" (67)

For all Lane's philosophical emphasis on the individual, this view does not take into account the differing circumstances and conditions that might constrain an individual. Lane's ideology of freedom expects all men to respond the same way, no matter their circumstances or abilities, and privileges the individual over any group or any practical relationship or responsibility. As she writes in 1943's *The Discovery of Freedom*, "So long as I live, I am self-controlling and responsible for what I do" (149). In addition, she argues, "No one and nothing but I, myself, can be responsible for what I do. I can not crawl out from under, saying, 'I have to do this, if I don't I'll lose my job,' or, 'We've got to, we can't afford to lose the contract,' or, 'I have a family to support,' or, 'We have a responsibility to the stockholders,' or, 'It's the Party Line; the end justifies the means.' Liberty is inalienable. I can not transfer my responsibility to anyone or anything" (15). According to Lane, no family unit, no social unity, no community bears the responsibilities that an individual American citizen does, and from her philosophical if not practical perspective, all individuals have equal opportunity if they are self-governing.

Lane incorporated ideals of individual hard work, responsibility, and self-sufficiency into her writings well before *The Discovery of Freedom*. The edited version of *Farmer Boy* (1933) underwent multiple difficult revisions, a process discussed in detail by Miller, Holtz, and Hill. *Farmer Boy* contains evident political and economic discourse that fleshes out Lane's "free and independent" philosophy. In the "Independence Day" chapter, ten-year-old Almanzo witnesses the excitement of the town's Fourth of July celebrations. He also learns an important lesson in economics, paving the way for his own independence. After Almanzo requests a nickel to buy pink lemonade, Almanzo's father instead gives him a half dollar, along with an economics lesson: "'You know what half a dollar is? . . . It's work, son,' Father said. 'That's what money is, it's hard work'" (182). Father asks Almanzo to explain how to raise potatoes, and Almanzo describes the plowing and harrowing of a field, the sowing of the seed potatoes, the hoeing and harvesting and the eventual sale of the potatoes raised. When Father asks, "If you get a good price, son, how much do you get to show for all that work? How much do you get for half a bushel of potatoes?" Almanzo answers, "Half a dollar" (184).

> "Yes," said Father. "That's what's in this half-dollar, Almanzo. The work that raised a half a bushel of potatoes is in it."
>
> Almanzo looked at the round piece of money that Father held up. It looked small, compared with all that work.
>
> "You can have it, Almanzo," Father said. " . . . You could buy a sucking pig with it, if you want to. You could raise it, and it would raise a litter of pigs, worth four, five dollars apiece. Or you can trade that half-dollar for lemonade and drink it up. You do as you want, it's your money." (184–85)

Father gives Almanzo not only money and an economics lesson but seemingly the individual freedom to decide how to use it.

Here and throughout, *Farmer Boy* promotes a certain kind of work ethic, American individualism, and sense of duty. The Fourth of July has been preceded by an unseasonable frost that leaves the Wilder family's cornfield in danger of ruin. Father, Mother, and the four children get up in the middle of the night and pour water over each cornstalk to thaw it before sunrise, saving almost all of the corn. After breakfast, they dress in their Sunday best for the Independence Day festivities in town, which are bookended with celebrations of the American work ethic. This is consecrated when Father says, "Don't forget it was axes and plows that made this country" (188). The chapter ends with Father's words to Almanzo: "It's the biggest country in the world, and it was farmers who took all that country and made it America, son. Don't you ever forget that" (189).

The Independence Day events also reveal a unique kind of privatized political discourse, arranged in an elaborate framework of private and public spheres that lends levels of authenticity to the themes expressed. In *Farmer Boy*, the discussion is established within specific conditions and dimensions of social life. The fact that the town can hold such a celebration intimates an established community, a bourgeois society, as well as a potential marketplace and economic system that reflects Lane's laissez-faire view of commerce, free from government interference. Father's half-dollar lesson to Almanzo takes place in the presence of other respected townspeople, particularly the merchant, Mr. Paddock, whose assessment that "The boy's too young, Wilder. . . . You can't make a youngster understand that" (183) is proven wrong. The book's unspoken storekeeper-versus-farmer conflict concludes in the last chapters, when Mr. Paddock facilitates Almanzo's two-hundred-dollar reward for responsibly returning a lost wallet containing more than a thousand dollars. Mr. Paddock offers Almanzo a position as apprentice in his buggy-building business, but Almanzo wants to use his reward to purchase a colt, deciding that he would rather "be just like Father" instead of like Mr. Paddock or even his own brother, Royal, a merchant in training. Father admits to Almanzo that as a town businessman, he would "have an easy life, in some ways" and would "always have plenty to eat and wear and money in the bank" (370). But Father tells Almanzo that "there's the other side, too": "You'd have to depend on other folks, son, in town. Everything you got, you'd get from other folks. A farmer depends on himself, and the land and the weather. If you're a farmer, you raise what you eat, you raise what you wear, and you keep warm with wood out of your own timber. You work hard, but you work as you please, and no man can tell you to go or come. You'll be free and independent, son, on a farm" (370). The text advocates the philosophy an adult Almanzo will share with Laura in *The First Four Years*, emphasizing self-sufficiency and the family as economic space.

However, Wilder's original, unmediated version of *Farmer Boy*'s Fourth of July events contrasts strikingly with the finished version that has been structured as a vehicle for Lane's political discourse. The earlier draft is written in straightforward, journalistic prose and is not imbued with any deeper meaning, nor does it constitute a separate chapter. Wilder places more weight on the unseasonable frost and the family's struggle to save the corn. Much of the emotion in this section of her handwritten draft is devoted to family members' anxiety about their crop. The actual account of the town celebration is spare: in fact, by the time the family arrives for the festivities, "the reading of the Declaration of Independence was over and most of the speeches. Almanzo was glad of that. He got to listen to one speech. Father said the speaker 'twisted the lion's tail and made the eagle scream,' but Almanzo couldn't see any lion, nor hear the eagle, and when he asked where they were, Father only laughed. He liked to see the band as it marched through the street ... [and] what fun it was to watch the men load and fire the two brass cannons" (Lane Papers, Box 16, Folder 2/7). Wilder then devotes a page and a half to description of the cannons and the noise they made when fired, and there the scene ends. Almanzo is detached from the political happenings around him, and there is no implicit economic lesson or explicit celebration of individualism. Comparing Lane's edited version of the same chapter to her mother's original manuscript, the difference between their perspectives is evident, even in this early volume of the series.

Similar contrasts are evident in the only other Fourth of July community gathering depicted in the series. In *Little Town on the Prairie*, teenaged Laura and her family become active in De Smet's civic community, and the book's overall theme is how Laura negotiates her increasingly curtailed physical freedoms. Laura is not comfortable at first with living in town, but she gradually learns how to negotiate social situations at school, during Ladies' Aid parties, and while being courted by Almanzo. Laura balks at the physical restrictions of her corsets and hoopskirts, the trappings of a young lady. But at this age, she must learn to adjust and accept them or risk social shame. Lane's edited version constructs an ideological and moral realization that corresponds with Laura's maturity but diverges significantly from Wilder's original manuscript version of events.

While Lane was working on *Little Town on the Prairie*, she was, as Miller acknowledges, experiencing a time of great personal political questioning and was "struggling with conflicting attitudes and points of view" (178). Lane's letters to Dorothy Thompson reflect this fluctuation, how she was "working her way toward a view [of humanity] that accepted the primacy of the individual and a society of dynamic inequality" (Holtz, "Dorothy" 137). By 1943, just two years after revising *Little Town on the Prairie*, Lane writes that the inalienable fact of liberty "is not recognized when individuals submit to an Authority that grants them 'freedoms.' Implicit in that plural is the belief that individuals are not free, that adult men and women must be controlled and cared for, as children are, and that, like children, they are naturally dependent and naturally obedient to an Authority that is responsible for their acts and their welfare" (150). This philosophy of individualism is anticipated in the alterations Lane makes in *Little Town on the Prairie*'s Independence Day celebration and shows how Lane's ideology had evolved beyond what she added to the Fourth of July scene in *Farmer Boy*.

In the published, Lane-influenced *Little Town on the Prairie*, the Fourth of July celebration in town is attended only by Pa, Laura, and Carrie. Ma, Mary, and Grace prefer to stay at home, where it is quiet, and Ma is adamant about ladies not attending rough activities such as horse races. Laura and Carrie watch the celebration primarily from Pa's store building and muse about events from American history rather than mingling with the noisy crowds. The published version of *Little Town on the Prairie*'s Fourth of July contains overt patriotic ideology, presented through songs, comments, and several detailed speeches, experienced firsthand by Laura. The celebration is the first event in a Wilder book whose primary plot is centered on community integration, and it takes place in a book that features as its climactic scene Laura's recitation of a hundred years of American history to a town audience (resulting in her receiving a teaching certificate). Laura is initially uncomfortable because of the noise and proximity to strangers, but when someone steps up to read the Declaration of Independence—excerpted in two pages of incorporated text—Laura listens with solemn, rapt attention even though she "knows every word" of it "by heart" (73). After the reading, in the hushed silence that ensues, Pa leads the assembled citizens in "My Country Tis of Thee." Laura "had a completely new thought" as the "Declaration and the song came together in her mind" (75): "She thought: God is America's king. She thought: America won't obey any king on earth. Americans are free. That means they have to obey their own consciences. No king bosses Pa; he has to boss himself. Why (she thought), when I am a little older, Pa and Ma will stop telling me what to do, and there isn't anyone else who has a right to give me orders. I will have to make myself be good.... This is what it means to be free. It means you have to be good.... The laws of Nature and of Nature's God endow you with a right to life and liberty. Then you have to keep the laws of God, for God's law is the only thing that gives you a right to be free" (75–76). Fictional Laura's mind becomes a kind of publicized sphere of political discourse, doubly emphasized by the textual repetition of "she thought." Protagonist-Laura clarifies and experiences Lane's ideologies, emphasizing individual, personal responsibility for being free and independent. Laura reflects on but also personifies how family, a community, a country, are all dependent on individuals upholding their personal responsibilities to "make themselves be good." Where young Almanzo had a firsthand practical application of Lane's social economics in *Farmer Boy*, here, Laura's experience is philosophical, mirroring Lane's own authorial shift from practical actions to abstract ideals of the individual.

In Lane's edited version of *Little Town on the Prairie*, Almanzo Wilder enters the buggy race, his team pulling his brother's heavy peddler's cart. As Laura watches, agonizing that it's "not *fair*!" that the beautiful Morgan team hasn't a chance at winning against all the other light buggies, she overhears some men talking. Mr. Boast comments that Almanzo "might've rousted out a buggy somewhere" to race with, but another man responds, "He's an independent kind of a young cuss.... He'd rather lose with what he's got than win with a borrowed buggy" (81). Of course, Almanzo nevertheless wins the race, and his victory and five-dollar prize are consecrated in part by his independence in using his own family resources. He demonstrates the responsible self-governance and liberty Lane espouses in her political writings of the same time.

In significant contrast, Wilder's manuscript for this episode again demonstrates her tendency to report personal, familial details rather than to pontificate. Chapter 3 of the manuscript, "Getting Ready for the Fourth," describes preparations for the town's celebration, focusing on the Ingalls family's special foodways and dress. Mary walks eagerly to town with the rest, enabling the sisterly interaction that Wilder commonly injects into her work. Someone reads the Declaration of Independence with theatrical waving arms, and then there are several political speeches, but Laura fidgets until Mary pinches her arm and hisses, "Sit still!" This time, Carrie does not understand the phrases about "twist[ing] the lion's tail and ma[king] the eagle scream," and although Laura tells her sister that "they meant lawyer Barnes praised the United States and the other speakers said mean things about England ... Carrie still looked puzzled" (Wilder Papers, folders 4 and 5). The Ingalls and Boast families, including Ma and Mrs. Boast, watch several races, and after a humorous sack race that leaves the contestants crawling on the ground, Laura sees Almanzo win the buggy race despite his heavy cart. The celebration continues with a town square dance on the bandstand, and, while the family doesn't stay, Ma and Mary nevertheless talk about how nice it is to live near town, ostensibly to take part in such celebrations (Wilder Papers, folders 4 and 5).[3]

In the Little House books, ideas about American independence and freedom as individual responsibility, often in opposition to government/administrative authority, are usually presented through Laura herself or through her future husband, Almanzo. Analysis from earlier drafts reveals that the source for these ideological assertions is indisputably Lane rather than Wilder.[4] Fictional Laura, like fictional Almanzo in *Farmer Boy*, is fully invested in the book's political belief system, not a detached, uninterested observer. With Lane's editorial revisions, the community events in *Little House*'s Fourth of July scenes become not about town or community but about American individual autonomy, freedom from moral dependence on governing systems. In Wilder's original versions, however, freedom is emphatically linked to physical and personal space. Interestingly, both authors' versions reject community participation and integration, even as they resist—or are oblivious to—how the family ultimately depends on the community.

The effects of such discourse within the context of a children's book are complex enough, but in the case of the Wilder-Lane collaborations, many additional circumstances and elements must be taken into account. The relationships among author, text, and reader are more intricate than in other works written by Wilder or Lane individually. The "problem of fictionality," as Maria Nikolajeva identifies it, suggests that in literary criticism, the characters being analyzed are "always a social and cultural construct" (164). In the Little House books, Laura Ingalls is simultaneously real and fictional. She is Wilder and Lane's construction, the reclamation of Bessie Wilder (as Almanzo referred to his wife), Rose Lane's vehicle for political and economic ideology. This, combined with Wilder's idealized, even mythologized reputation as a beloved author of all-American children's classics, provides the books' political discourse with slippery, elaborate, (and often protective) cushioning. Readers and scholars will always need to be vigilant as they read, understanding that each of the texts' authors has a distinctive purpose and agenda.

Lane's philosophies regarding what it means to be free and independent may well have succeeded *because* they were presented within the authoritative yet unthreatening framework of the child-protagonist Laura herself, ostensibly penned by the beloved American pioneer author Laura Ingalls Wilder. Lane's ideology resonated more widely because it was grounded not just in philosophy but in the secure, detail-rich, all-American home space contributed by Wilder. Both versions of these scenes affirm specific national visions and ideological ideas of family and community, even as they seem to promote American individualism. For generations, readers' responses emphasize their love of the characters and their close family bonds; readers came to think of the fictionalized Ingallses and Wilders as family. While Lane's and Wilder's individual contributions demonstrate the values associated with the Little House series, their combined achievement has endured. Like the fiction itself, the close family bond between the authors has had the most lasting impact. And, as their writings, letters, and other evidence continues to demonstrate, neither really could be entirely free and independent—economically, psychologically, familially—of the other. As the scholarship on their complex relationship and accomplishments continues to reveal, the ideology of the Little House series is thus complex and layered and sometimes paradoxical, fueled by writers with similar but also quite different concerns and perspectives.

NOTES

1. While fictional Laura does not express dissatisfaction with the Ingalls family's farming, in *The First Four Years* she explains, "Now Laura had always been a pioneer girl rather than a farmer's daughter, always moving on to new places before the fields grew large" (25). And in *By the Shores of Silver Lake*, she and Cousin Lena often sing a song about how they "wouldn't marry a farmer, he's always in the dirt" (93). She is aware of and apparently resistant to the demands that farming would make on her as a woman and wife.

2. According to Donald Zochert, Laura's school salary was "the $30 that bought the colt, that was sold to buy the sheep, that with their increase were sold for the money that bought Rocky Ridge" (186). However, Rose wrote in the 1950s that the hundred dollars that bought Rocky Ridge was earned by Laura "sewing in a dressmaker's shop" in De Smet (see "She Can Stand On Her Own Feet," in Anderson, *Little* 175). Either way, Rocky Ridge Farm was likely the result of Laura's economic profits, not Almanzo's. Later, after decades of economic struggle, the Wilders' late-in-life solvency is again provided by Laura, via her career as the beloved author of the Little House books. For further discussion of Wilder's increasing financial autonomy, see Fraser 179.

3. In *Pioneer Girl*, the descriptions of town Fourth of July events are even less political or ideological, although Wilder reuses and expands these events in *Little Town on the Prairie* and *These Happy Golden Years*. She includes little description in the first one, calling it "a tiresome day" (236); in the second, she mentions only that for the holiday, "Manly and I did not go to hear the speeches" (304) but instead indulged in one of their long buggy rides.

4. Of Lane's increased involvement in *The Long Winter* and *Little Town on the Prairie*, Miller notes, "The story and most of the language were Laura's, but Rose went further in rewriting and expanding this draft than she had done in most of the other volumes. For example, she expanded her mother's brief one-page description of storekeeper Daniel Loftus's effort to profit from Almanzo and Cap Garland's brave dash to get the wheat into a much more elaborate five-page scenario" (237). Lane's polished version also includes discourse, this time from Pa, about what it means to be free and independent, emphasizing multiple individuals' collective bargaining power against Loftus but never going so far as to overtly suggest a collective stand against the shopkeeper currently in a position of economic dominance. Woodside goes even further: "The Fourth of July story in the published version of *Little Town on the Prairie* goes on for five dramatic pages.... The final portrayal of the Fourth of July reflects Rose's evolving attitudes about individual freedom as being uniquely available in the United States" (128).

WORKS CITED

Anderson, William, ed. *A Little House Reader*. HarperCollins, 1998.
Anderson, William. *The Story of the Wilders*. Anderson Publications, 1983.
Fraser, Caroline. *Prairie Fires: The American Dreams of Laura Ingalls Wilder*. Metropolitan/Henry Holt, 2017.
Hill, Pamela Smith. *Laura Ingalls Wilder: A Writer's Life*. South Dakota Historical Society Press, 2007.
Holtz, William, ed. *Dorothy Thompson and Rose Wilder Lane: Forty Years of Friendship: Letters, 1921–1960*. University of Missouri Press, 1991.
Holtz, William. *The Ghost in the Little House: A Life of Rose Wilder Lane*. University of Missouri Press, 1993.
Lane, Rose Wilder. *The Discovery of Freedom: Man's Struggle against Authority*. John Day, 1943.
Lane, Rose Wilder. *Free Land*. University of Nebraska Press, 1938.
Lane, Rose Wilder. Rose Wilder Lane Papers. Box 16, Folder 2/7. Laura Ingalls Wilder Series, Manuscripts, Notes, and Resource Material, Herbert Hoover Presidential Library-Museum, West Branch, Iowa.
Lane, Rose Wilder. *Young Pioneers*. Harper, 1976.
Lane, Rose Wilder, and Roger Lea MacBride. *Rose Wilder Lane: Her Story*. Stein and Day, 1977.
Miller, John E. *Becoming Laura Ingalls Wilder: The Woman behind the Legend*. University of Missouri Press, 1998.
Moore, Rosa Ann. "Laura Ingalls Wilder and Rose Wilder Lane: The Chemistry of Collaboration." *Children's Literature in Education* 11, no. 3 (September 1980): 101–9.
Moore, Rosa Ann. "Laura Ingalls Wilder's Orange Notebooks and the Art of the Little House Books." *Children's Literature* 4 (1975): 105–19.
Moore, Rosa Ann. "The Little House Books: Rose-Colored Classics." *Children's Literature* 7 (1978): 7–16.
Nikolajeva, Maria. *Reading for Learning: Cognitive Approaches to Children's Literature*. John Benjamins, 2014.
Wilder, Laura Ingalls. *Farmer Boy*. Harper, 1933.
Wilder, Laura Ingalls. *The First Four Years*. Harper, 1971.
Wilder, Laura Ingalls. Laura Ingalls Wilder Papers, folders 4 and 5, Pomona Library.
Wilder, Laura Ingalls. *Little Town on the Prairie*. Harper, 1941.
Wilder, Laura Ingalls. *Pioneer Girl: The Annotated Autobiography*. Edited by Pamela Smith Hill. South Dakota Historical Society Press, 2014.
Wilder, Laura Ingalls. *The Selected Letters of Laura Ingalls Wilder*. Edited by William Anderson. HarperCollins, 2016.
Woodside, Christine. *Libertarians on the Prairie: Laura Ingalls Wilder, Rose Wilder Lane, and the Making of the Little House Books*. Arcade, 2016.
Zochert, Donald. *Laura: The Life of Laura Ingalls Wilder*. Avon, 1976.

THE COMPLICATED POLITICS OF DISABILITY

Reading the Little House Books and Helen Keller

Keri Holt and Christine Cooper-Rompato

Disability plays a central role in Laura Ingalls Wilder's work. Wilder writes about people with physical and cognitive disabilities, including the "idiot boy" she encounters in Iowa, numerous "crippled" or "lame" children, and neighbors and acquaintances disabled by illness or accidents. In the context of disability, Wilder is primarily remembered for the depiction of the blindness of her sister, Mary Ingalls, as a result of viral meningoencephalitis contracted in 1879 and depicted in both Wilder's autobiography, *Pioneer Girl*, and the fictional Little House series (see Allexan et al.). Significant differences emerge, however, in the way Wilder represents Mary's blindness in these two works, and this contrast provides a new framework for examining Wilder's political perspectives.

In *Pioneer Girl*, Mary's blindness is not a dominant part of the story, and her experiences are referenced only briefly. Wilder represents Mary's blindness as a disempowering experience that resigns her to a sedentary and dependent role. In the Little House series, by contrast, Mary's blindness receives more focused attention. Rather than representing Mary as passive, Wilder recasts her as a dynamic, independent person who voices opinions and actively contributes to the household. Instead of representing Mary's blindness as an isolated state of dependence, Wilder describes it as an experience that involves the whole family, rewriting disability in terms of relationships of interaction and interdependence.

Wilder's deliberate revision of the experience of blindness in her fiction marks an important political dimension of her work that critics have not examined. Discussions involving the politics of the Little House series typically focus on Wilder's emphasis on independence and critique of government intervention. As Anita Clair Fellman writes, Wilder's works promote "an individualistic, antistatist perspective [that] contributed to a renaissance in antigovernment thinking" (246), ideas that are often examined in relation to the Libertarian politics of her daughter and coauthor, Rose Wilder Lane. Critics have failed to address the politics of disability in Wilder's work, a surprising oversight given Wilder's attention to Mary's blindness and the growing influence of disability studies in the field of children's literature. As Kathy Saunders writes, "The insight that disability scholars can bring to analysis of children's literature lies in their understanding of 'disability' not as a personalised, wholly biological and medically mediated characteristic, but as a social construction" (4); critics have increasingly pushed scholars to recognize "the potency of children's texts as an agent in creating, preserving and reflecting cultural attitudes" about disabilities (3).

Drawing on the insights of disability studies, this chapter examines the disability politics in Wilder's work, focusing specifically on the way her representation of disability changed between the *Pioneer Girl* manuscript and the published series. Wilder's strategic revision of Mary's blindness becomes particularly compelling when we situate her writing in relation to the political activism surrounding disability in the early twentieth century. As Wilder and her daughter were drafting the Little House series, radical changes were taking place in public perceptions of disability and in the government's role in providing resources. Before the twentieth century, disability was largely viewed as a private issue. Care was relegated to families, churches, or private organizations, and people with disabilities were often kept out of the public eye. In the aftermath of World War I, however, disabilities became more visible as injured veterans returned, resulting in greater public awareness and arguments for government support. During this period, perceptions of disability were also transformed through the work of Helen Keller, whose fame and lifelong activism redefined people with disabilities as active and contributing members of society.

Wilder's fictional representation of Mary aligns in many ways with Keller's arguments, particularly with regard to efforts to promote the agency of people with disabilities and redefine their experiences of dependency. These alignments might seem surprising considering that Wilder and Keller were at opposite ends of the political spectrum. A self-avowed socialist and strident critic of capitalism, Keller's politics differed sharply from those of Wilder. Nevertheless, their efforts to represent the blind as independent, productive individuals reveal a shared engagement with the politics of disability that offers a new lens for considering the cultural and political influence of Wilder's work as well as the complicated consequences of her representations. Wilder's representation of Mary's self-sufficiency aligns with the ideology of independent individualism for which the Little House series is so well known, but the fact that Wilder attributes these qualities to a person with disabilities invites reevaluation of her politics. Drawing attention to Wilder's representation of Mary and to parallels between her writing and Keller's opens new avenues for considering Wilder's work. At the same time, Wilder and Keller's representations of disability are at times somewhat problematic, and their writings also feature some contradictory and limiting dimensions.

In *Pioneer Girl*, Wilder treats Mary's blindness as a factual event in her life rather than a focus for extended attention. She reports the loss of Mary's sight with sympathy, writing that "the last thing Mary ever saw was the bright blue of Grace's eyes as Grace stood holding by her chair, looking up at her" (142). Wilder does not mention Mary's blindness again until the family's departure from Walnut Grove five months later (145). Wilder primarily represents Mary's experiences in terms of loss and limitation—what she can no longer do, such as cooking, sewing, or helping with outdoor chores (183, 186, 213). Instead of actively participating in the household, Mary takes on a sedentary role, sitting "in her big rocking chair in the warmest corner" (178).

In *Pioneer Girl*, Mary remains dependent on family members, who are always doing things "for Mary." Knitting a pair of socks, Wilder comments that she and Ma help Mary with the "hard places" (185); when Mary goes to bed without Laura, Carrie must accompany her oldest sister upstairs (189). Mary's circumstances change when she attends school in Vinton, Iowa, and learns to sew, read Braille, and play the organ. Mary returns home "much happier than when she went away" (295). Despite this brighter disposition, Wilder continues to represent Mary as a solitary figure, mentioning her only a few times in the remainder of the autobiography. When she goes on a short drive with Laura and Almanzo, for example, we are told that Mary "did not care to go far" (302). We never hear what she did care to do.

A different picture of Mary emerges in the Little House series. Lane initially advised cutting references to Mary's blindness because young readers might find it too sad. Wilder, however, insisted on making it prominent: "A touch of tragedy makes the story truer to life and showing the way we all took it illustrates the spirit of the times and the frontier" (qtd. in Hill 35). Wilder's interest in showing "the way we all took it" highlights an important new focus. Instead of representing Mary's blindness as separating her from the rest of the family, Wilder now represents it as an interactive and interdependent experience involving the entire family. This approach may have been influenced by

Wilder's continued engagement with disability through the experiences of her husband, who suffered temporary paralysis and permanent nerve damage after contracting diphtheria in 1888. Almanzo's disability had lasting effects on the Wilders' day-to-day life and likely inspired Laura to represent disability differently in her fiction.

While the Mary of *Pioneer Girl* sits in the rocking chair for much of the book, her fictional counterpart joins in the household work, becoming, as Lois Keith observes, "a vital member of the family" (201). In *The Long Winter*, Wilder describes Mary setting the table by herself: "'I don't need any help,' Mary said happily. 'The cupboard is in a different place, but Ma put all the dishes in the same places in the cupboard, so I find them just as easily as ever'" (72–73). In *Pioneer Girl*, Mary is not allowed to help twist hay for the stove during the terrible winter, and Wilder writes, "Mary had never been strong and we would not let her stay out in the cold storm shed" (213). However, in *The Long Winter*, Laura teaches Mary to twist hay, and the sisters sit side by side, working together. At one point it is so cold, Wilder writes, that "neither could twist more than two or three sticks of hay without going to thaw their hands over the stove" (260). In contrast to the passive figure in *Pioneer Girl*, the Mary of the Little House books says she can "see with her fingers" (*Winter* 146) and becomes an active presence in the Ingalls household. Wilder also emphasizes Mary's independence outside the home: for example, Mary visits the home of her friend, Ida, during college break, and they ride the train by themselves (*Happy* 123–38). Wilder thus transforms Mary's disability into an experience that no longer separates her from society or limits her involvement within it.

Wilder's emphasis on Mary's agency and self-sufficiency makes sense considering the thematic focus of the Little House series, which, as John E. Miller writes, promotes "self-reliance, individual initiative, frugality, hard work, and personal responsibility" (*Laura* 183). But attaching these characteristics to a blind individual takes Wilder's work in a new political direction since in her era, people with disabilities were not typically described in these terms. By associating Mary with the same values of individualism, independence, and self-sufficiency that Wilder credits to her able-bodied characters, Wilder offers a more progressive political agenda than is often attributed to her work. (For further discussions of the politics typically associated with Wilder's work, see Fellman; Hill; Holtz; Woodside.)

Wilder's revised representation of Mary also marks a significant change from traditional representations of disability in children's literature. Disability was a prominent theme in many nineteenth- and early twentieth-century children's books, such as *What Katy Did* (1872), *Heidi* (1881), or *The Secret Garden* (1911), in which children with disabilities largely played symbolic roles as "helpless, pitiable creatures or as saintly invalids" who were meant to serve as moral role models (Dowker 4). Emiliano C. Ayala examines how such depictions were perpetuated by ensuing representations of children with disabilities as "poor little things" and "brave little souls" (104), characterizations that removed them from active engagement with the world and required readers to respond to them solely in terms of sorrow and sympathy.[1]

Wilder's emphasis on Mary's activity and independence diverges from these sentimental stereotypes, and her work largely stands alone in making this shift. The Little House books were published between 1932 and 1943, and although American children's books showed a heightened attention to realism during this period, few represented disabilities; those that did offered "bland depictions of disability with predictable outcomes, one-dimensional characters, and sermon-like content" (Beauchamp, Chung, and Mogilner 56). Not until the 1970s did children's books published in the United States begin to emphasize experiences of disability, largely as a result of the Rehabilitation Act (1973) and the Education for All Handicapped Children Act (1975), which helped integrate children with disabilities into schools. Wilder's early and extended attention to disability thus establishes her as a pioneering voice in the history of children's literature and the politics of disability writ large. (For the history and transformation of disability in children's literature, see Quicke; Beauchamp, Chung, and Mogilner.)

Wilder's transformative revision of Mary's blindness finds a parallel, however, in the work of Helen Keller, whose fame and influence overlapped with the publication of the Little House series. Although it is difficult to determine whether Wilder and Keller ever met, Keller's speeches and activities were covered in Wilder's local newspapers, including the *Mansfield Mirror* and the *Daily Missourian*. Keller traveled throughout Missouri from 1910 through the 1940s and spoke in the towns of Lexington, Columbia, and Mexico, all of which are near Wilder's hometown, Mansfield (Hermann; Lash; Nielsen, *Radical*). Wilder's involvement with Mansfield social clubs likely brought her into contact with Keller's ideas since these groups focused on local speakers and current events (Miller, *Becoming* 114–40; Hill 115–26).

It is difficult to overstate Keller's impact on public views of disability in the late nineteenth and early twentieth centuries. Born in 1880, Keller became deaf and blind as a toddler and rose to fame when she learned to communicate using a manual alphabet with the aid of her lifelong teacher, Anne Sullivan Macy. Keller lived nearly all her life in the public eye, making appearances throughout the United States, publishing books and articles, and eventually serving as the official spokesperson for the American Foundation for the Blind from 1924 to 1964 (see Hermann; Lash; Keller, *Story*).

Keller's political advocacy, particularly her arguments that people with disabilities could live and work successfully in the world of able-bodied individuals, is echoed in Wilder's work. In contrast to prevailing assumptions that deaf and blind individuals were entirely dependent on others, Keller argued that people with disabilities could support themselves in the able-bodied world using modified methods. Describing her experiences attending school "with seeing and hearing girls" at the Cambridge School for Young Ladies and later Radcliffe College, where she graduated cum laude in 1904 (Keller, *Story* 59), Keller took pride in having her academic skills evaluated "by the standards of those who see and hear" (68). Although she acknowledged that her disabilities presented "peculiar difficulties," she averred, "I have the consolation of knowing that I overcame them all" (68).

After graduation, Keller became more vocal in her arguments about the independence and self-sufficiency of deaf and blind individuals. "They do not want to be fed and clothed and housed by other people. They want to work and support themselves," wrote Keller in 1904 ("Our Duties" 39). Keller pushed the public to regard disability not as a lamentable condition of limitation but as an experience of agency: "We know that the blind are not debarred from usefulness solely by their infirmity" ("Unemployed" 22). Instead of characterizing people with disabilities as inferior individuals, Keller asserted "their sense of equality as citizens" ("Fair" 46). "A blind man can do nothing less and nothing more than what a person with five senses can do, minus what can be done only with the eye," wrote Keller ("Our Duties" 43), and these arguments for equality laid the groundwork for more aggressive advocacy for people with disabilities throughout the twentieth century.

Keller's arguments for equality align with Wilder's representation of Mary's agency and self-sufficiency in the Little House books. Like Keller, Wilder insists that Mary's work be treated with equality and respect. When Mary helps with twisting hay, for example, Laura remarks, "it took her some time because she could not see how Laura twisted and held the strands and tucked in the ends, but at last she did it well" (*Winter* 235). Wilder also notes how Mary's disability sometimes enabled her to complete her work faster and more efficiently, as when Mary completes her braided rugs faster than Laura finishes her own sewing: "The dark doesn't bother me," Mary states with pride in her ability to work later hours than her sisters (*Winter* 146). Whereas *The Long Winter* certainly showcases Ma's domestic skills, it also celebrates Mary's ability to flourish in an oppressive climate that daunts the rest of the family.

Keller and Wilder also focus on the close, interdependent relationships that define experiences of disability. Perhaps the greatest transformation between *Pioneer Girl* and the Little House series concerns Wilder's representation of

Mary and Laura's relationship. In *Pioneer Girl*, Wilder notes a few moments when she "told Mary about everything I saw," but this relationship is not a significant focus, and the narrative concentrates primarily on Laura's experiences. In the Little House series, however, Wilder describes a complex relationship of interdependency between Laura and Mary when Laura agrees to serve as Mary's "eyes." Although this might initially seem to be a relationship of dependence, where Mary relies on Laura to represent the world she cannot see, over time, the relationship becomes mutually beneficial. Laura's descriptions help her develop skills as a careful observer (which will aid in Wilder's later career as a writer) as well as perceive the world from different perspectives. Instead of placing Laura and Mary in the hierarchical roles of caretaker and recipient, Wilder shows them engaging on equal terms that continue to reflect their different temperaments and opinions, as evidenced when they disagree about Laura's descriptions of the world around them. At one point, Laura tells Mary, "The road pushes against the grassy land and breaks off short. And that's the end of it." Mary disagrees: "It can't be. . . . [T]he road goes all the way to Silver Lake"; "I don't think you ought to say things like that. . . . [W]e should always be careful to say what we mean" (*Shores* 58). Though Laura and Mary are closely connected and Mary depends on Laura's visual perceptions of the world, they still have very different views of the best way to represent that world. Laura concludes this exchange by drawing attention to the equal value and legitimacy of their views: "I was saying what I meant . . . but she could not explain. There were so many ways of seeing things and so many ways of saying them" (58). Here, Wilder redefines traditional perceptions of dependency by showing how Mary's blindness enables an empowering and collaborative relationship in which Mary and Laura operate as independent individuals who can nevertheless understand, accept, and draw on one another's differences.

These dynamics align closely with Keller's accounts of the interdependent relationships that define the experiences of all people with disabilities. Keller depended on people who could use the manual alphabet to communicate, and for most of her life, this role was filled by Macy, who served as Keller's teacher, collaborator, and companion. Keller was candid about her dependence: "My teacher is so near to me that I scarcely think of myself apart from her," she wrote. "How much of my delight in all beautiful things is innate, and how much is due to her influence, I can never tell. I feel that her being is inseparable from my own and that the footsteps of my life are in hers" (*Story* 27; see also Hermann 115–23, 189–93, 245–48).

The closeness of this relationship, however, often undermined Keller's claims of independence and self-sufficiency, and critics argued that Keller's ideas and accomplishments represented the work of her teacher rather than her own. Addressing this criticism, Keller challenged her audiences to revise their understanding of dependency: "I have heard that some people think the views I am expressing on this subject, and indeed on all subjects, are not my own, but Miss Sullivan's" ("Our Duties" 38), and she asked her critics to evaluate her relationship with Macy the way one would evaluate a person with healthy vision and hearing: "I express ideas which I have been fortunate enough to gather from other wise sources from the books I have read, from the friends with whom I talk, even from the poets, the prophets, and the sages. It is not strange that some of my ideas come from the wise one with whom I am most intimate and to whom I owe all that I am. I rejoice for myself and for you if Miss Sullivan's ideas are commingled with mine" (38). Here, Keller recasts her dependency as a condition that enables her to exercise her own authority and agency. Even though she depends on Macy for information, she is not a passive recipient but retains the ability to evaluate and use these ideas on her own terms—an argument that Wilder similarly conveys through her representation of Mary's relationship with Laura. Keller takes her argument a step further by insisting that her process of acquiring information through Macy is no different than the way able-bodied individuals consult books and advisers. If able-bodied people can without question form credible and independent views under the influence of other sources, then deaf and blind people should be granted the same agency.

Like Wilder, Keller emphasized how relationships with people with disabilities could be productive and mutually beneficial. Keller's descriptions of her interactions with Macy characterize both women as active, contributing participants, and Keller's writings consistently describe their relationship as collaborative: "I saw more clearly than ever before how inseparably our lives were bound together," wrote Keller (*Midstream* 143).² Rather than presenting her dependence as a sign of weakness or inferiority, Keller recasts their relationship as an equal and productive partnership, and Keller's empowering representation of dependency provides an important framework for evaluating Wilder's revision of Mary's dependent relationships in the Little House series. Keller's success in transforming the way the public viewed her dependence on Macy is evident in the way popular magazines covered their relationship, with John Albert Macy writing in the *Ladies' Home Journal*, "The two are naturally responsive, they stimulate each other" (October, 12) and "Miss Sullivan says that both she and Miss Keller remember 'in their fingers' what they have said" (November, 11).

Keller showed that she could cultivate productive relationships with many people, redefining her dependencies as experiences that promoted action rather than passivity. In describing the many friends to whom she is "deeply indebted," Keller concludes, "In a thousand ways they have turned my limitations into beautiful privileges, and enabled me to walk serene and happy" (*Story* 101). Rather than reinforcing her limitations, Keller's dependent relationships provide opportunities for movement and agency. Revising public perceptions of the dependencies that define the lives of people with disabilities, Keller, like Wilder, made it possible for audiences to recognize people with disabilities as active and influential participants in the world. Furthermore, as Keller often remarked in her lectures, this collaborative and generative understanding of dependency had benefits not just for people with disabilities but for the general public: "Alone we can do so little," she often stated at the end of her performances, "together we can do so much" (Lash 489).

A final parallel between Keller's and Wilder's work concerns their persistent optimism. Keller and Wilder transformed the prevailing pre-twentieth-century representations of disabilities as debilitating forms of loss by refusing to portray people with disabilities as pitiable victims and representing their experiences in positive terms. Keller led the way in promoting this affirmative outlook, believing that optimism was the best way to depict disability as offering action and opportunity. "Optimism is the faith that leads to achievement," wrote Keller (*Optimism* 67). "If I regarded my life from the point of view of the pessimist, I should be undone. I should seek in vain for the light that does not visit my eyes and the music that does not ring in my ears. . . . But since I consider it a duty to myself and to others to be happy, I escape a misery worse than any physical deprivation" (54). Keller's optimism became one of the most recognizable features of her activism, and this positive attitude was instrumental in garnering support for her causes, particularly when she became the spokesperson for the American Foundation for the Blind.

Wilder likewise represented disability in optimistic terms, using rhetorical strategies similar to Keller's. Throughout the Little House books, Mary retains an upbeat attitude about her blindness. She always responds to her challenges "cheerfully" and "brightly." As Laura describes her, "Her face was so serene . . . and her voice so gay that she did not seem to be walking in darkness" (*Town* 11). Rather than express sorrow about the things she cannot do, Mary faces these moments "happily" and focuses on her ability to engage in alternative activities, such as tending her younger sisters or sewing (*Winter* 73). "She had never cried," reports Laura in *By the Shores of Silver Lake*, "she was still patient and brave" (2). This positive attitude becomes a source of admiration for those around her. "Mary is a great comfort to me . . . She has never once repined," Ma tells Rev. Alden later in the book, to which Alden replies, "Mary is a rare soul and lesson to us all" as a consequence of her ability to "turn [her] afflictions to good" (217).

These optimistic representations of disability have drawn criticism from contemporary scholars and activists, particularly in regard to Keller's work.

By representing disability as a celebratory "triumph over adversity," writes Kim Nielsen, Keller's activism becomes "mired in the performance and ideology of perpetually overcoming her disability," an argument that limits discussions of disability to the accomplishments of specific individuals rather than advocating for people with disabilities as a collective group ("Helen Keller" 283). Others argue that Keller's perpetual optimism obscures the difficulties of disability that need to be publicly addressed. Keller's positive rhetoric, writes Liz Crow, presents disability through "an image of super-human attainment ... with all the complications and compromises tippexed out" (853). By failing to recognize or accurately represent the challenges associated with disability, Keller's positive attitude does not create conditions for strengthening the rights of people with disabilities, particularly with regard to equalizing forms of access and educational support. (For the problematic politics of Keller's work, see Nielsen, *Radical*; Kleege; Crow; Kudlick.)

Wilder seems to have been aware of the drawbacks of the optimistic approach. As much as Mary exemplifies Keller's idealized optimism, Wilder complicates her characterization of the fictional Mary's sunny disposition by having her sister admit that she is not always cheerful about her condition. In *Little Town on the Prairie*, Laura and Mary go for a walk and discuss Mary's "goodness," and Mary confesses that she often has negative feelings: "If you could see how rebellious and mean I feel sometimes, if you could see what I really am, inside, you wouldn't want to be like me" (11). Mary's reference to "rebellious" feelings is noteworthy since it suggests that Mary did at times feel constrained by her disability and desire to push back against the expectations that shaped her experiences. This moment marks a compelling departure by acknowledging that Mary's positive attitude is to some extent a performance that masks harsher realities.

Wilder does not dwell on this moment. Mary and Laura's conversation quickly returns to the importance of being "good" despite these challenges, and they end their discussion by reasserting their faith in "the goodness of God" (*Town* 12). Nevertheless, this exchange provides realistic insight into Mary's struggles. Juxtaposing Mary's performance of optimism with her real feelings of anger and rebellion, Wilder acknowledges the limitations of representing disability solely through feelings of hope and good cheer. Even though Mary's optimism proves constructive in enabling her action and independence, Wilder also recognizes that optimism obscures some challenging realities.

Keller and Wilder unquestionably broke new ground in asserting the agency, self-sufficiency, and equality of people with disabilities as well as in redefining their relationships of interdependency, but the legacy of their representations remains complicated. A case in point concerns their positions regarding state and private support. Both Keller and Mary received funding and educational resources provided by the government or private donors to people with disabilities. However, Keller and Wilder took pains to distance themselves from this support in their writings to avoid undermining their arguments about independence and self-sufficiency. Throughout her life, Keller insisted that she could support herself through her work as a professional speaker and writer, but the expenses associated with her disabilities, which included supporting her teacher and subsequent companions, were a continual source of hardship. At various points, she accepted financial support from philanthropists such as Andrew Carnegie but went to great lengths to downplay this assistance. She never spoke of these grants publicly and often made a great show of refusing them, only to quietly accept them later while continuing to assert her ability to support herself (Hermann 108–9, 168–71). This emphasis on personal independence often conflicted with Keller's public advocacy. Throughout her life, she argued for state-sponsored resources for people with disabilities, but she carefully disassociated herself from any direct involvement with these programs, choosing to emphasize her independent accomplishments. Keller's decision to obscure or limit her relationship to external resources did little to promote public services during her lifetime. As Kleege observes, Keller's self-focused arguments served to "increase the visibility of people with disabilities but g[a]ve them no real authority" (108). By failing to associate herself with any form of state or private support, Keller did little to support people with disabilities as a collective group.

Like Keller, Wilder also distanced her experiences with disability from any public forms of assistance. In the Little House books, Wilder stresses that the members of the Ingalls family managed Mary's blindness on their own. Wilder represents Mary's education as paid for solely by the family and emphasizes the sacrifices made to support Mary's education, including when Pa decides to sell the family's calf after blackbirds destroy the corn crop (*Town* 106–7). In reality, Mary's enrollment at the Iowa College of the Blind was entirely funded by a government tuition grant. At $216 per year, the out-of-state tuition was unaffordable for the Ingalls family, and they applied to the South Dakota territorial government for financial support in 1881. Because South Dakota did not have its own schools for the blind, the territorial legislature appropriated funds to educate its blind residents in other states, and the state covered the tuition costs for Mary's entire education, leaving the Ingalls family responsible only for her transportation and clothing (Hill 58; Fellman 80; Koupal).

Wilder and Lane deliberately cut any reference to this state support in the Little House books, a decision that allowed them to reinforce the ideology of independence and individualism and the opposition to government intervention that were central to the series and to Lane's evolving politics. Wilder's refusal to acknowledge this support, however, obscures an important and necessary dimension of the family's experience with disability that enabled Mary to achieve precisely the independence and agency that Wilder goes on to celebrate. Like Keller, Wilder believed she needed to distance her representation of disability from any association with external support to protect her arguments about independence and self-sufficiency, but this distancing has problematic effects, particularly with regard to illuminating the interdependent relationships that define the experiences of those with disabilities.

Ironically, Keller's and Wilder's efforts to downplay reliance on state and private forms of support came at a time when government resources and social services for people with disabilities were expanding. As disabilities became more visible following the two world wars, considerable growth occurred in state-sponsored schools and programs providing education and vocational training for those with physical and mental disabilities as well as in institutions designed to provide housing and daily care. As Nielsen writes, between 1900 and 1950, "the management of disability became increasingly built into national structures" (*History* 99), and by transforming disability from a private "problem" into a central concern for the state, these developments helped promote equality for people with disabilities in ways that were more effective than Keller's and Wilder's narratives of personal triumph.

Keller is a complicated figure whose legacy is defined by contradictions. As we situate Wilder within disability studies, similar conclusions about her work will surely arise. Like Keller, Wilder drew attention to the equality and agency of people with disabilities without necessarily modeling effective forms of political advocacy or promoting collective rights. However, the fact that Wilder chose to engage with disability in the context of children's literature marks an interesting difference. Directed toward young audiences, children's literature plays a powerful role in transforming cultural ideas and attitudes. As John Stephens writes, "While children's literature is immensely enjoyable as art, it is also immensely powerful as ideology" (8), and scholars have noted how "children's literature can be instrumental in changing readers' attitudes about stereotypes" (Adomat 9; for more on the politics of children's literature, see Clark; Murray; McGillis). Addressing children and transforming the way children view disability, the Little House books take Keller's ideas in a new direction by targeting audiences of the present as well as of the future. In doing so, the Little House series argues for political change by encouraging young readers to reflect on characters such as Mary and find better ways to address the abilities and needs of individuals with disabilities as they grow up and enter the public sphere. Wilder's focus on personal independence might seem to undercut arguments for greater civil rights or state support for people with disabilities. Nevertheless, her characterization of Mary for young audiences suggests a bolder argument for political change than critics have acknowledged. While Wilder may not overtly promote political change, by writing for children, she may inspire readers to promote political change. Wilder's engagement with the politics of disability is decidedly complex. Nonetheless, much may be gained from this avenue of inquiry, particularly regarding the long-term political and cultural effects of Wilder's work on public perceptions of disability.

NOTES

1. Dowker notes that in some cases, disabilities were also represented as a form of "spiritual discipline" where bad children were punished by a debilitating affliction (2). For more on sentimental representations of children with disabilities, see Hughes; Keith; Rubin and Watson.

2. Cressman examines Keller and Macy's interdependent relationship in detail, describing it as a "collaborative consciousness" that benefited both (21). See also Kleege.

WORKS CITED

Adomat, Donna Sayers. "Exploring Issues of Disability in Children's Literature Discussions." *Disability Studies Quarterly* 34, no. 3 (2014): 9–19.

Allexan, Sarah S., Carrie L. Byington, Jerome I. Finkelstein, and Beth A. Tarini. "Blindness in Walnut Grove: How Did Mary Ingalls Lose Her Sight?" *Pediatrics* 131, no. 3 (2013): 404–6.

Ayala, Emiliano C. "'Poor Little Things' and 'Brave Little Souls': The Portrayal of Individuals with Disabilities in Children's Literature." *Reading Research and Instruction* 39, no. 1 (1999): 103–17.

Beauchamp, Miles, Wendy Chung, and Alijandra Mogilner. *Disabled Literature: A Critical Examination of the Portrayals of Individuals with Disabilities in Selected Works of Modern and Contemporary American Literature.* BrownWalker, 2015.

Clark, Beverly Lyon. *Kiddie Lit: The Cultural Construction of Children's Literature.* Johns Hopkins University Press, 2005.

Cressman, Jodi. "Helen Keller and the Mind's Eyewitness." *Western Humanities Review* 54, no. 2 (2000): 108–23.

Crow, Liz. "Helen Keller: Rethinking the Problematic Icon." *Disability and Society* 15, no. 6 (2000): 845–59.

Dowker, Ann. "The Treatment of Disability in 19th and Early 20th Century Children's Literature." *Disability Studies Quarterly* 24, no. 1 (2004): 1–8.

Fellman, Anita Clair. *Little House, Long Shadow: Laura Ingalls Wilder's Impact on American Culture.* University of Missouri Press, 2008.

Hermann, Dorothy. *Helen Keller: A Life*. Knopf, 1998.
Hill, Pamela Smith. *Laura Ingalls Wilder: A Writer's Life*. South Dakota State Historical Society Press, 2007.
Holtz, William. *The Ghost in the Little House: A Life of Rose Wilder Lane*. University of Missouri Press, 1993.
Hughes, Chloe. "Seeing Blindness in Children's Picture Books." *Journal of Literary and Cultural Disability Studies* 6, no. 1 (2012): 35–51.
Keith, Lois. *Take Up Thy Bed and Walk: Death, Disability, and Cure in Classic Fiction for Girls*. Routledge, 2001.
Keller, Helen. "A Fair Chance to be Independent and Self-Respecting and Useful." February 1915. In Nielsen, 45–47.
Keller, Helen. *Midstream: My Later Life*. In Nielsen, *Helen Keller*, 126–46. .
Keller, Helen. *Optimism: An Essay*. Merrymount, 1903.
Keller, Helen. "Our Duties to the Blind." 1904. In Nielsen, *Helen Keller*, 37–44.
Keller, Helen. *The Story of My Life*. 1904. Bantam, 2005.
Keller, Helen. "The Unemployed." *Zeigler Magazine for the Blind*. 1911. In *Helen Keller: Rebel Lives*, edited by John Davis, 20–23. Ocean Press, 2003.
Kleege, Georgina. "The Helen Keller Who Still Matters." *Raritan* 42, no. 1 (2004): 100–112.
Koupal, Nancy Tystad. "Mary Ingalls Goes to School." *The Pioneer Girl Project*. pioneergirl-project.org.
Kudlick, Catherine J. "The Outlook of *The Problem* and the Problem with *The Outlook*: Two Advocacy Journals Reinvent Blind People in Turn-of-the-Century America." In Longmore and Umansky, 187–213.
Lash, Joseph P. *Helen and Teacher: The Story of Helen Keller and Anne Sullivan Macy*. Delacorte, 1980.
Longmore, Paul K., and Lauri Umansky, eds. *The New Disability History: American Perspectives*. New York University Press, 2001.
Macy, John Albert. "Helen Keller as She Really Is." *Ladies' Home Journal*, October 1902, 11–12, 40, November 1902, 11–12, 55.
McGillis, Roderick. *The Nimble Reader: Literary Theory and Children's Literature*. Twayne, 1996.
Miller, John E. *Becoming Laura Ingalls Wilder: The Woman behind the Legend*. University of Missouri Press, 1998.
Miller, John E. *Laura Ingalls Wilder and Rose Wilder Lane: Authorship, Place, Time, and Culture*. University of Missouri Press, 2008.
Murray, Gail Schmunk. *American Children's Literature and the Construction of Childhood*. Twayne, 1998.
Nielsen, Kim. *A Disability History of the United States*. Beacon, 2013.
Nielsen, Kim. "Helen Keller and the Politics of Civic Fitness" In Longmore and Umansky, 268–90.
Nielsen, Kim, ed. *Helen Keller: Selected Writings*. New York University Press, 2005.
Nielsen, Kim. *The Radical Lives of Helen Keller*. New York University Press, 2009.
Quicke, John. *Disability in Modern Children's Fiction*. Croom Helm, 1985.
Rubin, Ellen, and Emily Strauss Watson. "Disability Bias in Children's Literature." *The Lion and the Unicorn* 11, no. 1 (1987): 60–67.
Saunders, Kathy. "What Disability Studies Can Do for Children's Literature." *Disability Studies Quarterly* 24, no. 1 (2004): 1–14.

Stephens, John. *Language and Ideology in Children's Fiction*. Longman, 1992.
Wilder, Laura Ingalls. *By the Shores of Silver Lake*. 1939. Harper and Row, 1971.
Wilder, Laura Ingalls. *Little Town on the Prairie*. 1941. Harper and Row, 1971.
Wilder, Laura Ingalls. *The Long Winter*. 1940. Harper and Row, 1971.
Wilder, Laura Ingalls. *Pioneer Girl: The Annotated Autobiography*. Edited by Pamela Smith Hill. South Dakota Historical Society Press, 2014.
Wilder, Laura Ingalls. *These Happy Golden Years*. Harper and Row, 1971.
Woodside, Christine. *Libertarians on the Prairie: Laura Ingalls Wilder, Rose Wilder Lane, and the Making of the Little House Books*. Arcade, 2016.

Part 2
WILDER AND CONSTRUCTIONS OF GENDER

NAKED HORSES ON THE PRAIRIE

Laura Ingalls Wilder's Imagined Anglo-Indian Womanhood

Vera R. Foley

The specter of Indian hostility looms large in Laura Ingalls Wilder's depiction of 1870s Kansas Territory in *Little House on the Prairie*. In the Osage Diminished Reserve, where Laura and her family are illegal intruders, violence seems imminent, especially to her mother, who repeatedly asserts, "I don't like Indians around underfoot" (Wilder, *Prairie* 229). For six-year-old Laura, this hostility is balanced by the potential that she sees for liberty in the nomadic lifestyle of her Indian neighbors. While Laura does not identify with Osage chief Soldat du Chêne as a fellow patriarch the way Pa does, she recognizes his access to freedom and mobility and sees these qualities not as alien but as fundamentally American attributes to which she also aspires. For Laura, the "happy pony" that has lent him its allegiance embodies the Osage leader's freedom and integrity (305). Much of Laura's elaborate description of du Chêne is, in fact, focused on his wild steed: "His black pony came trotting willingly, sniffing the wind that blew its mane and tail like fluttering banners. The pony's nose and head were free; it wore no bridle.... There was nothing to make it do anything it didn't want to do" (304). For the girl who hates to wear shoes and loves to let her sunbonnet "dangle down her back" (174), the Indian pony's mobility and seeming evasion of the trappings of servitude have a profound appeal.

Wilder's ongoing efforts to explain her heroine's preference for outdoor, active femininity in terms of Native cultural mores complicate what might otherwise be read as a traditional narrative of feminine acculturation in the

Little House series. Laura's fantasy of prairie femininity emerges in opposition to what Susan Naramore Maher calls "the walls and borders of civility" (113), which persist in Ma's parenting throughout the series. Wilder articulates Laura's rebellion against Ma's restrictive domesticity through a purposeful focus on equestrian liberty that emerges in *Little House on the Prairie* and recurs throughout the rest of the series.

Horses and the emotional bonds that Laura forms with them represent the gateway to a new American womanhood that Wilder constructs for Laura, one grounded in Native American iconography. From her first glimpse of the migrating Osage tribe in Kansas, "Laura was excited about the ponies" (*Prairie* 306). As with her illustration of du Chêne, which lingers lovingly on his "happy pony," her description of the rest of the Osage riders carefully enumerates the "black ponies, bay ponies, gray and brown and spotted ponies" that fill the trail across the prairie (306).[1] While more than a decade passes before Laura realizes that she may marry (a future that would have been obvious to her mother), Wilder's heroine is quick to imagine emotional alliances with "naked" Indian horses who wear neither saddle nor bridle (305). This predilection aligns Wilder's depiction of Laura with what Mary Trachsel calls the "girl-meets-horse story" (22), in which horses provide "a safe space apart from the culture of romance, in which girls can recognize and develop an authentic self" (34). Laura's emotional allegiance with the horses of Kansas Territory is doubly significant because of the intercultural solidarity that this connection allows her to imagine with their riders.

Although Wilder's depiction of feminine coming of age on the frontier is by no means egalitarian in its depiction of Native Americans, it does share significant commonalities with narratives by Native authors such as Charles Alexander Eastman, Zitkála-Šá, and especially Mourning Dove. The value that Wilder seems to see in such narratives, particularly the profound sympathy that Mourning Dove suggests may exist between girl and horse, indicates that Wilder was not, as scholars such as Frances W. Kaye, Sharon Smulders, and Bethany Schneider have argued, intentionally working to subvert Native rhetoric. Instead, by emphasizing perfect freedom on horseback—"going like music," "sailing over waves of rushing air," and so forth (*Shores* 53–54)—Wilder emulates the language that Zitkála-Šá and Mourning Dove use to depict idealized moments of unfettered youthful freedom on the frontier. Wilder uses these tropes to disrupt Ma's constrictive ideas about Anglo-American feminine propriety and reconstitute Laura not as unfeminine but instead as a cultural innovator whose enthusiasm for the bond she sees between the Osage riders and their naked horses reflects a capacity for emotional partnership.

The Osage mounts that Laura covets recur throughout the Little House series in the form of the black ponies of Silver Lake, Almanzo Wilder's driving horses in De Smet, and the gray mare, Trixy, who becomes emblematic of the freedom Laura finds in marriage. These echoes of the riders of Indian Territory repeatedly act as catalysts that help her express her values and desires as an "independent" Anglo-American girl coming of age on a transforming frontier. Historically, scholars have rightly read Wilder's depiction of the Osage Indians in *Little House on the Prairie* as symptomatic of the colonialist impulse that led the Ingalls family to settle in Indian Territory. As Ann Romines points out, when Laura demands that her father "give" her an Indian papoose, her "assertive, imperative, desirous demand for the baby taps an impulse that her Euro-American upbringing has offered no way for a girl to express" (78). In other words, Laura has no cultural tools through which to relate to this Native American child in a manner not reliant on racial hierarchy. Donna M. Campbell expands on this reading, arguing that Laura's labeling the object of her desire "a 'papoose,' not a baby" clearly demonstrates a "gesture of appropriation" that "follows logically from Pa's earlier racialized objectification" of such children (116). Similarly, Smulders worries that Laura understands the Osage papoose in terms of animal iconography, as a "fawn" rather than a person (194). Even Philip Heldrich, who reads *Little House on the Prairie* as Wilder's retrospective critique of her parents' "individualism and ethnocentric, racist behavior," admits that "she never fully recognized the Indians as human equals" (103, 106). The Osages are, for Wilder's purposes, symbols of perfect liberty as opposed to people in their own right.[2]

If Wilder's interest is not in representing authentic Indian experience, literary scholars must examine the purpose of including du Chêne and his people in the text. As Smulders points out, because the "real" Laura Ingalls was only three when her family illegally settled in Indian Territory, *Little House on the Prairie* "relies, more than the other volumes in the series, on imagination rather than memory" (192).[3] Heldrich, Pamela Smith Hill, and John E. Miller, among others, have traced Wilder's efforts to find a historical figure onto whom she could project her vision of du Chêne. Unfortunately, Wilder's identification of this man is entirely false. The real du Chêne "sat for his portrait in Philadelphia in the early 1800s" and was long dead by the time the Ingalls family arrived in Kansas (Hill 13 n. 28). It seems clear in light of such narrative liberties that Wilder's purpose in introducing du Chêne and his people is not to establish a historical record of events in Kansas Territory; rather, she uses such figures to signify aspects of her own emotional and psychological experience as a young girl caught between the influence of a genteel mother and an unstable frontier.

Whether such creative flights constitute cultural appropriation or a gesture toward genuine albeit limited cultural exchange remains open to debate. Miller, while acknowledging "Wilder's slighting of American Indians" in her fiction, emphasizes the celebrated passage in her published 1894 diary, *On the Way*

Home (24), in which she says of a former Indian territory near the Missouri River, "If I had been the Indians, I would have scalped more white folk before I ever would have left it" (320). Miller claims that Wilder retrospectively "transcended the standard prejudices and attitudes of the time," overtly aligning herself with oppressed Natives rather than with the colonialist enterprise of her parents (320). This stance is by no means inevitable; unlike the Little House series, *Pioneer Girl*, Wilder's original nonfictional record of her frontier coming of age, is an adult's recounting of the many anxieties attendant to a "timid" Anglo-American girl's experience on the edge of "civilization" (153). In *Pioneer Girl*'s depiction of Indian Territory, Wilder describes herself and her sister as "two scared little mites" cowering before their Native neighbors (11). For *Little House on the Prairie*, however, Wilder rewrote young Laura as the fierce child who "didn't move" or flinch under the gaze of Indian intruders though "her heart jumped in her throat" (140). Fictional Laura's bravery in the face of the Native denizens of the prairie foreshadows her growing affinity for racing ponies and sunburned skin. Further, it suggests Wilder's desire to utilize her perception of Indian mores to define her own version of American womanhood, in many ways so different from that of her more conservative mother.

"RIDING THOSE GAY PONIES": NAKED HORSES ON THE PRAIRIE

Tracing Wilder's equestrian imagery throughout the series reveals her larger narrative scope: the integration of fantasies of "Indian" freedom into her Anglo-American adulthood. In reality, such freedoms were rapidly eroding. By the time the fictional Ingalls family reached Indian Territory in approximately 1873, Westward Expansion was well under way. As turn-of-the-century Indian memoirs repeatedly noted, the frontier was by this time comparatively crowded. *Little House on the Prairie* is, of course, controversial in that it represents the Ingalls family's illegal occupation of lands still reserved for Indian use. The Homestead Act of 1862 and other legislation pushed reservations ever farther west, a circumstance that provokes Kaye to allude to Laura Ingalls as the "Little Squatter on the Osage Diminished Reserve." As the century progressed, Indian tribes were subjected to injurious legislation such as the Dawes Act of 1887, which eroded tribes' collective right to ancestral lands.[4] The Osages' decision "to sell their lands in Kansas and move to a new reservation in Indian Territory, which is now part of Oklahoma" (Hill 15 n. 28), represented an attempt to avoid precisely this situation. For Anglo-Americans and Indians alike, the postbellum West was growing ever smaller.

Wilder's reconstruction of a girlhood spent on the shrinking American frontier distinctly resembles earlier literary works that rely on a Native protagonist's connection to animals and the natural world more broadly. Popularized by Zitkála-Šá and Eastman, among others, at the beginning of the new century, Native American memoirs regularly associate childhood with unfettered liberty, with both boys and girls reveling in their "wild freedom and overflowing spirits" (Zitkála-Šá 8). At the same time, these narratives of Native freedom repeatedly acknowledge the looming constraints of adulthood, a state that reflects the oppressive controls imposed by colonizing influences. In language typical of the genre, Zitkála-Šá describes the days she spent racing her shadow on the prairie or communing with "a little ground squirrel" (36). She then juxtaposes this youthful frontier experience with the restrictions imposed by the "tightly fitting clothes" and rigid daily schedule of her boarding school days, which render her "only one of many little animals driven by a herder" (53, 56). Likewise, Eastman's account of his time as a "chil[d] of the wilderness" (4), "capable of holding extended conversations in an unknown dialect with birds and red squirrels" (8), incorporates the same outdoor imagery that Laura attributes to the Osage riders.

Reading the Little House books alongside such Indian coming-of-age narratives reveals Wilder's interest in constructing her own frontier genesis in similar terms. Schneider has gone so far as to call *Little House on the Prairie* a "cannibal" text that mines Zitkála-Šá's authentic frontier narrative for content and repurposes such material in the form of a "settler-colonial" plot (65–66). In more diplomatic terms, Romines notes that "Wilder joined a tradition that had persisted for at least several generations in the United States, that of children's literature responding to non-Indian children's interest in Native American cultures" (64). Unlike Zitkála-Šá's narrative, however, Wilder's novels utilize such iconography in symbolic rather than historical terms. Critiquing Wilder's description of "ponies [that] did not have to wear bridles or saddles" (*Prairie* 307), Smulders cites Donald Zochert's reference to "another Kansas settler" of the same period, Eliza Wyckoff, who describes the Osages as having "saddle-trees with sheepskin over them to ride on" (qtd. in Smulders 201 n. 16). Such an innovation would make sense, particularly in light of the Osages' frequent relocations. A saddletree protects a horse's back, allowing it to travel farther and bear heavier loads without injury. Wilder, constructing literary imagery rather than recalling actual experience, is more invested in casting the ponies and their riders as symbols of liberty than in conveying cultural accuracy.

Far from seeing this creative license as cultural appropriation, Wilder emphasizes the value that Laura sees in Indian versions of domesticity, which often take place in her preferred outdoor environment. As Maher has noted, "Laura coarsens up" during the time she and her family spend in Kansas Territory, and her "cultural allegiances blur" (133). The constrictions of shoes and sunbonnets that routinely plague Laura do not apply to the Osage children. Indeed, before she retreats into what Romines calls the "Euro-American" colonialist discourse that allows (and perhaps even encourages) her to imagine possessing not just the ponies but their papoose passenger as well (78), "she had a naughty wish to be a little Indian girl" herself (*Prairie* 307). In this reversed model of cultural exchange, Laura imagines herself participating in an alternative form of American childhood that seems to offer more freedom than does her own. While her "civilized" persona reasserts itself and she concedes, "Of course she did not really mean it" (307), Laura continues to search throughout the series for moments in which she feels, as she believes these Indian children do, "naked in the wind and the sunshine, and riding one of those gay little ponies" (307). Her imagined capacity to ride the prairie reflects a strategic design on Wilder's part. By clinging to the memory of the naked ponies and the freedom they represent, adolescent Laura demonstrates that she has not given up her childhood fantasies of freedom to become a mature, married woman like her mother. Instead, Wilder explains Laura's decision to marry Almanzo Wilder, the tamer of wild horses, as an action in keeping with her love of liberty rather than as what Smulders calls "a final emphatic rejection of the Indian and his appeal" (199–200).

"LIKE PRAIRIE BIRDS": LAURA'S DAY OF INDIAN LIBERTY

Soon after she and her family reach the South Dakota prairie, thirteen-year-old Laura encounters a sight that will remain with her for the rest of her life: two young riders who "rode crouching, their hair streaming back, their hands clutched in the flying black manes and their brown legs clasping the ponies' sides. The ponies curved and swerved, clashing each other on the prairie like birds in the sky. Laura would never have tired of watching them" (*Shores* 52). A reader could be excused for believing these fearless children to be Indians, with their wild hair, "brown" skin, and whooping cries of "Hi! Yi! Yi, yi, yee-ee!" (47). But these riders are Lena and Jean, the stepchildren of Laura's Aunt Docia.[5] While Laura is not allowed to so much as hold the reins of her father's driving horses lest they run away, her cousins, like the Indian children of Kansas, traverse the prairie without any fetters for their black ponies. Lena does not worry about becoming "brown as an Indian,"[6] one of Ma's recurring anxieties about Laura. Far from fretting about the need to renounce such unladylike behavior when she grows up, Lena declares, "I'm not ever going to get married, or if I do, I'm going to marry a railroader and keep on moving west as long as I live" (*Shores* 50). Here, Laura encounters a conception of American wifehood that capitalizes on rather than rejects her "naughty wish to be an Indian girl." Learning that a frontier girl named Lizzie has married at thirteen, Laura "soberly" reflects, "she can't play any more now" (*Shores* 50). Ma's example of patient indoor labor and uncomplaining devotion to domestic tasks has given Laura the impression that her temperament is incompatible with marriage. In Lena's imagination, however, romantic attachment need not impede "good times" (50).

Lena's experience of American girlhood appeals tremendously to Laura. When her cousins at last offer her a ride on one of the spirited black ponies, she finds herself awash in conflicting sensations: riding the "warm, slippery, moving mass of pony" is like "sailing over waves in rushing air"; yet at the same time, "the jolting rattle[s] her teeth" painfully (*Shores* 53–54). Far from retreating from this sensory onslaught, Laura concludes, "That was a wonderful afternoon" (54). Tellingly, the things that make it "wonderful" contrast significantly with other, more staid, moments of pleasure Wilder depicts in the novel. Riding the black ponies, Laura acquires a bloody nose; "her hair came unbraided and her throat grew hoarse from laughing and screeching, and her legs were scratched from running through the sharp grass and trying to leap onto her pony while it was running" (54). These physical realities pale before the sensation of perfect liberty that the galloping pony offers: "They were going like music and nothing could happen to her until the music stopped" (54). For a girl whose family has repeatedly encountered tragedy (Laura's sister, Mary, has gone blind and her family has fled Minnesota in poverty), this feeling of invulnerability is nothing short of miraculous.

Wilder ensures that echoes of the Osage riders of Kansas Territory remain conspicuous to readers of *By the Shores of Silver Lake*. When Ma sees the "scratched," bloodied visage of her second daughter, she immediately identifies the kind of liberty Laura has gained: "I don't know when Laura's looked so like a wild Indian" (54, 55). Because the sensations of "sailing" and "jolting" are so overtly physical, Ma believes that they require policing. Unlike Laura, Ma perceives as illicit what Trachsel pointedly calls "physically 'consummating'" the desire to ride a spirited pony (33). Laura, however, understands that she has not given up a part of herself but has instead gained something crucial: "a sense of agency" unavailable to many adolescent girls (Trachsel 34).

Such agency reflects the most obvious intersection between Wilder's Little House books and the Native American literature that preceded them. Although we cannot know which specific texts Wilder may have encountered, the commonalities her fiction shares with Native American representations of the last decades of the frontier are difficult to dismiss. In 1927, Mourning Dove, an Okanogan Indian from Washington State, used language very close to what Wilder later developed in *By the Shores of Silver Lake* to describe her Native American heroine Cogewea's almost spiritual connection to the American horizon, which she invariably experiences on horseback. Mourning Dove's semiautobiographical novel, *Cogewea: The Half-Blood*, describes a mixed-race Montana frontierswoman who must reconcile her love of liberty with the conflicting mores of the two cultures she inhabits. Like Laura, who loves to be "going like music" on Lena's black pony, "Cogewea's impulse was to be going, going, going," on the back of her "outlaw" steed, Wanawish (22, 23). In the saddle of her "bunch-grass cayuse," Cogewea narrates, "the whole universe is chock full of time; with all eternity awaiting us just over the Border" (22–23).

Mourning Dove emphasizes the unique freedoms available to her heroine on a small, hardy Indian steed, a "cayuse," as opposed to the thoroughbreds favored by white ranchers. Like Wilder, this Native author links American patriotism with the visceral connection to the natural world American readers commonly associated with Indian sensibilities. Creating a local Fourth of July celebration for her fictional Montana community, which includes both a "ladies' race" for the white, female population of the Great Cattle Range and a "squaw race" for their Indian counterparts, Mourning Dove gives herself the opportunity to represent the connection between her heroine's equestrian prowess and her authentic American roots. Cogewea considers it her right to ride in both Independence Day races—and wins both, once on the "brag thoroughbred," Diamond, and again on White Star, "the plumb good cayuse" who "moves like a shootin' sky-meteor" (58, 57). Like Wilder's imagined Osages, who sport head-dresses decorated with "eagle feathers" (*Prairie* 305), Mourning Dove's Cogewea adorns herself patriotically for her Independence Day rides, braiding "red, white and blue ribbons [into] her hair, which streaming to the racer's back, lent a picturesque wildness to her figure" (62). Being "wild," in Mourning Dove's feminine imagination, is inextricable from the American quality of the celebratory races.

Laura's wild gallop with Lena on the black ponies of Silver Lake, which so resembles Cogewea's exploits, exemplifies the strategic revisions that Wilder made in adapting her autobiography into fiction. These revisions allow her to access the same nostalgic experience of freedom forged on horseback in defiance of restrictive definitions of femininity that Mourning Dove describes. Wilder's original, nonfictional recollection of the scene features Lena and the black ponies but bears little resemblance to her fictional characterization of the wind-whipped Osage children. Instead, "I rode around with Lena a little, but I was timid for I had never ridden a horse" (*Pioneer* 153). Although Wilder recalls driving the ponies with her cousin "while we shouted and sang" (a scene that recurs in the fictional *Silver Lake*), the historical Laura Ingalls is "timid" about the might of the black ponies rather than intoxicated by it. Wilder's fictionalization of her life repeatedly relies on the symbolism of running horses in tandem with archetypal "Indian" images such as that of the noble chief in his "eagle feathers" or the racing ponies in the early volumes of the series. Such images contextualize Laura's desire for liberty and avoidance of social conventions even as she transitions toward adulthood and marriage in *These Happy Golden Years* (1943) and the posthumously published *The First Four Years* (1971).

"BROWN AS AN INDIAN": LAURA'S FRONTIER ROMANCE

Wilder's fictional Laura seems destined for Almanzo from her first glimpse of him in *The Long Winter* (1940) when she is no more than fourteen; she has no other romantic interests, nor does it occur to her at first to see "that Wilder boy" in this light. Her attraction to his "sleek brown horses," with "their dainty feet" and "perfect rhythm" (*Happy* 84) spurs Laura to anticipate his appearances. Wilder eliminates from her fiction the many suitors she describes in *Pioneer Girl*, including lawyer Alfred Thomas and Ernest Perry of the "kissing games" (257). This reflects Almanzo's singular status as the man who, with his horse, Prince, faced the elements during the Hard Winter to bring wheat to starving townspeople, including the Ingalls family. Like Laura, Almanzo's appeal as a character is tied directly to his sympathy for and alliance with his horses.

Visually, Almanzo's teams of driving horses do not resemble the Osage ponies of Kansas Territory. In all probability, the Indian ponies of Laura's early childhood resembled Mourning Dove's cayuses more than Prince and Lady or Barnum and Skip, the two teams that feature prominently in *Happy Golden Years*. Yet Wilder takes pains to align all of Almanzo's horses with the impulses for liberty and mobility that Laura first articulated in connection with the naked ponies of Indian Territory. Prince and Lady model for Laura the kind of playful partnership that she and Almanzo will eventually share; trotting through the winter chill, they "touched noses as though they whispered to each other," and Laura knows that their relationship is "beautiful" (*Happy* 84). As their courtship continues, Wilder's desire to represent the frontier as a shared cultural space in which a "tomboy" girl can thrive clearly informs her characterization of Barnum and Skip (*Town* 146), whose appeal to Laura echoes that of the Native ponies of Kansas Territory. Both are "wild" (in the sense of their behavior) despite the fact that they are in full harness and being trained as driving horses (*Town* 146; *Happy* 210). Appropriately "tall" and imposing, rather than light and quick (the qualities of a cayuse), they respond to being asked to pull the buggy in telling fashion: "the brown horse [Barnum] reared straight up on his hind legs, with front feet pawing the air, while the bay horse [Skip] jumped ahead" (*Happy* 187). Neither rearing nor jumping is permitted in harness; Barnum and Skip's actions are clear signs of resistance to their master's commands.

Laura's courtship with Almanzo, Barnum, and Skip is several steps away from the naked ponies of Kansas. The mismatched horses wear a full driving harness, and over the course of Laura and Almanzo's romance, they become increasingly accustomed to technological innovations, including Laura's hoopskirts and the raised top of Almanzo's buggy. (Laura, who resents her immobilizing hoopskirts, and the corresponding restriction of her corset, sympathizes with Barnum and Skip's objections to such unnatural constraints [*Happy* 186–87].) Yet the later Little House books continue to draw on the intersecting tropes of "runaway" horses and American independence as Laura forges new definitions of womanhood and propriety. When Wilder was writing *Little Town on the Prairie*, her daughter, Rose Wilder Lane, encouraged her to emphasize the patriotism of De Smet in a full chapter about their Fourth of July celebrations. Unlike Laura, who envisions freedom in the form of a ride behind Almanzo's prizewinning horses, Pa and his friends assert the connection between freedom and the right to hold property.[7] In their words, freedom enables "every man Jack of us" to claim land and thus shape his own fate in the American West (*Town* 73). The Laura that Wilder retrospectively constructs rejects this colonial, materialist model of patriotism in favor of emotional ties: her sympathy with Almanzo's "runaway" horses first allows Laura to imagine a liberating partnership with him (*Happy* 210).

Far from being frightened by the rebellious antics of Barnum and Skip, as is her rival, Nellie Oleson, Laura understands Barnum's impulse to rear in the face of authority. Although she and Almanzo are ostensibly attempting to "gentle" these "runaway" horses by taking them driving, Laura asserts that "they are not as much fun when they behave" (*Happy* 191). Hurtling across the grasslands, she identifies this madcap reimagining of the genteel Anglo-American courtship ritual of the buggy ride with the Little House series' earlier pinnacle of liberating transgression: "This was fun. It reminded her of a long time ago when she and Cousin Lena let the black ponies run away on the prairie" (144). While she still knows that she does not "really" want to be an "Indian girl" (*Prairie* 307), Laura's sympathy for Barnum allows her to gain an influence over him that even Almanzo cannot replicate. In the chapter triumphantly titled "Barnum Walks," Laura finds that when she "let[s] him carry the bit easily," the spirited horse "likes" to obey (*Happy* 210). The citizens of De Smet are awed by her mastery over Barnum; in Almanzo's words, "They never expected to see a woman driving that horse" (199). In this moment, Laura attains a new status as the driver of Barnum that empowers rather than limits her.

On the surface, Laura's gentling of Barnum might seem a triumph for Ma and the cult of domesticity. After all, Laura has apparently rejected the "fun" way of driving Barnum in favor of a safe, decorous manner. Yet her affinity for the "runaway" horse continues to reflect the same sympathetic tendencies that Mourning Dove's Cogewea expresses when she says of her temperamental, "pranc[ing]" steed, "Wanawish and I understand each other" (23). While du Chêne achieved this empathetic connection with his "happy pony" by dispensing entirely with bit and bridle (*Prairie* 304), Laura echoes this method of acknowledging Barnum's desire for liberty by "let[ting] him hold the bit easily" (*Happy* 210).

Laura's sympathy with Barnum also has much broader implications for her future as a wife and mother. As she becomes fonder of the "runaway" horse, Wilder maps a corresponding increase in her trust in Almanzo. Trachsel's study reveals the increasingly popular literary intersection between the rhetoric of romance and of "the special relationship between human and horse"; like romantic love, this bond "develop[s] through an intense physical interaction between horse and rider, through communication channels that are largely instinctive and deeper than words" (32). In light of the physicality with which Laura tames Barnum, it comes as no surprise when she agrees to enter into a marital union with Almanzo (*Happy* 210). Ma, an expert in matters of womanly sentiment, notices the increasingly blurred line between Laura's feelings for Barnum and for her human suitor. In response to the news of Laura's engagement, she tentatively replies, "If only you are sure, Laura.... Sometimes I think it is the horses you care for, more than their master" (216). Rather than allaying her mother's concerns with an unequivocal declaration of love for Almanzo, Laura insists on aligning man and horse, "shakily" declaring, "I couldn't have one without the other" (216). Braiding the presence of "wild" horses into Laura's proposed union with Almanzo, Wilder constructs a marriage imbued with the promise of "going like music": the sensation that she attributes to the black ponies of Silver Lake, who in turn reprised her original impression of "naked" liberty in the form of the Osage riders of her earliest memories (*Shores* 54; *Prairie* 305).

"SOMETHING FOR YOU TO PLAY WITH": PARTNERSHIP ON THE PRAIRIE

Wilder's narrative of the Anglo-American wife who becomes "brown as an Indian" galloping the prairies with her new husband is, of course, limited by the scope of events in her own life (*Happy* 283). The newly married Laura of the 1880s still rode the prairie fully clothed and shared in her husband's agricultural labors on their homestead (*First* 24). Nevertheless, Wilder repeatedly returns to the ethos of the "naked" Osage ponies in descriptions of her married life. This narrative continuity with the early books of the series reveals her desire to present her marriage not as a concession to her mother's efforts to domesticate her but instead as a means of accessing the freedom of fresh air and sunshine. (For additional analyses of Laura's transition to domestic womanhood, see Maher; Romines; Mowder.) Despite her hoopskirts and fashionable bonnets, Laura remains committed, in Wilder's retelling, to a form of American wifehood that shares common ground with her idea of Native American equestrian partnership.

In light of this model of partnership, the most significant figure in Laura's marriage may not be Almanzo himself but the gift he delivers soon after their wedding. Rather than presenting his new wife with a stove or a sewing machine (domestic appliances for indoor labor that Pa provides for Ma), Almanzo gives Laura "a small iron-gray pony" that he describes as "something for you to play with" (*First* 24). The pony, Trixy, bears a resemblance to both the Native ponies of *Little House on the Prairie* and the frontier cayuse of Mourning Dove's *Cogewea*: like the smaller Indian horses, Trixy's "feet were small and her legs fine and flat" (*First* 24); like du Chêne's "happy pony" (*Prairie* 304), her "ears [were] pointed and alert" and "her mane and tail ... long and thick" (*First* 24). As it turns out, the Laura of *Silver Lake* was wrong in assuming that a married woman cannot play. With Trixy, Laura can both fulfill a transgressive childhood dream—to be "riding one of those gay little ponies" of the Western prairie—and establish a relationship with her husband that is egalitarian rather than hierarchical. When Almanzo claims that his own pony, Fly, is fast enough to "run away from" Trixy (*First* 26), Laura has the opportunity to demonstrate her own mastery of skills that both she and her husband value: "Laura bent low over Trixy's neck, touched her with her whip, and imitated, as near as she could manage, a cowboy yell. Trixy shot ahead like a streak" (26–27). Racing the ponies "on a twenty-mile ride over the open prairie before breakfast" gives Laura a taste of the perfect mobility (Mourning Dove's "going, going, going" [22]) that she has long associated with freedom (*First* 27). Moreover, it enables her to triumph over her husband rather than bow to his authority; after all, "it was proven many times that Trixy was faster" than Fly (27).

Trixy, the Silver Lake ponies, Prince and Lady, and Barnum and Skip all represent answers to a very real need that both the child and adult Lauras feel for agency. By the end of *These Happy Golden Years*, Laura understands that play need not be sacrificed on the altar of marriage. Instead, Wilder uses her marriage to reconcile Laura's desire for both freedom and partnership, the same union that existed between du Chêne and his pony and between Prince and Lady. This *Prairie*-inflected play is the bedrock of her long, happy union with Almanzo. As such, Wilder asserts, the nostalgia Laura feels for *Little House on the Prairie*'s naked Osage children and their mounts serves as the basis for a productive American womanhood. Wilder's revelation of the agency Laura gains through her imagined solidarity with Native definitions of freedom reflects a growing trend in twentieth-century children's literature. From Walter Farley's privileged Alec Ramsay in *The Black Stallion* to Scott O'Dell's dispossessed Karana in *The Island of the Blue Dolphins*, American children must often look beyond their parents' definitions of propriety to surmount increasingly adult challenges. By constructing for herself an American legacy of freedom and partnership in the form of the naked Indian ponies of her childhood, Wilder models the process by which a girl on the frontier may reshape ideas about femininity and coming of age to honor the pursuit of liberty and happiness.

NOTES

1. When Wilder refers to *ponies*, she is not describing Shetlands or other modern breeds intended to be ridden by children. If the animal in question is less than 58 inches tall (14.2 hands) at the withers, it qualifies as a pony. The black pony of Kansas Territory would certainly have been large enough to bear an adult rider such as du Chêne.

2. Many scholars have expressed displeasure at Laura's undeniably racist understanding of Native American neighbors throughout the series. For important voices in this strand of Wilder scholarship, see Kaye; Smulders; Reese.

3. Scholars have noted the discrepancy between the fictional narrative and the true chronology of Wilder's early childhood travels, in which the family's sojourn in Indian Territory predated experiences depicted in *Little House in the Big Woods*. Romines calculates that "the actual Laura Ingalls moved to postbellum Kansas about 1869" (59), before the events of *Little House in the Big Woods*. Thus, *Little House on the Prairie* represents the genesis of Wilder's childhood memories, a circumstance that lends profound significance to Laura's often sympathetic depiction of her "wild" Indian neighbors (*Prairie* 137).

4. Callahan's *Wynema: A Child of the Forest* (1891), widely acknowledged as the first novel written by a woman of Native American descent, addresses at length the dire consequences of the Dawes Act.

5. Hill's annotations to *Pioneer Girl* reveal that Lena and Jean were the biological children of Docia (151). Although Wilder did not mention Docia's status as a divorcee, this breach of propriety may have prompted her willingness to recast her aunt as a stepmother to these wild cousins.

6. Ma's anxiety about Laura's disregard for her complexion and its potential to obscure her white racial origins is a recurring theme that culminates with the youngest Ingalls daughter, Grace, repeating Ma's caution to Laura on her wedding day (*Happy* 283).

7. Woodside (128) claims that Lane may have written this Fourth of July scene, which would account for Pa's very different definition of American freedom.

WORKS CITED

Callahan, S. Alice. *Wynema: A Child of the Forest*. Edited by A. Lavonne Brown Ruoff. University of Nebraska Press, 1997.

Campbell, Donna M. "'Wild Men' and Dissenting Voices: Narrative Disruption in *Little House on the Prairie*." *Great Plains Quarterly* 20, no. 2 (Spring 2000): 111–22.

Eastman, Charles Alexander. *Indian Boyhood*. McClure, Phillips, 1902.

Farley, Walter. *The Black Stallion*. Random House, 1941.

Heldrich, Philip. "'Going to Indian Territory': Attitudes toward Native Americans in 'Little House on the Prairie.'" *Great Plains Quarterly* 20, no. 2 (Spring 2000): 99–109.

Hill, Pamela Smith. "Introduction: 'Will it Come to Anything?': The Story of *Pioneer Girl*." In *Pioneer Girl: The Annotated Autobiography*, by Laura Ingalls Wilder, xv–lxi. South Dakota Historical Society Press, 2014.

Kaye, Frances W. "Little Squatter on the Osage Diminished Reserve: Reading Laura Ingalls Wilder's Kansas Indians." *Great Plains Quarterly* 20, no. 2 (2000): 123–40.

Maher, Susan Naramore. "Laura Ingalls and Caddie Woodlawn: Daughters of a Border Space." *The Lion and the Unicorn* 18, no. 2 (December 1994): 130–42.

Miller, John E. "American Indians in the Fiction of Laura Ingalls Wilder." *South Dakota History* 30, no. 3 (2000): 303–20.

Mourning Dove. *Cogewea, the Half-Blood: A Depiction of the Great Montana Cattle Range*. University of Nebraska Press, 1981.

O'Dell, Scott. *The Island of the Blue Dolphins*. Houghton Mifflin, 1988.

Reese, Debbie. "Indigenizing Children's Literature." *Journal of Language and Literacy Education* 4, no. 2 (2008): 59–72.

Romines, Ann. *Constructing the Little House: Gender, Culture, and Laura Ingalls Wilder*. University of Massachusetts Press, 1997.

Schneider, Bethany. "A Modest Proposal: Laura Ingalls Wilder Ate Zitkála-Šá." *GLQ: A Journal of Lesbian and Gay Studies* 21, no. 1 (2015): 65–93.

Smulders, Sharon. "'The Only Good Indian': History, Race, and Representation in Laura Ingalls Wilder's *Little House on the Prairie*." *Children's Literature Association Quarterly* 27, no. 4 (Winter 2002): 191–202.

Trachsel, Mary. "Horse Stories and Romance Fiction: Variants or Alternative Texts of Female Identity?" *Reader: Essays in Reader-Oriented Theory, Criticism, and Pedagogy* 39 (Fall–Spring 1997–98): 1–22.

Wilder, Laura Ingalls. *By the Shores of Silver Lake*. Harper, 1953.

Wilder, Laura Ingalls. *The First Four Years*. Harper, 1971.

Wilder, Laura Ingalls. *Little House on the Prairie*. Harper, 1953.

Wilder, Laura Ingalls. *Little Town on the Prairie*. Harper, 1953.

Wilder, Laura Ingalls. *On the Way Home: The Diary of a Trip from South Dakota to Mansfield, Missouri, in 1894*. Harper and Row, 1962.

Wilder, Laura Ingalls. *Pioneer Girl: The Annotated Autobiography*. Edited by Pamela Smith Hill. South Dakota Historical Society Press, 2014.

Wilder, Laura Ingalls. *These Happy Golden Years*. Harper, 1953.

Woodside, Christine. *Libertarians on the Prairie: Laura Ingalls Wilder, Rose Wilder Lane, and the Making of the Little House Books*. Arcade, 2016.

Zitkála-Šá (Gertrude Bonnin). *American Indian Stories*. Hayworth, 1921.

HER OWN BABY

Dolls and Family in "Indians Ride Away"
Jenna Brack

Perhaps the most discussed scene in Laura Ingalls Wilder's Little House series appears near the end of *Little House on the Prairie*, when the Ingalls family watches the Osage people withdraw during a fictionalized depiction of Indian Removal.[1] In a shocking outburst, Laura becomes fixated on an Osage infant, declaring that she "want[s] that one little baby" (308). Wilder's reductive depiction of Native culture and resettlement, along with the scene's problematic racialized and gendered subtexts, has provoked curiosity and critique. As well, critics have pondered the function of this scene within the series as a whole.

Nonetheless, space remains for readings that more specifically explain Laura's motivations and uncharacteristic intensity in this moment. In light of the racial subtexts of Laura's doll, Charlotte, and the racial, gendered, and familial dynamics of the Ingalls family, Laura's response to the Indian baby might be read as a desire for *her own* baby, in opposition to Ma's claim that the family has "*our* own baby" (*Prairie* 310; emphasis added). The phrase *her own baby* captures the contradictory and coexisting attitudes Laura exhibits: while her response treats the baby as no more than a doll, she also seems motivated by a conflicted sense of self within her family.

Some critics have condemned the Indian Removal scene. Waziyatawin Angela Cavender Wilson, for example, identifies it as "one of the most offensive passages" in the series, because Laura wishes for the baby "just as she would [for] a pet" ("Burning" 71). Sharon Smulders argues that Laura's decision to call the baby *it* "objectifies" the child and reveals Laura's attitude of "conquest and control" (198–99). And Frances W. Kaye labels Wilder's descriptions of the Natives—particularly their stoic faces—as representative of "false sentimentalism" and asserts that Laura even "savors [the Indians'] tragedy" rather than identifying with their suffering (136).[2]

Other scholars believe that this scene demonstrates Laura's attempt to identify with the Natives. Charles Frey asserts that Laura's longing for the baby "suggests a deep and mysterious affinity . . . with the Indian spirit and way of life" (128), while Elizabeth Segel claims that the Natives' appearance provides Laura with "freedom from deforming constraints" (69). Likewise, Louise Mowder sees Laura's response as "a surge of desire . . . for the emancipation that the baby embodies" (17; see also Foley, this volume). Extending the idea that Laura identifies with the Natives, Ann Romines writes that while the demand for the baby reveals Laura's "cultural entitlement," it also suggests her desire for a "shared life between the Euro-American and Native American children" (78).

My argument is inspired particularly by Smulders's assertion that Laura objectifies the baby and Romines's proposal that Laura embraces the baby as family, although these scholars interpret the moment in radically different ways. Smulders is correct that Laura "captures the child as 'it,'" especially in light of Laura's interactions with her doll, Charlotte. Yet underlying familial tension in the novel also suggests that, in Romines's words, Laura in a limited way may be "reaching toward an extended family," although the series ultimately fails to offer any vision of a "shared life" (78). Close analysis of Laura's interactions with Charlotte and with her siblings paradoxically supports both interpretations.

To better understand Smulders's assertion that Laura objectifies the Osage baby, we must turn to the scene in *Little House in the Big Woods* where Laura receives a doll for Christmas. The doll, which she names Charlotte, has curly black hair, a calico dress, red stockings, and "black button eyes" (75). When Laura sees Charlotte, she is speechless: "She was so beautiful that Laura could not say a word. She just held her tight and forgot everything else. She did not know that everyone was looking at her, till Aunt Eliza said: 'Did you ever see such big eyes!'" (*Woods* 76). Aside from superficially adhering to Ma's instruction to share the doll, Laura does not stop looking at or holding Charlotte: the doll instantly becomes the object of Laura's desire.

This episode appears to parallel Laura's fixation on the Indian baby in *Little House on the Prairie*. Laura immediately notices the Indian baby's eyes, which are "black as a night when no stars shine" (*Prairie* 308), reminiscent of Charlotte's black button eyes. In addition, Laura shares a prolonged gaze with the baby, paralleling her intense focus on Charlotte: "Those black eyes looked deep into Laura's eyes and she looked deep down into the blackness of that little baby's eyes, and she wanted that one little baby" (308). Finally, Laura becomes speechless as she watches the Indian baby: "'Its eyes are so black,' . . . She could not say what she meant" (309).

Incorporating strikingly similar components in these scenes, Wilder appears to align the Osage baby with Charlotte, by extension suggesting that Laura sees the Native child as a mere toy that can be gifted to her. Even worse, Laura names her doll, while the baby is referred to as *it* (*Prairie* 308).[3] Laura's outburst is disturbing and surprising. Although she expresses strong feelings elsewhere, in no other moment does she make an outright demand. Even when her desires do not conform to her family's standards, she outwardly submits to her parents' expectations. In this moment, Laura shows little restraint, offering no apology, attempting to "obey Pa" only after "tears and sobs" (310).

Perhaps the closest Laura comes to replicating this outburst happens in *On the Banks of Plum Creek*, where comparisons between Charlotte and the Osage baby are further extended. When Mrs. Nelson's daughter, Anna, visits, Laura allows her to play with the doll, believing that Anna "could not hurt Charlotte" (231). But Anna delivers a much worse blow, determining to keep the doll. Horrified, Laura cries, "I want my doll!" (232). Ma dismisses Laura's desire: "'For shame, Laura,' Ma said. . . . You don't want that doll'" (232). Obeying her mother, Laura watches Anna depart with beloved Charlotte but then experiences profound melancholy: "Laura quietly climbed the ladder and sat down on her box by the window. She did not cry, but she felt crying inside her because Charlotte was gone. . . . Everything was empty and cold" (232).

Laura's experience of losing Charlotte significantly parallels and evokes her response to the Native baby. Laura's cry for Charlotte—"I want my doll!"—is reminiscent of her behavior in Indian territory, when she repeatedly cries, "Oh, I want it! I want it!" (*Prairie* 308). Ma even counters Laura's protests over losing Charlotte and the Indian baby with the exact same phrases: "For shame, Laura," and "You don't want another baby" (309–10). Moreover, Laura's forlorn gaze while watching Anna take Charlotte mirrors her response as the Osage leave the prairie, when Laura "sat a long time on the doorstep, looking into the empty west where the Indians had gone" (311). Everything is "empty" after Charlotte is gone and "empty" when the Indians leave, and Laura feels profound sadness after both incidents: "nothing was left but silence and emptiness. All the world seemed very quiet and lonely" (*Prairie* 311).

The placement of the Indian baby scene between Laura's reception of and then loss of Charlotte, while not previously addressed by critics, does not seem coincidental. Laura's attitude toward Charlotte in *Little House in the Big Woods* and *On the Banks of Plum Creek* provides a frame within which to consider her attitude toward the Indian baby in *Little House on the Prairie*. This analysis extends Smulders's claim that the text objectifies the Osage baby, revealing that

Laura treats the baby not so much as "chattel" or "pretty beads scavenged from the Indian camp" (198) but more as a plaything. While fascinated by the baby's dark, beautiful eyes, Laura fails to register the baby's humanity.

Aligning a doll with a human character—especially a nonwhite character—has ample precedents. Robin Bernstein demonstrates in *Racial Innocence* how toys such as dolls have been used to construct and perpetuate racism, often covertly: "Dolls, as signs of childhood and property of many children, create propinquity between the idea of childhood and the racial project of determining who is a person and who is a thing; thus dolls tuck racial politics beneath a cloak of innocence" (18). Bernstein primarily explores dolls' roles in furthering racial narratives about African Americans, but her work is important to understanding how dolls, as a "genre of object," perpetuate harmful narratives about other communities of color (157).[4] Bernstein notes that the doll collections amassed by white children during the late nineteenth and early twentieth centuries rarely included soft Indian dolls (157).[5] I am not claiming that Charlotte is explicitly an Indian doll, but Bernstein's research lends credibility to literary associations of Charlotte with the Native baby, demonstrating that the seemingly white and "innocent" Charlotte can also be read as "racially complex" (186). Describing Laura's doll similarly to the Osage baby, the text conflates the doll and baby in ways that question the baby's personhood.

We know that Charlotte is present in Indian territory, as "Laura and Mary clung tight to their rag dolls" (*Prairie* 4) when leaving the Big Woods, yet Laura seems to pay little attention to Charlotte once they reach the prairie. Instead, she is consumed with the idea of seeing a "papoose," which Pa describes as "a little, brown, Indian baby" (6). The term *papoose* is itself objectifying language. As Debbie Reese has noted, such descriptions "subtly dehumanize American Indians and distance the reader from the human qualities they share with Native American people" (254).[6] It is possible that the idea of seeing a "papoose" replaces Laura's earlier fascination with her doll. Laura's lack of interactions with Charlotte on the prairie, then, suggest a further conflation of the baby and doll. Laura does not need her doll because she is instead waiting for an Indian baby—yet another "doll" to play with.

Wilder makes one other significant artistic decision in *On the Banks of Plum Creek* that further aligns Charlotte with the Indian baby and complicates how we are to interpret the alignment. Weeks after Anna takes the doll, Laura finds Charlotte "drowned and frozen in a puddle" in the Nelsons' barnyard (234). Surveying Charlotte's condition, Laura notices that Charlotte's black yarn hair is missing: "Anna had *scalped* her" (234; emphasis added). Wilder uses the word *scalp* in association with her fictionalized Indians in *Little House on the*

Prairie, where Indians are described as having "red-brown skin bright against the blue sky, and *scalplocks* wound with colored string" (227; emphasis added).

In this scene, the perpetrator of scalping is a young white girl of Scandinavian descent, a detail that is noteworthy in light of the fact that *On the Banks of Plum Creek* is set in Minnesota shortly after the US-Dakota War of 1862. This conflict has largely been viewed as a Native attack on white settlers rather than resistance resulting from white, colonial oppression, but as Wilson demonstrates through firsthand accounts, white settlers—particularly women—committed atrocities as the Dakotas were evicted from their land. Among many horrific examples, Natives were pulled "by the hair of the head" from wagons, a white woman killed a Dakota baby by throwing the child onto the ground, and white women hurled stones, weapons, and even boiling water at the Dakota people ("Decolonizing" 200, 205). Wilson provides evidence that "women led" these attacks: "The numerous accounts describing the role that white women (and their children) played in civilian attacks on the Indigenous prisoners challenge the notion that their participation in the processes of Dakota genocide and dispossession was benign or exculpatory" (204–5).[7]

The imagery surrounding Anna's treatment of Charlotte recalls the historical accounts of white women's abuse of Natives.[8] The doll has been "scalped," "drowned," and eye-gouged; she is described as "bleeding," "torn," and left in the "beating down" rain, all at the hands of a white female (234). Language of destruction permeates Anna's interactions with Charlotte; earlier Anna is said to have "banged [Charlotte] against the floor" (231–32). By contrast, when Laura sees Charlotte, she "snatche[s]" up the doll, shelters her inside her shawl, and runs "against the angry wind" back home (234–35).[9]

Anna's violent behavior and Laura's emotional response illuminate two different but coexisting realities of soft doll play: "Children embrace and cuddle soft dolls, and they violently abuse them" (Bernstein 185). Both types of play have problematic racial subtexts. In assessing white girls' interactions with black dolls, Bernstein shows how cuddle play with a "compliant, cottony, soft doll [can] transform a girl into a doting 'mistress'"; in other words, even affectionate doll play can act out racialized scripts of white dominance (186). Thus, Charlotte's loss and rescue reveal two equally problematic white responses toward Indian Removal. Anna manifests overt hatred and violence, while Laura demonstrates pity and sympathy toward Natives. Yet even Laura's sympathy ultimately reflects an attitude of possession and furthers a white savior narrative. After Laura rescues the helpless doll, she brings Charlotte back into *her* home and *her* culture, where the doll is remade to more closely reflect an Ingalls family ideal.

Applying Bernstein's work on racialized doll play to these scenes reveals another level on which Wilder perpetuates harmful racial narratives. This reading also provides additional motivation for Laura's demand for the Indian baby: her response reflects (and is influenced by) her past and future interactions with Charlotte. Laura reaches forcefully and emotionally toward the infant, perhaps because she sees the Indian baby as "her own" baby doll—in need of rescuing.

Associations between Charlotte and the Indian baby throughout the early books further expose the racism of Wilder's series and strengthen Smulders's argument that Laura objectifies the Osage baby. Yet Charlotte is aligned as well with Laura's family, and exploring Laura's conflicted feelings about her familial relationships provides another lens through which to read Laura's desire for "her own baby." While I do not agree that Laura finds "delight in difference" (Romines 78), Romines's assertion that Laura reaches toward the baby as "family" illuminates how Laura may be questioning her family's cultural narrative and negotiating her own identity.

Charlotte is merely a toy, but she does carry strong familial associations for Laura. When Anna takes Charlotte, Laura's sadness over the loss echoes her feelings about her father's absence, a comparison mentioned twice: "Pa was not there, and Charlotte's box was empty"; "her heart was crying all the time for Pa and Charlotte" (*Banks* 233). Assigning Charlotte's and Pa's absences comparable emotional weight is noteworthy. Pa represents Laura's closest family relationship; as Frey notes, the "wrenching alliance between father and daughter" (128) is a major theme in *Little House on the Prairie*.

The possessive tendencies that Laura exhibits toward both Charlotte and the Osage baby are also present in her relationship with her sister, Carrie. In *Little House in the Big Woods*, Laura squabbles with her cousin—the other Laura Ingalls—over which of their sisters is prettiest. When the other Laura claims that "her baby" is prettier than Laura's baby, Laura protests and declares, "Carrie's the prettiest baby in the whole world!" (142–43). Although Laura is not close to Carrie in the early books (their friendship develops later, beginning with *By the Shores of Silver Lake*), this disagreement conveys that Laura feels possessive not only of her dolls and the Indian baby but also of "her" family.

Romines perceptively demonstrates that Charlotte's creation is associated with Laura's family: "Every detail evokes a process and a craft.... Laura must already know that Charlotte is the product of woman's work" (165). As a product of domesticity, Charlotte represents Laura's connection to Ma, Aunt Eliza, and Wilder's maternal grandmother, whose name was Charlotte (265). Although I disagree with Romines's contention that "the new doll *initiates* Laura" into Ma's world (166; emphasis added) because Laura is hardly aligned with Ma's domesticity in the first books of the series, Romines's argument convincingly demonstrates that even as Charlotte carries problematic racial meaning, she also symbolizes familial connection.

In fact, Charlotte is such an important symbol that Garth Williams prominently featured her in his 1953 cover illustration for *Little House in the Big Woods*. The oft-reproduced image depicts Laura cradling and adoring Charlotte while the rest of the family watches. The illustration reinforces Charlotte's status as an object, emphasized by her facelessness, but Williams's decision to make Charlotte central to the cover also speaks of her importance to the series. Moreover, by isolating Laura and Charlotte from the rest of the family, Williams makes visible a significant tension: the relational displacement Laura feels within her own family.

Even as Laura exhibits affection toward her family, her sense of self within the family is complicated, providing another way to read Laura's desire for "her own baby." With the exception of Laura's defense of Baby Carrie in *Little House in the Big Woods*, Mary and Carrie are more closely aligned throughout the early books. Ma regularly places Carrie into Mary's arms, and Mary makes decisions with Carrie in mind. In *On the Banks of Plum Creek*, Mary "watche[s] Carrie to keep her from falling down into the creek" (12), even when friends are around: "Mary and the big girls came down slowly, bringing Carrie to play with" (172). In *Little House on the Prairie*, although Laura goes to pick blackberries with Ma, we are told that "Mary hardly ever went to pick blackberries. She stayed in the house to mind Baby Carrie, because she was older" (183–84).

It is logical that Mary spends more time with Carrie for precisely this reason, but other factors transcend matters of age. Throughout the series, Mary is seen as more "maternal" than Laura. Despite receiving domestic gifts from her mother such as dolls and ribbons, Laura rarely participates in womanly tasks early in the series. Rather, while Mary "sit[s] down to sew," Laura often is "bounding" outdoors to work next to Pa (*Banks* 134). Scholars have noted these alignments. Ellen Simpson Novotny writes that Mary "identifies more with Ma, prefers indoors, likes to sew, wears her sunbonnet, [and] likes to study," while Laura "identifies more with Pa, prefers outdoors, hates to sew, resists wearing a sunbonnet, [and] dislikes studying" (53). In addition, Mowder asserts that "Mary and Ma are parallel in their proper femininity, which is recognized both by its domesticity and its self-suppression" (15). Laura is neither domesticated nor "self-suppressed," preferring outdoor adventure to life inside the home. Thus, Laura's relationship to Ma and Mary is complicated; she is entwined in their maternal, domestic relationships yet cannot fully identify with them.

Because Mary is more closely aligned with both Ma and Carrie, a complicated sibling rivalry between Mary and Laura is woven throughout the series.

Mary and Laura seem to have an idyllic sisterhood in some moments, such as when they are catching gophers or sliding down Pa's haystacks. However, tensions between them are introduced in the first volume and are impossible to overlook. Janet Spaeth has even identified Mary and Laura's sibling rivalry as a "major motif" in the series (*Laura* 84). As Virginia L. Wolf explains, although security is a primary focus in *Big Woods*, "within the little house, [Laura's] security is somewhat threatened because her sister Mary is so much better than she" (111). After Laura's pocket rips because she collects too many pebbles, she thinks about how "nothing like that ever happened to Mary. Mary was a good little girl who always kept her dress clean and neat and minded her manners . . . Laura did not think it was fair" (*Woods* 175). Moments such as this one interrupt otherwise pleasant family-focused episodes, highlighting the internal conflict Laura often feels in her relationship with Mary.

Throughout the series' early books, underlying tensions between the sisters seem to disadvantage Laura more than Mary. In *Little House on the Prairie*, after the girls collect beads from the Indian camp, Mary wants to give them to Carrie, but Laura wants to keep them for herself:

"These are mine," [Laura] said.
   Then Mary said, "Carrie can have mine."
   Ma waited to hear what Laura would say. Laura didn't want to say anything. . . . [S]he wished with all her might that Mary wouldn't always be such a good little girl. (179)

Laura begrudgingly strings her beads onto a necklace for her baby sister, resenting Mary for forcing her to give the beads away: "When she looked at Mary she wanted to slap her" (*Prairie* 181). Carrie, however, is delighted with the gift and "clap[s] her hands and laugh[s]" (181). This incident reinforces the idea that Carrie is "Mary's baby" and emphasizes Mary's alignment with Ma, since Mary's idea receives Ma's approval. In fact, in *On the Banks of Plum Creek*, Mary and Laura make another necklace for Carrie, this time at Ma's suggestion, providing yet another significant alignment of Ma and Mary.

Mary and Carrie also share a physical quality: golden hair. The color of Mary's hair is a source of significant rivalry throughout the series, as Ma tells the girls to ask Aunt Lotty "which she likes best, brown curls or golden curls" (*Woods* 181). Despite Aunt Lotty's claim that she likes both, Laura feels certain that her brown hair is inferior to Mary's blond locks. Pa reminds Laura that he has brown hair, but Laura's sense of inferiority endures. Describing her family to friends at school in *On the Banks of Plum Creek*, Laura identifies them by hair color: "'That's Mary, and Carrie's the baby. She has golden hair, too'" (148).

Here and throughout the series, Laura implicitly reveals her feeling as Other within her family, especially among her sisters.

The importance of blond hair also illuminates a racial subtext that carries throughout the series: what is praiseworthy for females in this family is European whiteness. Mowder illuminates the racialization of Mary and Laura. Mary, like Ma, resembles the white, blond-haired china doll as a "model of femininity," while Laura "is continually chastised for her 'Indian-like' traits: her rambunctious noisiness and her refusal to maintain a pale complexion" (Mowder 16). (For more on Ma's association with the china doll, see Spaeth, "Over"; Segel.) Laura's supposed alignment with the Indians is unacceptable to Ma, and Mary, in turn, echoes Ma's racist sentiments. In *On the Banks of Plum Creek*, Mary's scolding of Laura for not wearing her bonnet could have come from Ma's mouth: "'For pity's sake, Laura,' said Mary, 'keep your sunbonnet on! You'll be brown as an Indian, and what will the town girls think of us?' 'I don't care!' said Laura, loudly and bravely" (143).

Such exchanges reinforce whiteness as an ideal standard for femininity and for acceptance both within the family (as a means of gaining Ma and Mary's approval) and outside of it (to earn the approval of the girls who live in town). Because Laura does not represent this womanly and racially appropriate ideal, she is often displaced by her mother and sister, at least until she begins to align herself more with her family's and her culture's normative ideals of womanhood in the later books.

Evidence of Laura's displacement within her family is highlighted by returning to the physical description of Charlotte. We are told in *Little House in the Big Woods* that just as Laura has brown hair, Charlotte's hair is also dark: "her hair was black yarn that had been knit and raveled, so that it was curly" (76). However, when Anna "scalps" Charlotte in *On the Banks of Plum Creek*, most of the doll's black hair is removed. After Laura rescues the damaged Charlotte, Ma volunteers to help Laura remake Charlotte "as good as new" (236).

But when Ma strips all of Charlotte's remaining dark hair, cleanses her, and reconstructs her, the doll undergoes what can be read as a reracializing process. "Ma ripped off the torn hair and the bits of her mouth and her remaining eye and her face ... washed her thoroughly clean and starched and ironed her while Laura chose from the scrap-bag a new, pale pink face for her and new button eyes" (236). The act of "ripping" Charlotte's dark hair, along with the subsequent cleaning, starching, and ironing, can be read as Ma's determination to separate the Ingalls family from the dangers of the Other. As Holly Blackford argues, in the act of ironing clothes throughout the series, Ma "establish[es] a symbolic border between the untamed and the tamed," thus creating racial order and distinguishing her family from the "threat" of Indians (180).

Accordingly, after Charlotte is reassembled, she retains most but not all of her original qualities: she still has eyes that "sh[i]ne black" and a "red mouth"; significantly, though, her dark hair has been replaced by "golden-brown yarn hair braided in two wee braids and tied with blue yarn bows" (236). Laura expresses neither pleasure nor disappointment about the condition of the revived Charlotte, but the doll has clearly undergone a transformation that makes her look less like Laura—and less like the Indian baby in *Little House on the Prairie*—and more like Mary, with lighter hair, orderly braids, and blue bows. We are told later in *On the Banks of Plum Creek* that "Mary had to wear blue [ribbons] because her hair was golden and Laura had to wear pink because her hair was brown" (180). Therefore, as Ma remakes Charlotte, Laura's treasured doll looks more like the Ingalls family ideal of fair-skinned, blond-haired femininity.

We might say that Charlotte has been remade in the same way that Mary and Ma wish to remake Laura. Indeed, the remaking of Charlotte seems to be an attempt to redefine Laura's character as well, as Ma actively enlists her daughter in the process. Miriam Formanek-Brunell explains that doll making was an important part of nineteenth-century girls' "informal apprenticeship for being a wife and mother" (10). She also traces how the function of dolls shifted during this time. In antebellum America (the era in which Ma came of age), dolls played a utilitarian role in providing opportunity to learn sewing skills, while in postwar America (when Laura was born), dolls were increasingly used for developing young women's emotional affinities. Enlisting Laura in the domestic task of reconstructing Charlotte, Ma attempts to integrate her "wild" daughter into an acceptable gendered and racialized role while minimizing Laura's emotional connection to a doll she is "too big to play with" (*Banks* 232).

Ma's remaking of Laura seems successful because she appears to lose interest in Charlotte after this moment. Although the "old rag doll, Charlotte" is mentioned during Laura's packing before marrying Almanzo in *These Happy Golden Years* (274), we do not see Laura playing with her again. One explanation is that Laura is simply growing older. More significantly, Charlotte has lost some of the qualities that connected her to Laura and the Indian baby. Thus, rather than playing with her remade doll, Laura places the lighter-haired Charlotte "in her box" and then falls asleep "cuddled against Mary," a detail that signifies the closer alignment between the two sisters throughout the rest of the series (236).

Tracking these familial complications—Laura's loyalty to as well as relational displacement in her family, particularly in relation to her sisters and Ma—we return to the scene with Laura and the Indian baby. In light of Laura's conflicted position as a sister and daughter, this moment may be read not only as Laura's demand for a toy but also as her desire for familial and cultural connection.

That Laura imagines a family connection with the Indian baby is seen through the gaze they share. When Laura sees the baby, she is not merely looking at Charlotte's static black button eyes; instead, the baby looks back at Laura, a fact reinforced twice: "Those black eyes looked deep into Laura's eyes"; "Its head turned and its eyes kept looking into Laura's eyes" (*Prairie* 308). Moreover, the description of the baby's eyes as "bright" mirrors descriptions of Laura's favorite family members. Pa's eyes often are characterized throughout the series as "shining," and Laura notices the same spirit in her grandmother's eyes, which "sparkled just like Pa's when he laughed" (*Woods* 35, 150). Laura also recognizes the eyes of the other Indians in the parade as "alive," a characterization that associates them with some of her most beloved family members (*Prairie* 305). This contradicts Kaye's analysis that the Indians' eyes have a "stoical depthlessness" (136) and gestures toward Laura's desire for another family member who might identify with her rather than Ma, Mary, or Carrie. Thus, Laura does reach toward an "extended family," as Romines suggests, but not one to "share with ... her white sisters" (78); rather, she hopes for a sibling who could be her own.

The text also explains that Laura "looked straight into the bright eyes of the little baby *nearer her*" (*Prairie* 308; emphasis added). This commentary on the spatial relationship between Laura and the baby not only indicates their connection but implies that this baby is "nearer" to Laura than to Mary, Ma, or Carrie. Just as Carrie is Ma's and Mary's baby, Laura wants a companion who can identify with her dark hair, love for the outdoors, and free spirit. If Laura cannot actually "*be* a little Indian girl" (307; emphasis added), as she initially wishes, then she wants the Indian baby to become part of her family. Laura's expression that the baby "wants to stay with me" (308), then, becomes Laura's projection of her desire.

Laura cannot explain this desire to Ma: "'Why on earth do you want an Indian baby, of all things!' Ma asked her. 'Its eyes are so black,' Laura sobbed. She could not say what she meant" (*Prairie* 309). Ma insists that the family already has a baby, "our own baby" (310). This phrase not only describes Carrie's biological status but also carries racial subtexts. The Indian baby is not one of the family's "own" white race, making Laura's desire for her to become part of the family completely unthinkable to Ma. Ma refuses to acknowledge Laura's desire for a nonwhite sibling, rejecting her statement: "Why Laura ... you don't want another baby" (310). But although she cannot offer an explanation, Laura does not immediately submit to Ma's rewriting of her desire, as she does in other instances. Instead, Laura restates it with even more force: "I want the other one, too!" (310). Laura thus resists inclusion in the phrase *our own baby*, instead asking for what we might call "*her* own baby"—a sibling who can identify with her in ways her white family does not. Of course, this desire falls short of any mutual "shared life" with the Natives, for Laura would like the baby to join *her* family, not the other way around (Romines 78).

Neither Ma nor Pa understands Laura's desire for the Indian baby in this moment, nor does Laura fully understand her own feelings. Yet as a young girl negotiating her identity, Laura feels these conflicts keenly. Novotny points out that the tension Laura feels in relationship to her familial identity has a profound influence on her throughout the series: "Laura must reconcile her family's attitudes toward both race and gender to her sense of self. This tension affects Laura deeply, altering her thoughts and behaviors. It disrupts her sense of self as same, inviting a sense of self as other because she now has difficulty identifying with Ma and Mary—her teachers, models, protectors, and socializers" (49). In other words, Laura's near tantrum can be read as a child's response to her inner negotiation of identity. Laura's response to the baby is complex because her own identity is complex; although she places high value on family, her own position within that family is at times difficult to negotiate. As Spaeth suggests, throughout the series Laura is "intensely alert," frequently feeling "not the way good little girls are 'supposed' to feel ... making her character multifaceted or multidimensional and always interesting" (*Laura* 65).

Although we cannot tell exactly what Laura feels as she cries over the Indian baby, I see a multidimensional Laura in this passage. Her demands are selfish, yet she seeks relationship. She is motivated by egocentrism, yet she questions the ethnocentric expectations of her family. Her possessive desire would displace the Osage baby, yet she feels misplaced. Acknowledging this complexity does not diminish the abundant racial and gendered problems in the series; rather, it deepens our awareness of how profoundly they operate—even implicitly, as with Charlotte—and reveals how Laura perpetuates her family's negative beliefs while navigating her position within the family.

Reading this moment as Laura's desire for her own baby gestures toward the moment's duality: Laura participates in the Osage baby's objectification by longing to possess it as she does her doll (her *own* baby), and at the same time she looks for connection (*her* own baby). That these layers operate simultaneously is part of what creates such a troubling scene, one that does not resolve the series' many tensions but instead illuminates them.

NOTES

1. The historical inaccuracy and literary embellishment of Wilder's Indian Removal scene has been well noted. As Bethany Schneider writes, "Wilder rearranges family and national history in order to make her series march westward with the fantasy of the frontier into the fantasy of the future" (82).

2. Schneider generally aligns herself with these scholars but finds this particular scene "illegible to everyone.... I think it is best to allow the child character to be, in fact, dumbfounded" (71).

3. Laura even names her corncob doll Susan (*Woods* 21).

4. Bernstein's research focuses on actual artifacts of culture, sometimes produced as an extension of literature (for example, a topsy-turvy doll or Raggedy Ann). I do not focus here on material Charlotte dolls, although many have been produced and sold. I merely apply Bernstein's theory to the literary references to Charlotte.

5. While soft Indian dolls did not appear during this time, Indian figurines did appear in "floor games" that "modeled imperialist visions" for boys (Bernstein 185).

6. Smulders points out that words such as *papoose* and *Indian* act as "white ideological construct[s] delimiting the native as deficient, generic, and static" (193). See also Berkhofer.

7. Such historical accounts also reinforce larger issues in Wilder's depictions of frontier settlement and Indian Removal. As Kaye and others have noted, the narrative of westward expansion chronicled by dominant white culture has vilified native people while blatantly ignoring the crimes of white settlers, including the Ingalls family.

8. To be clear, the Osage described in *Little House on the Prairie* are not the Dakota of Minnesota. I agree with Schneider that Wilder uses the generic term *Indian* to represent all Native characters, conflating regional differences (83).

9. Whether Wilder is intentionally aligning the Native baby with Charlotte and making a veiled statement about the treatment of indigenous people is unclear. Historian John E. Miller has credited Wilder with a view of Indians that is "well-meaning, if often ambivalent" (206). Yet if Wilder aimed to critique Indian Removal in her books, she certainly could have done so more explicitly. While not old enough to remember living in Kansas, Wilder "absolutely smelled and touched ... settler-colonial violence" in De Smet, yet she writes about those years rather "bucolically" (Schneider 89, 83).

WORKS CITED

Berkhofer, Robert F., Jr. *The White Man's Indian: Images of the American Indian from Columbus to the Present*. Random House, 1979.

Bernstein, Robin. *Racial Innocence: Performing American Childhood from Slavery to Civil Rights*. New York University Press, 2011.

Blackford, Holly. "Civilization and Her Discontents: The Unsettling Nature of Ma in *Little House in the Big Woods*." *Frontiers: A Journal of Women Studies* 29, no. 1 (2008): 147–87.

Formanek-Brunell, Miriam. *Made to Play House*. Johns Hopkins University Press, 1993.

Frey, Charles. "Laura and Pa: Family and Landscape in *Little House on the Prairie*." *Children's Literature Association Quarterly* 12 (1987): 125–28.

Kaye, Frances W. "Little Squatter on the Osage Diminished Reserve: Reading Laura Ingalls Wilder's Kansas Indians." *Great Plains Quarterly* 20, no. 2 (2000): 123–40.

Miller, John E. *Becoming Laura Ingalls Wilder: The Woman behind the Legend*. University of Missouri Press, 1998.

Mowder, Louise. "Domestication of Desire: Gender, Language, and Landscape in the Little House Books." *Children's Literature Association Quarterly* 17, no. 1 (1992): 15–19.

Novotny, Ellen Simpson. "Shattering the Myth: Mary and Laura as Antagonists in *Little House in the Big Woods, Little House on the Prairie*, and *On the Banks of Plum Creek*." *Heritage of the Great Plains* 28, no. 2 (1995): 48–64.

Reese, Debbie. "Proceed with Caution: Using Native American Folktales in the Classroom." *Language Arts* 84, no. 3 (2007): 245–56.

Romines, Ann. *Constructing the Little House: Gender, Culture, and Laura Ingalls Wilder.* University of Massachusetts Press, 1997.

Schneider, Bethany. "A Modest Proposal: Laura Ingalls Wilder Ate Zitkála-Šá." *GLQ: A Journal of Gay and Lesbian Studies* 21, no. 1 (2015): 65–93.

Segel, Elizabeth. "Laura Ingalls Wilder's America: An Unflinching Assessment." *Children's Literature in Education* 8, no. 2 (1977): 63–70.

Smulders, Sharon. "'The Only Good Indian': History, Race, and Representation in Laura Ingalls Wilder's *Little House on the Prairie*." *Children's Literature Association Quarterly* 27, no. 4 (2002): 191–202.

Spaeth, Janet. *Laura Ingalls Wilder.* Twayne, 1987.

Spaeth, Janet. "Over the Horizon of the Years: Laura Ingalls Wilder and the Little House Books." PhD diss., University of North Dakota, 1982.

Wilder, Laura Ingalls. *Little House in the Big Woods.* Harper, 1932.

Wilder, Laura Ingalls. *Little House on the Prairie.* Scholastic, 1935.

Wilder, Laura Ingalls. *On the Banks of Plum Creek.* Harper, 1937.

Wilder, Laura Ingalls. *These Happy Golden Years.* Harper, 1943.

Wilson, Waziyatawin Angela Cavender. "Burning Down the House: Laura Ingalls Wilder and American Colonialism." In *Unlearning the Language of Conquest*, edited by Wahinkpe Topa AKA Don Trent Jacobs, 66–80. University of Texas Press, 2006.

Wilson, Waziyatawin Angela Cavender. "Decolonizing the 1862 Death Marches." *American Indian Quarterly* 28, no. 1 (2004): 185–215.

Wolf, Virginia L. "The Symbolic Center: *Little House in the Big Woods*." *Children's Literature in Education* 13, no. 3 (1982): 107–13.

LAURA'S LINEAGE

The Matrilineal Legacy of Laura Ingalls Wilder's Little House Narratives

Sonya Sawyer Fritz

In her 1937 Detroit Book Fair speech, Laura Ingalls Wilder, famous child pioneer who grew up in the US western territories, frames herself as a pioneer of genre as well: "I thought of writing the story of my childhood in several volumes—an eight-volume historical novel for children. . . . I was told that such a thing had never been done before, that a novel of several volumes was only for grown-ups. . . . Someone has to do a thing first; I would be the first to write a multi-volume novel for children" (qtd. in Fatzinger 30). Wilder's original series is now just one of many sets of "multi-volume novel[s]" that extend the Little House narrative: Melissa Wiley's Martha books (1999–2003) and Charlotte books (1999–2004) detail Wilder's great-grandmother's and grandmother's childhoods, respectively; Maria D. Wilkes's and Celia Wilkins's Caroline books (1996–2005) follow Wilder's mother before she became Ma; and Roger Lea MacBride's Rose books (1993–99) portray Wilder's only daughter and collaborator, Rose Wilder Lane.[1] Altogether, the four series include nearly two dozen books, but critics have not yet considered how these spin-offs affect the sociocultural and political shape of Wilder's novels. Drawing on Sanne Parlevliet's definition of historical fiction, I argue that these texts constitute "a cultural practice that brings images of the past into circulation" in the present (354). How, then, do the images of the past that these texts circulate interact with Wilder's presentation of history to shape American collective memory and reinforce or revise Wilder's place in the story of America's origin?

The spin-off series strengthen the Little House dynasty by emphasizing Anglo-American national identity while simultaneously creating a matrilineal history. Each little girl protagonist becomes the adult mother in a subsequent series, allowing mothers to become more important to their daughters' stories than would otherwise be the case and encouraging young readers to consider how the recurring transitions from daughter to mother shape our definitions of history. Particularly in Wilkes's Caroline books and MacBride's Rose books, Native Americans continue to be framed as Other, perpetuating the troubling ethnocentrism of Wilder's original texts.[2] In so doing, these texts cast Anglo-American mothers and daughters as active participants in the narrative of American history and settling the American frontier while foregrounding their whiteness.

Launched in the early 1990s by HarperCollins, these spin-offs celebrate Wilder's narrative and recognize its importance as a commercial enterprise. But they were also explicitly conceived to mimic more contemporary popular historical fiction for girls. Subsequent editions of these works have been abridged, for example, presumably to render them as accessible as the American Girl books, which are typically short and episodic. MacBride's Rose books were the first to be published, and MacBride, who was Lane's beneficiary and (unofficially) adopted grandson, undertakes a deeply personal project in telling her story while leveraging the familiarity of the Little House brand to build a lucrative franchise. The spin-offs do this in part by using titles similar to those of Wilder's original books. The title of the first book in each new series replicates Wilder's formulaic *Little House* phrasing: the Martha Years' *Little House in the Highlands* (1999); the Charlotte Years' *Little House by Boston Bay* (1999); the Caroline Years' *Little House in Brookfield* (1996); and the Rose Years' *Little House on Rocky Ridge* (1993). Similarly, the illustrations, particularly those in the Rose series, are black-and-white drawings evocative of the iconic pictures Garth Williams created for Wilder's books. Like the original Little House books, these new series are episodic, offering fictionalized accounts of Wilder's relatives' lives. For example, Wiley's Martha books portray Wilder's great-grandmother growing up on a Scottish estate, having adventures, learning from her experiences, and growing closer to family members and friends. The Charlotte books, also written by Wiley, follow Martha's daughter (Wilder's grandmother), who lives with her immigrant parents and siblings in Boston during the War of 1812. Wilkes's and Wilkins's books focus on Caroline Quiner, Wilder's mother, tracing her life as one of six children raised by a widow on the Wisconsin frontier. MacBride's Rose books follow Wilder's daughter, who grew up in Missouri with Laura and Almanzo on their Rocky Ridge farm before traveling to Louisiana for schooling and later to Kansas City.

The spin-offs' mother-daughter relationships also relate to aspects of the original series. Scholars have defined mother-daughter connections as a significant component of Wilder's narratives; matrilineage in general and the relationships between both Wilder and Caroline and Wilder and Rose inform the texts implicitly and explicitly. Ann Romines identifies Wilder as "the beneficiary of a knot of Euro-American women's cultural traditions" (14), noting that Wilder's mother "had compiled her own handwritten and handsewn book of original and collected poems as a girl and had preserved it to pass on to her daughters" (14), thereby giving "her daughter an example of a writing woman" (17). Romines additionally notes that "one of the attributes repeatedly associated with Ma is her pen, its pearl handle carved in the shape of a feather.... [Y]oung Laura connected her mother with that pen, which evokes a quill and thus a long history of writing women" (14). Other scholars argue that Wilder's texts paint a more complicated picture of her relationship with her mother and the emotional and psychological legacies passed down between mothers and daughters in the family. Anita Clair Fellman claims that as Wilder re-created her childhood for consumption as fiction, she "settled old scores and came to terms with a childhood in which she had played second fiddle to a good, beautiful sister, 'the bright one,' who was much like their mother" (43). Wilder accomplished this not only by centering the story on herself and legitimizing her own perspective but also by "elaborat[ing] her father's role at the expense of her mother's, claim[ing] his admiration and approval, and celebrat[ing] her childhood rebelliousness without ever denouncing—or acknowledging—the power of her mother's gentle repressiveness" (43). Indeed, Wilder's novels represent Ma, "more subdued in personality ... than her husband" (25), with "exacting standards of behavior that young Laura could not always meet" (26), as both fundamentally different from Laura and distanced from her daughter's perspectives by her identity as an adult. Unlike Pa, whose enduring boyishness makes him empathetic to children's attitudes and struggles, Ma rarely hints at the young girl she used to be or suggests that she remembers the feeling of being a child.

Following Caroline's death, Wilder corresponded with her aunt, Martha Carpenter, and these letters suggest that Caroline seemed aloof because she avoided speaking about a childhood that was fraught with hardship. According to Carpenter, "I do not wonder that your Dear Mother and My Dear Sister did not like to talk about it. It made ones heart ache too" (Jameson 45–46). Regardless, Wilder's characterization of Caroline does little to humanize her. As Holly Blackford contends, Ma is "so mythic, so complete, so far above [Laura], and so untouchable that Laura can never compete with or replicate Ma's goddess-like powers" (147). The dance scene in *Little House in the Big Woods*, which offers the novels' most iconic description of Caroline, substantiates this: "Ma was beautiful, too, in her dark green delaine...so rich and fine that Laura was afraid to touch her" (141–42). Caroline is beautiful, as the ideal mother always is, but her beauty renders her alien and untouchable. Likewise, as Blackford notes, the delaine dress Caroline wears itself "achieves enormous significance, alluding to an inverse myth of Ma's fashionable past and 'fall' into Pa's preferred lifestyle" (150)—it had been made by a dressmaker back east, as had all of Ma's clothes "before she married Pa" (*Woods* 128). This highlights the distance between Caroline and Laura, whose wild, tomboyish inclinations tie her to the frontier and her father. Overall, the Little House books do not encourage readers to see special bonds between Wilder and her mother, to consider the maturation process by which a girl becomes a woman and a mother, or to interpret Wilder's mother as an especially heroic protagonist in the stories.[3]

In contrast, the Martha, Charlotte, Caroline, and Rose books, written by authors who are not directly related to the characters and who are distanced from their relationships, emphasize mother-daughter intimacy and matrilineal history. Each girl's series enshrines her mother's adulthood; juxtaposed with one another, the stories suggest there may have been various ways to be an American girl but just one way to be an American woman. Regardless of what kind of girl one is when young, these four series suggest, one becomes a certain kind of mother: strong and firm yet gentle; wise, moderate, nurturing, and kind, with a special tenderness just for one's daughter. Each mother's life is fraught with hardship but inflected with racial privilege.

Typically each series' first book includes a foundational description of the girl protagonist's mother that echoes the glorified image of Laura's Ma presented in *Little House in the Big Woods*. For example, in Wiley's *Little House in the Highlands*, Martha's mother, whom we know only as an adult, is characterized as beautiful, warm, cheery, and lively: "Her hair was a rich golden brown.... She wore it piled high on her head in a mass of shining waves. Her blue eyes always had a laugh peeking out of them" (6).[4] As a mother herself in Wiley's Charlotte books, Martha is the lively heart of the Tucker home, with a "quick tongue" that is full of humor and "a different song for every task" (Wiley, *Boston Bay* 8, 9). In Charlotte's eyes, her mama "is so beautiful in her fine black linen that Charlotte almost wished she were old enough to stay home and take care of [her baby sister, Mary], so that Mama could go to meeting where all the town could see her" (16). In time, Charlotte becomes just as beautiful to her daughters: when the family attends a party in Wilkes's *Little Town at the Crossroads*, a rare event for the Quiners, Caroline marvels at how beautiful her mother is in her party dress: "Mother was standing on the far side of the hearth, where the soft glow of firelight made her gold-colored dress shine richly...."

As Mother glided across the room to help the girls brush and braid their hair, Caroline thought she looked just like an angel" (221–22). In MacBride's *Little House on Rocky Ridge*, Wilder becomes the same kind of beautiful mother: "Mama was the most beautiful of her sisters" (186).

In each of these characterizations, the protagonist's mother offers both perfection and accessibility, highlighting the crucial role of mother-daughter intimacy in the image of the ideal Anglo-American family the new series seek to portray. Even for Caroline's mother and Rose's mother, both of whom are described simply as beautiful, intimacy with their daughters is implied instead of the fear and awe Wilder evokes when describing her mother. Significantly, intimacy is often represented through the rituals of hairdressing. Just as Charlotte is "an angel" who tends her daughters' locks (Wilkes, *Crossroads* 222), Rose "thought Mama was most beautiful in the morning, when her hair fell over her back, with the light racing through it.... Rose loved the silky, smooth feel of it right after Mama brushed it out" (MacBride 186). With Martha's mother and Charlotte's mother—the mothers of the most heavily fictionalized series, in which the authors had the most freedom to imagine an ideal mother—warmth and joy are more explicit in their personalities and relationships with their children; each cultivates adoration and intimacy. In *The Far Side of the Loch*, for example, when Martha's mother travels to help Martha's aunt and uncle settle into their new home, Martha longs for her mother. And when they are reunited, "Martha's first sight of [Mum] was like catching the first scent of heather on the wind in the spring.... Martha wanted to run to Mum and hug her and tell her everything that had happened during the week" (192–93). Similarly, as Charlotte's mother, Martha functions regularly as comforter and confidant, becoming a particularly heroic figure in *Across the Puddingstone Dam*, the final book in this series. Following the tragic death of Charlotte's nine-month-old brother, Martha comforts Charlotte, telling her a secret: George is the fourth child that Martha has lost. The revelation that Martha silently copes with the loss of three other infants, all dead either before Charlotte was alive or before she was old enough to remember, allows the narrative's focus to shift temporarily from Charlotte and her grief over George's death to Martha's loss and courage: "Mama had carried a sorrowful secret beneath her merry smile.... Mama was even braver than Charlotte had guessed. But she was not bitter, not even now, when the merry light had been quenched by grief. And suddenly Charlotte had a flash of understanding. That light had been quenched before, three times at least, and it had always come back. She thought of what her life would have been like without that light, without the laughter in Mama's eyes, and she shuddered. She clung to her mother, feeling a wave of love" (196). Charlotte's celebration of Martha and the bond that mother and daughter share demonstrates the way in which Charlotte's story extends Martha's story, revealing the heartbreak she has experienced in adulthood and highlighting the hardships that wives and mothers have so often suffered throughout history.

In the Caroline books, Charlotte has an even harder adult life than Martha. Charlotte endures her husband's death and the loneliness and stress of raising six children with few resources. The story of Caroline's childhood, with all its small victories and frustrations, its rivalries and joys, is then also the story of grown-up Charlotte's recovery from "the dark days after they had learned that [her husband] had been lost at sea and was never coming back" and the new life she forges with her children as she moves them to a new home, works to provide for them, and eventually remarries (Wilkes, *Clearing* 11). The Charlotte series primes readers to feel sympathy for her as an adult, when Caroline describes her as "weary," as well as love for a woman who maintains "her kind, gentle voice" and "make[s] everything all right" (Wilkes, *Clearing* 9; Wilkins 301). That Charlotte represents an ideal mother despite the extreme hardships she experiences emphasizes how invested the Caroline books are in celebrating the mother—whether realistically or not—in the process of telling her daughter's story.

The losses that punctuate Martha's and Charlotte's stories also highlight how, as fictionalized matrilineal history, these works represent women's homemaking on the American frontier in much the way that Janet Floyd describes it: "The emigrant home ... is a space quintessentially unstable in meaning: like all homes it is, at some level, 'euphemistic,' yet the association of emigration with loss and dislocation gives the emigrant home a particular intensity of meaning" (3). Each series portrays the members of this matrilineal family as growing up in one place and then, in the subsequent book series, living as an emigrant somewhere else: Martha transitions from girlhood in Scotland to adulthood in America; Charlotte from girlhood in Boston to adulthood in Wisconsin; Caroline from girlhood in Wisconsin to adulthood in Kansas, Minnesota, and South Dakota; and Laura from girlhood on the frontier to adulthood in Missouri. While Wilder's original series highlights the pioneer girl and the frontier family as American icons, the spin-off series focus on the emigrant woman as central to American culture, history, and national identity. The five series combine to advance a striking subtext of loss, transition, and/or suspension of the home through migration as key to American womanhood. That these are fictionalized characterizations of real mothers makes them even more telling. Free to shape these women and their relationships with their daughters, the spin-off authors reinforce discourses on motherhood that idealize the white American pioneer mother and the expectations of the nineteenth-century

Cult of True Womanhood. This domestic ideology's general exclusion of all but white middle- and upper-class women is replicated in MacBride's, Wiley's, Wilkes's, and Wilkins's texts as they present white families and white women's homemaking and parenting practices as central to American history.

Even though these texts engage and expand on the narrative of white American female identity constructed by Wilder's original Little House series, and although they are written in a more contemporary era, they nonetheless reinforce ethnocentric values evident throughout Wilder's original series. In particular, *Little House on the Prairie* has long been critiqued for its representation of the Osage Indians as barbaric and dangerous. As Fellman notes, a "fair amount of ink has been spilled over whether Wilder was a critic of prevailing attitudes toward Indians or was a racist herself" (89). Frances W. Kaye and Philip Heldrich, among others, argue that Wilder's Little House books are racist in their representations of Native Americans. Kaye describes *Little House on the Prairie* as "a book that lulls us into believing that the dispossession of the Osage people from Kansas was sad but necessary and even 'natural,' like all losses of the innocence of childhood and other primitive ways of being" (124), while Heldrich offers a milder interpretation of the novel as a "complex text" that tempers Ma's straightforward racism with Pa's and Laura's more nuanced appreciations of the indigenous peoples with whom white settlers competed for land (107). In *Pioneer Girl*, Wilder's descriptions of Native Americans and her discussions of their interactions with whites are less dramatically developed and more ambiguous in their exoticization and vilification. Still, *Pioneer Girl* editor Pamela Smith Hill finds it necessary to offer missing context for the Osage Indians' behavior in the scenes that became part of *Little House on the Prairie*. As Hill notes, "Settlers were 'obliged to secure consent from the Indians' before occupying a 'squatter's claim' such as the Ingalls claim and ... individual Osages made frequent visits to their tenants' property to ensure ongoing payment"; moreover, the Osages "were impoverished and hungry" after white settlers destroyed the Natives' farmlands and the US government ended annuity payments (9 n. 22). Overall, the Little House stories are generally understood as texts that are ethnocentric as a result of the historical context in which they were written and the ethnicity and identity of those who produced them.

Of all the new series, only Wilkes's and Wilkins's Caroline books, set in Wisconsin territory during the 1840s and 1850s, attempt to complicate the white settler narrative. In the years leading up to Caroline's 1839 birth, Wisconsin was the site of significant exploitation of and attacks against the local tribes, as represented in the 1829 Treaties of Prairie du Chien, in which the Chippewa, Ottawa, Potawatomi, and Winnebago tribes were pressured to cede their land to the United States. The 1832 Black Hawk War followed, pitting the US military against Sauk tribe members who were attempting to return peacefully to lands they had lost in the controversial 1804 Treaty of St. Louis. These are important events that impacted the Quiners' lives in Wisconsin, and alluding to them might have enabled the Caroline books to directly address injustices suffered by the indigenous tribes of the region while focusing on the struggles of life on the frontier.

But the series instead chooses to frame Native Americans as Other, highlighting their marginalized minority status without acknowledging the roles that whites played in creating this status. Wilkes's *Little House in Brookfield* offers the most sympathetic portrayal of a Native American, but the portrayal is still problematic because readers perceive Native Americans exclusively through the Quiners' eyes. In that novel, during the long winter when the members of Caroline's fatherless family are struggling to feed themselves, a Native American man who knew Caroline's father gives them a deer. While the family acknowledges Crooked Bone's kindness, they view him as a strange and exotic specimen, with "black and sparkling" eyes and "a jagged scar [that] stretched from the corner of his left eye all the way down his red-brown cheek to the side of his chin" (193). Caroline's mother is horrified when Crooked Bone and his companion try to bring the carcass into the house to butcher it; Caroline's brother makes them take it to the barn. Despite their need and their gratitude, the Quiners see Crooked Bone and his friend through the lens of white privilege and ethnocentrism.

In the series' second book, *Little Town at the Crossroads*, Wilkes represents Native Americans as either volatile barbarians or tragic yet inevitable victims of progress, replicating *Little House on the Prairie*'s problematic stereotyping. Here, Caroline witnesses an angry Native American man whose brother was murdered accuse a townsperson, Mr. Carleton, of committing the murder. The white townspeople perceive this indigenous man as extremely dangerous: Caroline's mother "whisper[s] frantically" that they must get away from the man quickly (94), and he corroborates this view when he "whip[s] a thin silver knife out of his boot" and holds "the flashing blade up against Mr. Carleton's neck" (95). Mr. Carpenter, a Quiner family friend, sends away the Indian before he harms anyone, asserting that he wasn't dangerous because "one lone man can't stand up against a whole pack of townsfolk, no matter how crazed with anger he is" (96–97). Mr. Carpenter also denies claims that he effectively defused the situation because "that poor Indian didn't understand one word I was saying" (97), highlighting the man's Otherness; he is a bizarre spectacle rather than a complex individual.

Above all, however, this angry Native American man is frightening, and the incident casts a pall over the Quiner family's life for weeks: the children refer to him as "too scary to think about," and they notice that Mother "insisted on knowing the whereabouts of the children every time they left the house. . . . [S]he had stopped singing at night as she sewed in her rocker. She sat quietly now. Listening" (Wilkes, *Crossroads* 104–5). Ultimately, Mrs. Quiner's fear is justified when, paralleling events from *Little House on the Prairie*, the Native American enters the Quiner home uninvited, terrifying the family and taking some of their possessions, including peacock feathers that he puts in his hair, giving him "a wild and exotic look" (109). Much to the family's relief, he leaves after demanding, in broken English, to see the "man of house" and discovering that there is none (110). However, once the intruder has left, Caroline's two youngest siblings are discovered missing—kidnapped or otherwise harmed, the family assumes, by the Native American. Cries Mrs. Quiner, "There's no telling what he's done with them!" (111). Both children are found safe, but no one acknowledges facts that could complicate their understanding of this man as a dangerous savage: (1) his hostility stems from a long history of attacks on his people, including but not limited to the killing of his brother, and could easily be interpreted as justified; (2) his entrance into the Quiner home and appropriation of their belongings reflects cultural differences that nineteenth-century white settlers seldom tried to understand; (3) Mrs. Quiner's fears that the man had kidnapped the children are unfounded, and it is unlikely that he was interested in taking or harming two white children; and (4) the children would have been safer had they remained in the yard instead of running away from the man they perceived as dangerous. In other words, their fear of the Other caused more problems than it solved.

When the Quiners encounter additional Native Americans later in the novel, readers are offered representations that only ostensibly contrast with this angry, dangerous man. Caroline and her family meet a woman with a "drawn face and tired eyes" who is traveling with her son and her dying father (Wilkes, *Crossroads* 185). They are in search of the elderly man's birthplace, "where boulders and firs stand watch by running water," so that they can fulfill his wish to die and be buried there (185).[5] Taking pity on the trio, the Quiners accompany them and ask for help locating the landmark, and two men eventually load the Native American family into a sled, taking over the search. But Mrs. Quiner's dedication to helping these hapless strangers forces her children to consider how they should feel about and treat Indians in the wake of their home invasion experience. Caroline's brother, Joseph, refers to "the Indians who keep coming back and roaming through the countryside, helping themselves to folks' crops and running off with their livestock," asking "What about the Indian who came to our house?" (187–88). Mrs. Quiner quiets Joseph: "These people have done no such thing[s]," thus distancing this family from the villains Joseph describes without rebutting his characterization (188). Regardless, both versions of the Native are merely spectacles. The Caroline books imply that there is more than one way to be an "Indian": generous and honorable, like Crooked Bone; dangerous and barbaric, like the angry man seeking vengeance; or poetically tragic, like the family Caroline's mother helps. But the texts always cast Indians as the primitive Other or employ ethnocentric stereotypes.

In addition, Native Americans are peripheral figures in the Caroline novels, there to advance this white family's story and to underscore its heroism. Each Native American character highlights some admirable aspect of the Quiners' lives. Crooked Bone's generosity emphasizes the hardships they suffer without a father/provider as well as the greatness of the late Henry Quiner, whose friendship motivates Crooked Bone to help the family: "Red-Hand friend," Crooked Bone tells the family multiple times, describing Caroline's father by his burn scars (Wilkes, *Brookfield* 196, 197). Likewise, the family's encounters with Native Americans in *Little Town at the Crossroads* affirm the Quiners' courage and open-mindedness; juxtaposed with the family's terrifying experience with the angry Indian's home invasion and theft, Caroline's mother's attitude toward the Native American mother, son, and grandfather seems particularly noble: "There are good and bad men of all kinds, Caroline.... The woman and her boy need our help, same as we have needed other folks' help. 'Freely ye have received, freely give.' So shall it be" (189). We never find out whether this Native American family finds the land or the closure for which they search, and the novel does not explore the courage and desperation that inflect their pilgrimage.

The same is true of Crooked Bone's situation in *Little House in Brookfield*; Joseph explains that "Father told us that [Crooked Bone] and his people lived here long before us or any of our neighbors. Now Crooked Bone only comes back to hunt and fish" (194). For young readers, this statement glosses over its own implications: Crooked Bone's people were coerced into ceding land that was rightfully theirs, and their new home has fewer resources, motivating them to return when they can to hunt and trap. The dangers faced by tribes seeking peacefully to return to their homelands go unmentioned as well. Because of such representations, the more recent Little House narratives are complicit in Wilder's "tendency to make Native peoples disappear" in her original texts (Fellman 91). Whether kindhearted, enraged, or sad, Native Americans are characterized as fading from a landscape that now belongs to white settlers. Wilkes's novels also support Kathryn Shanley's claim that "Euro-Americans continue to retreat from the ambiguity inherent in recognizing how difficult it is to determine who or what one is observing and how one affects someone or something by observation" (41). Rather than foreground the understandably fraught subtext of the Quiners' interactions with Native Americans—and, indeed, of any white Wisconsin settlers' interactions with indigenous peoples during this historical period—and acknowledge the difficulties and limitations of observing Native Americans from an Anglo-European perspective, the Caroline books do not analyze the tensions and injustices surrounding Anglo relations with indigenous peoples in nineteenth-century Wisconsin.

As "The Indian Story" in MacBride's *Little House on Rocky Ridge* reveals, this impulse to engage stereotypical images of Native Americans without problematizing Anglo-Americans' perceptions of and interactions with indigenous people recurs throughout the spin-offs.[6] Traveling to Missouri, Rose's Papa tells the story of a railroad doctor who found an "Indian mummy"—the mummified body of a Native American infant—placed in a tree as part of a burial rite. The doctor removes the body from the tree, planning "to send it to the Smithsonian Institution in Washington, or maybe sell it to Barnum's Museum" (30–31), but when tribal members discover the baby's body is missing, they threaten to attack the railroad camp unless the body is returned. The doctor is reached by telegraph before he sells the body, and it is returned to the tribe. The chapter concludes with Rose noting that she "wanted to see an Indian mummy" and "was sorry there weren't Indians to see. . . . But Mama said she had seen enough Indians in her lifetime, thank you" (33). Papa's story, which Mama is concerned will "giv[e] her nightmares," is meant to enliven Rose's journey (30). The story's description and suspense hinge on casting Native Americans as spectacles of grotesquerie and violence. In other words, the representation of this event as a story worth telling rises out of a perception of the Indian as Other. Even Mama's concern that the story is inappropriate to share with a child is informed by this perception. Mama's suggestion that the story is not nice and could give a young girl nightmares is metonymic, representing her belief that Indians are not nice and could give a young (white) girl nightmares—a perspective that the novel does not challenge. Similarly, Papa's attitude about the story, although it appears to bear Native Americans no real ill will, relegates the real-life people involved in the event to a sort of bogeyman status—perhaps scary but also entertaining, and safely contained within the story. The oversimplification and demonization of Native Americans that occurs through this story may not seem as egregious as the problematic representations of American Indians in earlier twentieth-century children's works such as Wilder's *Little House on the Prairie* or Robert Lawson's *They Were Strong and Good* (1940), but it is equally dehumanizing in the subtle ways that it exploits a Native American family's grief over the death of a child and the subsequent horror of the desecration of that baby's burial site, all while winking at the monstrosity of a doctor who robs a grave for personal profit.

"The Indian Story" in *Little House on Rocky Ridge* also signifies Laura's own maturation. Laura begins as a girl who is fascinated with Indians and whose perspective "reflects a middle ground between her mother's and father's positions" on Indians (Heldrich 100). As a woman, though, she shifts entirely to her mother's side, finding Native Americans as distasteful as Ma did. Thus, the change in Laura's response as she moves from the position of daughter to that of mother demonstrates how the matrilineal history of these narratives and their sustained ethnocentrism can be connected. Because of Laura's whiteness, adopting her mother's xenophobic views becomes a "natural" part of growing up and becoming a mother herself. In this way, the intersections of race and gender represent for young readers the (white) female faces of American history through Wilder's iconic books and these new series. Even the series and novels that do not feature problematic representations of Native Americans privilege whiteness. For example, in the first Charlotte book, Wiley's *Little House by Boston Bay*, in which the Tucker family survives the War of 1812, Charlotte's mother notes that "America had no choice but to stand up to England and tell her she'd better think twice about tryin' to bully us—stealin' our sailors, sellin' guns to the Indians, and such" (182). The novel subtly associates Americanness and American patriotism with white settlers rather than indigenous peoples. The historical backdrop that highlights Charlotte's place in American history is articulated at the expense of non-Anglo-Europeans. Traces of the same ethnocentrism are present in the Martha books, which foreshadow her immigration to the United States through pointed references to "America, the brand-new country across the sea [that] had won its War for Independence in the year 1783, just one year after Martha had been born ... a whole country that was nearly the same age as a little girl!" (Wiley, *Highlands* 23). Wiley makes a familiar assumption here—no "real" nation existed in North America until Anglo-Europeans settled there and fought for their political autonomy; America's history begins only with white people's presence, a position that obscures and discounts the reality that numerous sovereign indigenous nations comprised North America for centuries before Anglo-Europeans arrived.

In her discussion of Caroline Ingalls's elusiveness in Wilder's original series, Jameson points out that "the problem" with Wilder's original Little House books is that "we must stop the story before [Laura] can grow up and become Ma, or Caroline, or maybe even Laura" because an adult Laura "would have to be enclosed by family and work; she would have to deal with failure and loss. Her adult life would violate the conventions of both Cinderella and the Pioneer Dream" (50–51). Jameson notes that "stories of adult women take us past the frontier, past the adventure, past childhood, past the fun" (50) and that we need more "accurate Western stories, in which adult women play important roles, in which family settlement is not the end of the frontier adventure but the beginning of the important task of building human social relationships. We need to imagine stories in which our real mothers and grandmothers helped create the West we inherited. We need to hear their stories" (51).

Overall, the spin-off Little House books do share women's stories, and they recast a portion of American history that has traditionally been traced through men and their public and political relationships, framing it instead as a matrilineal narrative. Yet like so many other stories of American history, these stories ignore intersections of race and gender by privileging the views of Anglo-American mothers and daughters. In doing so, these new series relinquish one mythic version of history so that another can take its place; together, they amplify and crystallize the notion, latent in Wilder's fictionalized accounts of her own girlhood, that the history of America is comprised of the girlhoods of its white mothers.

NOTES

1. MacBride previously collaborated with Lane on her biography.

2. While neither Wiley's Martha books nor her Charlotte books explicitly portray Native Americans, these series implicitly contribute to the characterization of American national identity as singularly Anglo-European.

3. This is also corroborated by details shared by Hill in the annotations to *Pioneer Girl* regarding Wilder's composition of her memoirs and the editorial process by which she and her daughter adapted these memoirs into the Little House novels. Hill's notes trace several instances when Wilder consciously revised statements originally attributed to one parent as having been made by the other. For example, in *Pioneer Girl*, when Laura begs her parents to get her an Indian baby as they watch the Osage Indian procession, her father scolds her; in *Little House on the Prairie*, her mother admonishes her (*Pioneer* 19 n. 41; *Prairie* 309), framing Ma in this moment as the parent who does not understand or empathize with her child's desires. At the same time, scholars such as Romines have recognized Caroline's increasing significance and closer relationship with Laura, particularly in *The Long Winter* and ensuing volumes.

4. Based on Martha's age in 1788, when her series begins, her mother would have been a child in the 1750s and 1760s.

5. Wilkes's narrative does not identify the particular tribe to which this family belongs, suggesting obliquely who they are through descriptions of clothing and names: the woman's son is described as wearing his hair "tightly wrapped in a pale-colored cloth that was twisted and folded high on top of his head," a headdress that resembles Potawatomi regalia, and his name, No-taw-kah, is also the name of a nineteenth-century Potawatomi chief (Wilkes, *Crossroads* 184).

6. MacBride lifted this story from Wilder (*Pioneer* 227–29).

WORKS CITED

Berg, Carol S. "Black Hawk War." *Salem Press Encyclopedia*. Salem Press, 2016.

Blackford, Holly. "Civilization and Her Discontents: The Unsettling Nature of Ma in *Little House in the Big Woods*." *Frontiers* 29, no. 1 (2008): 147–87.

"The Black Hawk War." *Wisconsin Historical Society*. https://www.wisconsinhistory.org/turningpoints/tp-012/#tid3.

Fatzinger, Amy. "'Indians in the House': Revisiting the American Indians in Laura Ingalls Wilder's Little House Books." PhD diss., University of Arizona, 2008.

Fellman, Anita Clair. *Little House, Long Shadow: Laura Ingalls Wilder's Impact on American Culture*. University of Missouri Press, 2008.

Floyd, Janet. *Writing the Pioneer Woman*. University of Missouri Press, 2002.

Heldrich, Philip. "'Going to Indian Territory': Attitudes toward Native Americans in *Little House on the Prairie*." *Great Plains Quarterly* 20, no. 2 (2000): 99–109.

Jameson, Elizabeth. "In Search of the Great Ma." *Journal of the West* 37, no. 2 (1998): 42–52.

Kaye, Frances W. "Little Squatter on the Osage Diminished Reserve: Reading Laura Ingalls Wilder's Kansas Indians." *Great Plains Quarterly* 20, no. 2 (2000): 123–40.

Lane, Rose Wilder, and Roger Lea MacBride. *Rose Wilder Lane: Her Story*. Stein and Day, 1977.

Lawson, Robert. *They Were Strong and Good*. Viking, 1940.

MacBride, Roger Lea. *Little House on Rocky Ridge*. HarperCollins, 1993.

Parlevliet, Sanne. "Is that Us? Dealing with the 'Black' Pages of History in Historical Fiction for Children (1996–2010)." *Children's Literature in Education* 47, no. 4 (2016): 343–56.

Romines, Ann. *Constructing the Little House: Gender, Culture, and Laura Ingalls Wilder*. University of Massachusetts Press, 1997.

Shanley, Kathryn. "The Indians America Loves to Love and Read: American Indian Identity and Cultural Appropriation." *American Indian Quarterly* 21, no. 4 (1997): 675–702.

"Treaty Councils, from Prairie du Chien to Madeline Island." *Wisconsin Historical Society*. https://www.wisconsinhistory.org/turningpoints/tp-013/?action=more_essay.

Wilder, Laura Ingalls. *Little House in the Big Woods*. Harper Trophy, 1971.

Wilder, Laura Ingalls. *Pioneer Girl: The Annotated Bibliography*. Edited by Pamela Smith Hill. South Dakota Historical Society Press, 2014.

Wiley, Melissa. *Across the Puddingstone Dam*. HarperCollins, 2004.

Wiley, Melissa. *The Far Side of the Loch*. HarperCollins, 2000.

Wiley, Melissa. *Little House by Boston Bay*. HarperCollins, 1999.

Wiley, Melissa. *Little House in the Highlands*. HarperCollins, 1999.

Wilkes, Maria D. *Little Clearing in the Woods*. HarperCollins, 1998.

Wilkes, Maria D. *Little House in Brookfield*. HarperCollins, 1996.

Wilkes, Maria D. *Little Town at the Crossroads*. HarperCollins, 1997.

Wilkins, Celia. *A Little House of Their Own*. HarperCollins, 2005.

LAURA'S "FARMER BOY"

Fictionalizing Almanzo Wilder in the Little House Series

Melanie J. Fishbane

In her Detroit Book Fair speech on 16 October 1937, Laura Ingalls Wilder claimed that the events described in her award-winning Little House series are all true: "Every story in this novel, all the circumstances, each incident are true. All I have told is true but it is not the whole truth" (Wilder and Lane 220). Numerous scholars have nevertheless contradicted these assertions, including with regard to her representation of her husband, Almanzo Wilder. To be sure, Laura Ingalls Wilder's second novel, *Farmer Boy*, which fictionalizes Almanzo's childhood in Malone, New York, draws on several letters and includes material such as his descriptions of his mother's sewing. Laura and Almanzo's daughter, Rose Wilder Lane, also interviewed her father for historical material for her novel, *Free Land*, and used these materials in her nonfiction (Anderson, *Story* 4).[1] As "postmodernists argue that history can only be contested versions of the past," so historical fiction demonstrates a biased and revisionist history, raising questions as to what decisions were made when the writer crafted a fictionalized version of a real person (Cooper and Short 5).

Wilder's depiction of Almanzo blurs the lines between fact and fiction. As a result, different versions of Almanzo emerge in the various volumes of the Little House series, in Wilder's journalism, and in Wilder's letters. Through these writings, readers come to know a variety of Almanzos, but Wilder carefully constructs each version to represent a man who wants an equal partnership with his wife above all else. In creating a husband who values and trusts his wife's opinion and sees her as his equal, Wilder provides readers with a feminist intervention, a counternarrative to the traditional frontier wife, such as her mother, Caroline Ingalls, who—except when she demands that Charles promise to send the girls to school and refuses to move further west—is seemingly comfortable with her position as an obedient wife and mother. Indeed, Wilder encourages readers to redefine traditional notions of marriage, showing them a relationship in which a husband and wife have equal say in the outcome of their lives and where a husband sees his wife as his equal as opposed to as property or as a lesser being.

Wilder crafts numerous versions of Almanzo, using his name to tie him to different identities. When he first appears in her journalism for the *Missouri Ruralist* and *McCall's*, he is the "Man of the Place," an intelligent, creative, and equal partner on the farm. Later, in the Little House series, he is "Almanzo," the heroic young man who saves the town from starvation in *The Long Winter*. With the publication of Wilder's posthumous *The First Four Years* in the 1960s, Almanzo's character is rechristened "Manly." More of a dreamer than the practical Almanzo of the novels, this figure is comparable to the equivalent figure in *Pioneer Girl*, where he is often called the Wilder Boy until he becomes Laura's suitor. Thus, these diverse texts offer sometimes consistent but sometimes conflicting glimpses of who Almanzo Wilder was, what sort of relationship he had with his wife, and how—and why—Laura Ingalls Wilder was purposefully crafting the way she depicted him. I focus first on Almanzo's character and his courtship of Laura, drawing on materials published during her lifetime. I then examine details that have emerged with the posthumous publication of other writings, such as *Pioneer Girl* and William Anderson's edition of *The Selected Letters of Laura Ingalls Wilder*, paying particular attention to Laura and Almanzo's courtship to consider how and why Laura's representations of him shift.

Almanzo James Wilder was born on 13 February 1857 in Malone, New York, one of six children (Anderson, *Story* 4). Almanzo attended the one-room Skeelsboro School and then the Franklin Academy in Malone. As *Farmer Boy* details, Almanzo's first childhood home was a comfortable, self-sustaining farm. But when Almanzo was seventeen, after his family had experienced several crop failures, the family started over in Spring Valley, Minnesota (5). Almanzo helped on the Spring Valley farm until he was twenty-two, when he traveled west with his brother, Royal, and his sister, Eliza Jane. In the Dakota territory, he filed a claim in Kingsbury County (which later became De Smet, South Dakota) on 21 August 1879 and filed a timber claim on the south edge of the claim (Hill 52, 73). The siblings returned to Spring Valley for a year before heading back to the De Smet area in 1880, when Anderson suggests Laura describes seeing the Wilder boys' wagon at the end of *By the Shores of*

Silver Lake (*Story* 6). Almanzo (with Cap Garland's assistance) helped save the town from starvation during the Hard Winter of 1880–81, traveling through a blizzard to bring back wheat. Almanzo subsequently worked his claim, courted Laura, and worked on timber claims and the railroad (Hill 54–55; Miller 67). Laura and Almanzo became engaged in 1884, and at the end of the year, Royal and Almanzo planned to go to the New Orleans Exposition and spend the winter in the South, returning just in time for planting. Almanzo and Royal changed their plans, however, traveling through Nebraska and Iowa instead; Almanzo then returned sooner than initially anticipated (Anderson, *Story* 7; Miller 69). Laura and Almanzo married on 25 August 1885.

Shortly after settling into their new home, while Almanzo was also working on the tree claim, Laura discovered that he had borrowed five hundred dollars on the homestead (Miller 74). Uncontrollable variables (including the weather) aside, he unquestionably was a hard worker. Their daughter, Rose, was born in December 1886, but the next few years were difficult. Both Laura and Almanzo contracted diphtheria. As Laura recovered, Almanzo returned to work too soon and suffered a stroke, leaving him paralyzed and weak. Their troubles continued: their son died soon after he was born, their house burned down, and the debt just increased. They regrouped while living with Almanzo's parents in Spring Valley before moving to Florida, hoping the climate would help Almanzo's health. After a year, the Wilders returned to De Smet and ultimately settled in the Ozarks, where they spent the rest of their lives. These trials brought the couple together, working side by side. As John E. Miller writes about the early years of their marriage, Laura "acted as a full partner, as responsible as Manly for making important decisions and securing their economic success" (78). After their decades of hard work, Rocky Ridge became a successful farm, and the couple lived the latter part of their lives in relative comfort. After years in poor health, Almanzo had a heart attack in July 1949 and died on 23 October (251).

Although we cannot fully know who the historical Almanzo was, his personality can be gleaned from primary sources such as interviews and letters. When Rose asked him specific details about homesteading, his detailed responses show a "keen memory" (Wilder and Lane 201–3). Further, Miller's interviews with people who knew the Wilders offer a version of Almanzo that is contradictory. Some commented that he was a "quiet type, not very talkative around people" and that his white moustache sometimes gave him a "stern appearance," so he seemed "grouchy and unapproachable" (248). However, another woman who knew Almanzo stated that he would "clown around with her mother," and Anna Gutschke reflected, "He had great humor, he enjoyed entertaining. . . . He had lots of fun, he was a joy" (248–49). Showing that he had ambition but never quite achieved what he had hoped for, Almanzo told Rose in 1937, "My life has been mainly disappointments" (Wilder and Lane 213).

This circumspect man is not the Almanzo that has been enshrined in Wilder's fiction. Many positive personality traits make Almanzo a desirable suitor for Laura, including his resourcefulness, bravery, sex appeal, strength of character, and willingness to see Laura as his equal. As Hill notes, "Almanzo Wilder was Laura's future husband; he had to be appropriately heroic to be worthy of her—and even of Pa" (51). For example, his ambition becomes clear when he argues with Royal about storing the seed wheat behind the wall so that he will have it for when planting time comes: "I'm going to run my own business my own way. I'm nailing up my seed wheat so nobody'll sell it. . . . [I]t'll be right here when seedtime comes" (*Winter* 166). Almanzo shows courage when he and Cap Garland brave a blizzard to save the starving town. In *Little Town of the Prairie*, when Laura is feeling overwhelmed at the revival and trying to get out of the church without speaking to anyone, she feels Almanzo's hand on her arm, helping her get outside (276–79). In *These Happy Golden Years*, he picks Laura up at the Brewsters' place each Friday so that she can spend the weekend with her family, particularly when it becomes clear that her situation at the Brewsters' is potentially dangerous (64–65). What particularly sets him apart is his open-mindedness when he agrees to strike the word *obey* from the marriage vows (269–70). Almanzo will not completely domesticate the free-spirited Laura, "embod[ying] the values of the 'free and independent' self-sufficient person, which Laura has been schooled to admire but is finding difficult to achieve herself," but he also has to show that he is a man of good character (Romines 230). In her fiction, Wilder shows that Almanzo is worthy because he can be counted on to be there when Laura needs him and because he understands the importance of her having an equal voice in their relationship.

In *Constructing the Little House*, Ann Romines discusses how historians traditionally saw settling the West as a male exercise because women were not perceived as having voices (159–60). Wilder's characterization of her husband is a counternarrative and a "feminist intervention" because she is giving women a voice in the history of the West as well as writing a relationship desirable from a woman's perspective—perhaps providing her younger readers with a notion of what an equal relationship could look like (Cooper and Short 2, 6). As Nicole Mancino discusses, Wilder demonstrates an awareness of being excluded from the traditional male sphere, and to counter that exclusion, she gives women voice (65). Although Laura may not see herself as a feminist, by telling Almanzo that she is uncomfortable with the term *obey*, she bravely voices her concerns. If feminism seeks an end to sexual oppression as well as equality, empowering oneself to have a voice within a relationship constitutes an important feminist goal. As bell hooks notes in "Feminism: A Movement to End Sexist Oppression," women may not be comfortable with the *feminist* label but may still want to change their position (52). When Laura is demanding that *obey* be struck from the marriage vows, she is telling Almanzo that she refuses to be put in a situation where she would not be able to stand up for herself, where her personal safety would be put in danger: she must be able to protect herself and her future children. Arguing for equality between the sexes, Wilder might then be seen as creating a feminist intervention. Along with emphasizing the fictional Almanzo's willingness to have an equal partner in marriage, Wilder made the fictional Laura a more active character who could make a living and contribute to the family home (Romines 194).

Wilder's non-Little House writings depict subtle distinctions in the development of her relationship with Almanzo and the evolution of their marriage. *Pioneer Girl, The First Four Years*, Wilder's journalism, and her letters give further insight into how well they worked together and how much she loved him. In fact, *The First Four Years* is arguably not only about Manly proving to Laura that he could be a successful farmer but also about how two people come together to create a prosperous future after facing misfortune. Manly wishes to build a beautiful home for his young bride, so he stretches his credit; goes into business with Laura's cousin, Peter; and buys her a pony (*First* 24). Even when the wheat is destroyed by hail, Manly is "cheerful and planning for the year ahead," pushing himself so hard that after being sick with diphtheria, he suffers two strokes (21, 89). Despite all these hardships, Manly remains a dreamer. Even after all the losses and trials of the first four years, he believes that "[e]verything will be alright, for it will all even up in time" (132). At the beginning of the novel, Laura allows Manly to dictate certain things, not necessarily including herself in discussion on the farm's finances, but by the end of the novel, she reflects on their hardship and how they were now making a "fresh start": "She was still the pioneer girl and she could understand Manly's love of the land through its appeal to herself" (133). One of the last things she observes is Manly singing, showing she is contentedly resolved to share in the struggles with him.

The most striking differences between *Pioneer Girl* and the Little House fiction involve Wilder's introduction of Almanzo, the way that she shifts the dynamics between Laura and Almanzo during their courtship, and the responses she attributes to Almanzo, all of which give readers new insight into who Almanzo was and how Wilder crafted his fictional counterpart. In a 1938 letter, Wilder told her daughter that readers "all seem wildly interested and want to know how, where and when Laura met Almanzo" (*Selected* 152–53). Despite readers' interest, Wilder and Lane debated several scenarios, including one where Laura and Pa meet Almanzo while they are hunting or stumbling on an envelope with his name and "puzzling over" it (*Pioneer Girl* 242 n. 41). Indeed, naming becomes an important factor in introducing Almanzo and the development of the couple's courtship. In *Pioneer Girl*, Wilder creates a sense of mystery by referring to Almanzo as "the Wilder Boy" (219) and the "younger Wilder boy" (243 n. 41) before briefly mentioning that the "same driver that had taken me so many times" (275) is at her door. Only after Laura explains, "I'm tired of saying Mr Wilder and then explaining that I mean the youngest Wilder boy and the crowd will laugh at me if I call you Mr Wilder to them" (277) is he dubbed "Manly" (277). Although Wilder does not use this naming technique in the Little House series, she foreshadows the fictional couple's meeting when Laura is moved by the young man—or the horses—at the end of *By the Shores of Silver Lake* and when she and Carrie overhear Royal call the young Wilder boy "Manzo" at the beginning of *The Long Winter* (23). In the same novel, Wilder builds tension by shifting points of view, giving readers more details about and from Almanzo's perspective. Still, Laura thinks of him only as one of the Wilder boys until *Little Town on the Prairie*, when Pa points him out during the Fourth of July race (80).

In *Pioneer Girl*, Mr. Wilder drives Laura to and from the Bouchie place during the winter, and she tells him that she is driving with him only because she wants to get home (264). When Laura returns home and sees her friends going sleigh riding, "the driver" swings by and asks her if she would like to go; she accepts (275). In this scene, Almanzo and Laura move to less formal address, (a significant step in Victorian courtship) choosing special names, "Manly" and "Bess," that are eventually woven into their partnership as a symbol of their affection to one another (277 n. 8).

Conversely, in *Little Town*, the first conversation between Laura and Almanzo takes place before she starts teaching. Laura has just picked up her freshly printed name cards, and Almanzo offers her a ride to school. The two talk briefly, and because she is not sure what else to do, she gives him a card; he reciprocates. In this scene, both characters' full names appear: Laura's in Garth Williams's illustration, and Almanzo's in the body of the novel (197–98). The exchange of name cards is significant because this is the first time Laura truly sees Almanzo as himself rather than as merely one of the Wilder boys, as her teacher's brother, or as her father's friend. She notices that "his hair was not black, as she had thought. It was dark brown, and his eyes were such a dark blue that they did not look pale in his darkly tanned face. He had a steady, dependable, yet light-hearted look" (200). The name card exchange becomes a more dramatic moment when Laura begins to see Almanzo as a potential suitor. It also demonstrates Wilder's purposeful control of the development of Almanzo and Laura's courtship.

While scholars have commented on how Wilder uses this detail to showcase Almanzo's masculinity as well as to convey Laura's growing attraction to him, Wilder also uses such episodes and others involving Almanzo's horses to show how well the couple will eventually learn to work together. In *Pioneer Girl*, Wilder describes how Laura learned how to jump into the buggy because to slow Barnum and Skip down would cause a "circus" (302). At one point, Lee Whiting, the husband of her cousin, Ella, warns, "Don't trust the driver too far, Laura. It isn't always safe," she laughs and says, "If the driver fails me, I can do the driving myself" (304). The innuendo here might reflect not just safety but also Manly's intentions, and Laura's reaction shows that she trusts him and could handle herself. Similarly, in the corresponding scene in *These Happy Golden Years*, Laura hops into the buggy, complaining about her hoopskirt. Laura recognizes Almanzo's need to keep control of the horses, so she tries to stay out of his way. Laura also manipulates the horses to scare off Nellie Oleson, who is clearly attracted to Almanzo, proving that Laura herself can handle the team (181–83). Learning to tame these horses shows the best in Laura and Almanzo's characters, giving them an outlet to learn how to work together.

Even if the historical Almanzo is shy, in *Pioneer Girl* he says what he thinks. For example, when Laura tells him that she is driving with him only to get home, he says, "Well . . . It is quite a while before school will be out anyway" (264). But in a similar scene in *These Happy Golden Years*, Wilder pauses for a beat to show Laura's emotional reaction to what she said—and what it would mean for her. She also shows Almanzo's feelings: "After a startled moment, Almanzo said slowly, 'I see'" (62). The brevity of the statement shows how much Laura has hurt his feelings; in the previous version, by contrast, Almanzo seems hopeful that she will change her mind. In *Pioneer Girl*, Wilder twice reveals that Almanzo initially courts Laura because of a dare. Almanzo's friend, Oscar Rhuel, bet that Almanzo would not see home the girl who walked behind Wilder but did not specify which girl; despite his awareness that Rhuel had been referring to the other girl, Almanzo chose to ask Laura instead (259–60). This is omitted from the fiction.

In addition, "Wilder" picks Laura up during a particularly bad blizzard and tells her that he had "hesitated to go, but that, as his team stood blanketed at a hitching post in town, Cap Garland had passed him, looked at the team and simply [said], 'God hates a coward,' and passed on. Then he had taken the blankets off the horses and gone" (*Pioneer Girl* 267). However, in *These Happy Golden Years*, Almanzo tells Laura that Cap Garland had egged him on to pick her up in the blizzard but explains that he did so because he "figured [Cap] was right" (77). In the fictional version, Almanzo shows that there was a moral reason to bring her home, while in the autobiography it could be surmised that he went because he did not want to be seen as a coward. In the novel, Almanzo mentions that Cap said she would not accept the ride, and Laura asks if he "bet" that she would; Almanzo responds, "I didn't, if that's what you want to know.... I wouldn't bet about a lady" (189). It is possible that between when she wrote the autobiography and the fiction, Wilder learned more about her husband's thoughts, but the example again demonstrates Wilder's emphasis on the fictional Almanzo's altruism and chivalry.

Miller argues that the real Almanzo may have been attracted to Laura's more lively personality because he was quiet (63–64). He also suggests that the Wilders' "quiet, sturdy affection and mutual sharing" was atypical of the period and that "if there was a dominant partner, it was Laura" (105). Given Wilder's tumultuous relationship with Rose, Almanzo became more of a supporting player, the outsider in the family trio (105). Almanzo's health and the needs of the farm dictated that he stayed closer to home. Nevertheless, his "supporting player" role may be viewed not as a negative trait but as demonstrating his backing of his wife's ambitions and dreams for traveling, giving her room to do the things that he might not be able to do.

Many of the articles Wilder wrote show how much the Man of the Place supports her efforts both on and off the farm. For example, a piece Wilder published in the *Missouri Ruralist* in July 1917 was inspired by a moment when her husband brought her cut flowers. The article contains reminisces from her childhood as well as a meditation on the simpler things in life (Wilder and Lane 16–19). Wilder's articles often include conversations and stories that show how much the Wilders worked together, as Wilder often credited her husband for his cleverness in finding new ways to modernize the home, as in 1925's "My Ozark Kitchen" and "The Farm Dining Room," both of which appeared in the *Country Gentleman* (*Selected* 137). In her weekly column, Wilder often argued that farming success required an equal partnership between a man and a woman In "The Woman's Place" (1922), Wilder writes, "In these days of women's clubs from which men are excluded, and men's clubs that permit women to be honorary members only, I'm glad to know [there is a club] whereby farm men and women work together on equal terms and with equal privileges" (*Ozarks* 199).Wilder's letters to her husband similarly demonstrate her deep affection for him. Writing home from San Francisco, where she was visiting Rose in 1915, Wilder addressed her husband "Manly Dear" (*Selected* 11). In a letter commemorating their thirtieth anniversary on 25 August 1915, she wrote, "I wish you were here. Half the fun I lose because all the time I am wishing for you" (11). And on 1 February 1950, a few months after Almanzo's death, Wilder wrote to a friend, "I do not mind living alone except for missing Almanzo. I am very lonely for him, but would be so wherever I am" (317). The letters and writings portray a man and a woman who had a deep mutual affection, who valued partnership, and who encouraged one another to explore their varied interests.

Today, Almanzo Wilder has become more than the young man of the Little House books. He is a hardworking, heroic, and handsome suitor, ready to work alongside Laura to create a life together. In popular culture, Almanzo is often included in online "book boyfriend" lists and historical blogs featuring "hot men from history." One blogger, for example, includes a photo of the real Almanzo Wilder on a list of characters who would play her book boyfriends, captioning the photo, "Kind of easy to see why Laura Ingalls fell madly in love with him! Dude is smoking hot right?!" ("Fangirl Friday"). In *My Life as Laura*, Kelly Kathleen Ferguson mentions that she broke up with a boyfriend in part because he lacked some of Almanzo's characteristics (29). In the author's note to her fictional account of Almanzo Wilder's journey to Spring Valley, *Farmer Boy Goes West*, Heather Williams (Tui Sutherland) writes that Almanzo is "an honest-to-goodness hero and genuinely good guy—and for me, he's always been the most believable, real characters in literature. Laura clearly loved him ... so it's no wonder that we all do, too!" (302).[2] According to Williams, her novel enables Almanzo to become the "bold, courteous suitor" he is in *These Happy Golden Years* (307). Williams's confession speaks to how well Wilder crafted a fictional version of her husband as a handsome, dependable, and courageous suitor—a person who would be worthy of Laura.

Almanzo also looms large because of various movie and television adaptations of the series, particularly the 1970s television version, in which Dean Butler played Almanzo. While this Almanzo is hardworking and a dreamer, he is also shy and a bit old-fashioned (see Fishbane). This version of Laura and Almanzo's road to romance is often reposted on YouTube, highlighting the moment she met him, her attempts to win him over, and his realization of how much he loves her in the "Sweet Sixteen" episode. Its popularity complicates the "true story" of Laura and Almanzo's real-life romance. Using a Jordin Sparks song, "Worth the Wait," for example, catchingraindrops24 suggests that Almanzo was worth waiting for because he proves his love for Laura by being a hardworking and kind man. Butler has created documentaries about Almanzo and Laura, narrating both *Almanzo Wilder: Life Before Laura* and *Little House on the Prairie: The Legacy of Laura Ingalls Wilder*, and titles his eBay store Call me Manly. Butler personifies Almanzo and therefore has become synonymous with the actual Almanzo Wilder, once again blurring the lines between history and fiction.

Although the husband-wife relationship depicted in Wilder's writings reflects an image carefully crafted by the author, biographical materials suggest that she indeed lived with a man who saw her as his equal. As neighbor John F. Case wrote in 1918, Wilder "is her husband's partner in every sense and is fully capable of managing the farm" (21). By making Laura's ideal fictional suitor handsome, hardworking, heroic, and most importantly able to see his future wife as an equal partner, Wilder offers a feminist intervention, purposefully delineating for younger readers what an equal heterosexual relationship could and should look like long before that subject became an explicit cultural conversation.

NOTES

1. Lane also included Almanzo's descriptions of his mother's love for homespun cloth in *Woman's Day Book of American Needlework*.

2. Williams is also the author of another Little House spin-off, *Nellie Oleson Meets Laura Ingalls*.

WORKS CITED

Anderson, William. *The Story of the Wilders*. Anderson Publications, 1973.
Butler, Dean. *Almanzo Wilder: Life before Laura*. Legacy Documentaries, 2012.
Butler, Dean. *Little House on the Prairie: The Legacy of Laura Ingalls Wilder*. Legacy Documentaries, 2014.
Case, John F. "Let's Visit Mrs. Wilder." In Wilder, *Little House in the Ozarks* 21–23.
catchingraindrops24. "Laura & Almanzo//Worth the Wait." *You Tube*, 4 April 2012. https://www.youtube.com/watch?v=2yhdpeGYF94.
Cooper, Katherine, and Emma Short, eds. *The Female Figure in Contemporary Historical Fiction*. Palgrave Macmillan, 2012.
"Fangirl Friday: Book Boyfriend Edition," *whatsarahreads.com*, 18 July 2014. https://whatsarahread.com/2014/07/18/fangirl-friday/.
Ferguson, Kelly Kathleen. *My Life as Laura: How I Searched for Laura Ingalls Wilder and Found Myself*. Salem Press, 2011.
Fishbane, Melanie. "Almanzo Wilder: A 'Very Special' Perfect Young Man." *Little House on the Prairie.com*, 1 December 2015. http://littlehouseontheprairie.com/almanzo-wilder-a-very-special-perfect-young-man.
Hill, Pamela Smith. *Laura Ingalls Wilder: A Writer's Life*. South Dakota Historical Society Press, 2007.
hooks, bell. "Feminism: A Movement to End Sexist Oppression." In *Feminist Theory Reader: Local and Global Perspectives*, edited by Carole R. McCann and Seung-Kyung Kim, 50–56. Routledge, 2003.
Lane, Rose Wilder. *Woman's Day Book of American Needlework*. Simon and Schuster, 1963.
Mancino, Nicole. "Woman Writes Herself: Exploring Identity Construction in Laura Ingalls Wilder's 'Pioneer Girl.'" PhD diss., Bowling Green State University, 2010.
Miller, John E. *Becoming Laura Ingalls Wilder: The Woman behind the Legend*. University of Missouri Press, 1998.
Romines, Ann. *Constructing the Little House: Gender, Culture, and Laura Ingalls Wilder*. University of Massachusetts Press, 1997.
Wilder, Laura Ingalls. *By the Shores of Silver Lake*. HarperCollins, 1971.

Wilder, Laura Ingalls. *Farmer Boy*. HarperCollins, 1953.
Wilder, Laura Ingalls. *The First Four Years*. HarperCollins, 1971.
Wilder, Laura Ingalls. *Little House in the Ozarks: The Rediscovered Writings*. Edited by Stephen W. Hines. Nelson, 1991.
Wilder, Laura Ingalls. *Little Town on the Prairie*. HarperCollins, 1968.
Wilder, Laura Ingalls. *The Long Winter*. HarperCollins, 1968.
Wilder, Laura Ingalls. *These Happy Golden Years*. HarperCollins, 1968.
Wilder, Laura Ingalls. *Pioneer Girl: The Annotated Autobiography*. Edited by Pamela Smith Hill. South Dakota Historical Society Press, 2014.
Wilder, Laura Ingalls. *The Selected Letters of Laura Ingalls Wilder*. Edited by William Anderson. HarperCollins, 2016.
Wilder, Laura Ingalls. "The Woman's Place." In Wilder, *Little House in the Ozarks* 199.
Wilder, Laura Ingalls, and Rose Wilder Lane. *A Little House Sampler*. Edited by William Anderson. HarperCollins, 1989.
Williams, Heather [Tui Sutherland]. *Farmer Boy Goes West*. HarperCollins, 2012.
Williams, Heather [Tui Sutherland]. *Nellie Oleson Meets Laura Ingalls*. HarperCollins, 2007.

Part 3

WILDER, PLAINS STUDIES, AND THE AMERICAN LITERATURE CANON

MOBILE STICKERS AND THE SPECTER OF SNUGNESS

Pa's Place-Making in Dakota Territory

Lindsay R. Stephens

In this essay, I trace Charles "Pa" Ingalls's place-making in Dakota Territory via his pursuit of snugness, community, and mobility. Pa's place-making contrasts with the strategies of characters in other twentieth-century settler narratives, particularly Per Hansa's monomaniacal pursuit of his so-called kingdom in O. E. Rølvaag's *Giants in the Earth* (published in Norway in 1924; English translation 1927). Laura Ingalls Wilder and her daughter/collaborator, Rose Wilder Lane, represent Pa's aims as modest and relatively selfless. I explore these representations through Diane Quantic's lenses of space and place on the Great Plains as well as Wallace Stegner's foundational classifications of westerners, or what I call the boomer/sticker divide. According to Quantic, Plains narratives hinge on a tangle of mythologies, and these myths influence and often delude settlers, who face the challenge of turning unforgiving, contested land into their home. Quantic frames the settler colonial project by emphasizing place: "To be usable, it must be occupied and transformed into identifiable places—farms and towns—by people who come from somewhere else" (xvi). In the Dakota novels, the Ingallses' attempts to transform space into place are particularly complex and often involve motion and relocation.

Stegner's boomer/sticker dichotomy provides succinct language for divergent philosophies that underpin the messy complexities of American settler colonialism. In *Where the Bluebird Sings to the Lemonade Springs*, Stegner famously coins these terms: western hopefulness "is the product not of the boomers but of the stickers, not of those who pillage and run but of those who settle, and love the life they have made and the place they have made it in" (xxvii). In contrast to stickers, boomers do not adapt to their surroundings, so they flee. According to Stegner, "Whatever it might want to be, the West is still primarily a series of brief visitations or a trail to somewhere else; and Western literature . . . has been largely a literature not of place but of motion" (72). In Wilder and Lane's Dakota novels, Pa Ingalls's adaptability, continuous movement, and ongoing place-making blur the lines of Stegner's boomer/sticker binary opposition.

Critical readings of Pa's character by children's literature scholars, including Katharine Slater's excellent study of Pa's ideology in *Little House on the Prairie*, underscore his initial commitment to forward motion. In the early volumes, he has little interest in sticking. However, in the Dakota novels, Pa's actions complicate Stegner's categories. I therefore place Wilder and Lane's texts into conversation with Stegner's theory alongside Bonney MacDonald's problematization of it, particularly her assertion that "mobility, temporary settlements, and continual movement over land may, in fact, be the best way to adapt" (506). While the Ingalls family stays in the De Smet area, they do not remain rooted in a singular place, nor do they decamp to more promising territory at the first sign of hardship. Instead, they purposefully move from homestead to town and back again. Pa Ingalls, then, is not strictly a boomer but rather a place-making opportunist with boomer tendencies—in other words, what I conceive as a sticker in motion, seeking refuge for his family even as his area of influence expands to encompass the De Smet community. Pa's place-making strategies uniquely negotiate the divide between boomer and sticker, transforming the daunting space of Dakota Territory. Viewing Pa through a Plains literature lens offers new and important readings of his character development, as these later texts illustrate the full breadth of his fallibility, tenacity, and adaptability.

Wilder and Lane's Dakota texts denote the series' transition from children's to young adult literature and its increasingly sophisticated approach to space and place. Ann Romines emphasizes this shift, explaining that even the appearance of the books changed: "The earlier books were large and squarish, with generous illustrations. But the last four took on the standard shape, thickness, and print size of novels for adults" (139). Thinking of audience, Wilder felt strongly that *By the Shores of Silver Lake* needed to bridge the gap between Laura's childhood and adulthood, writing to Lane on 26 January 1938,

> Just a word more about Silver Lake. You fear it is too adult. But adult stuff must begin to be mixed in, for Laura is growing up. In three years she will be teaching school and we can't jump into grown up stuff all at once. . . . [Our readers] seem

wildly interested and want to know how, where, and when Laura met Almanzo and about their getting married.... Surely Laura will have to be rather adult then. And I think it will be more reasonable and easier to begin mixing it in, in Silver Lake.... We can't spoil this story by making it childish. (*Selected* 151)

Issues of audience, however, extend beyond aesthetics and adolescence. The earlier books promote sticking in one place or westward motion, while the Dakota texts promote more complex themes of adaptive place-making. As Wilder sternly reminded Lane on 25 January 1938, "the theme of Silver Lake is *homesteading*" (*Selected* 148). Sticking and place-making are central concerns in the Dakota novels, with Pa's strategies of music, snugness, mobility, and community becoming markedly more complex.

Marital tension, present throughout the series, boils over in *Silver Lake* when an opportunity arises to leave grasshopper-infested Minnesota for Dakota Territory. Caroline Ingalls typifies a Stegner-esque sticker who hopes that her girls might become educated ladies with Victorian pallor and sterling deportment. While opportunist Pa argues for Dakota, Ma defends staying in Minnesota even though their experiences on Plum Creek have not gone well (4). Ma's desire to stick vis-à-vis invocation of her girls and kitchen echoes many gendered western narratives that connect staying in one place to home and to child rearing. But sticking need not be so oversimplified or so gendered, as demonstrated by Willa Cather's fiercely independent, childless Alexandra Bergson in *O Pioneers* (1913) or perhaps the gruffest, most obdurate sticker of all, the father in Mari Sandoz's *Old Jules* (1935).

Pa does not exemplify Stegner's pillaging boomer but does demonstrate boomer tendencies. In *Little House in the Big Woods*, Pa seems to be a sticker; the family leads a comfortable life in Wisconsin, living frugally on a small but sustainable farm that Pa supplements through fishing, hunting, and trapping. But after the family leaves Wisconsin, Pa chases irresistible opportunities and works a variety of jobs without success. Part of Pa's rationale for leaving Minnesota is the job offered by Aunt Docia at the opening of *Silver Lake* (4). Pa later attempts other ventures, such as running a makeshift boardinghouse, carpentry, and realty. These boomeresque efforts supplement Pa's homesteading; farming and hunting, meanwhile, remain his preferred activities and sources of income, and his approach to these two activities blurs the distinction between boomer and sticker.

Pa's penchant for hunting emerges as a fraught practice: by hunting he can feed his family and thus stick in one place, but hunting reduces animal populations—the actions of a boomer. Wilder and Lane foreshadow the family's eventual relocation to Dakota Territory with Pa's seemingly biocentric view of human settlement in *Little House on the Prairie*: "Wild animals would not stay in a country where there were so many people. Pa did not like to stay, either. He liked a country where the wild animals lived without being afraid" (1–2). Pa makes this argument again early in *Silver Lake*, but this time Wilder and Lane emphasize that Pa likes sparsely populated areas because the hunting is better. Beseeching Caroline to "listen to reason," he claims, "the hunting's good in the west, [and] a man can get all the meat he wants" (4). Later, the De Smet building boom in which Pa participates takes its toll, frightening game from the area (244–45). Hunting no longer seems a viable means of putting food on the table. Yet the family stays in Dakota, and Pa regretfully adapts, developing his homestead and fulfilling his promise to Ma that their daughters will attend school.

We might expect that Pa's other favorite occupation, farming, would necessitate sticking, but this enterprise, too, demands boomeresque opportunism. In Kansas, Pa spends his time hunting and trapping, although he does hope to farm the following year. After a wildfire consumes the tall grass on their homestead, Pa was "glad of it, because plowing would be easier" (284). He never gets to plow, however, since the Ingalls family leaves Kansas before the military ejects them. In Minnesota, Pa hitches his family's fortunes to his wheat crop, but the harvest never materializes: grasshoppers devour the crop, and Pa becomes a farmhand, walking "three hundred miles" before finding work (*Banks* 227). In *On the Banks of Plum Creek*, we see the scope of Pa Ingalls's adaptability via this mobility, which aligns with Stegner's claim that Western literature addresses motion rather than place (105).

Place-making, or the transformation of space into place on the prairie, was surely daunting. Stegner proclaims that "especially in the West, what we have instead of place is space" (72). The seemingly featureless landscapes east of the 100th meridian pose their own challenges: as Quantic points out, "the creation of a place is not a simple act for the plains pioneer" (2). This vast space bewildered newcomers; even seasoned stickers were not immune to its seeming infinity. Rølvaag gestures toward temporality and space in *Giants*, beginning book 2 with an ominous description of "an endless plain. From Kansas-Illinois, it stretched far into the Canadian north, God alone knows how far; from the Mississippi River to the western Rockies, miles without number.... endless ... beginningless" (249; ellipses in original). Rølvaag's attention to scale suggests that settlers who decided to claim so-called free land in this region had little to orient them, and comparisons of this landscape to the sea have become a worn Great Plains trope in countless works, including Wilder and Lane's.

Arriving in Dakota, the Ingalls family enters stark, featureless land. Contextualizing the bewilderment experienced by new arrivals, Quantic explains, "On the Great Plains, space and place were at first indistinguishable. On a purely physical level, where there were no landmarks to delineate direction or distance, men and women became disoriented" (1). Without markers of geographic progress, temporal and spatial disorientation overwhelm Laura (*Shores* 59). The openness later becomes more familiar, and the threat of agoraphobia lessens, but this familiarity does little to diminish the scale of Dakota's vast expanse. When the family first views the newly constructed homestead shanty, Laura muses that it "looked like a yellow toy on the great rolling prairie covered with rippling young grass" (263). While Wilder and Lane's simile gestures to younger readers, the landscape's scale also serves to defamiliarize the new abode, making it seem more fanciful than inviting. This contrast between space and home is absent in Rølvaag's *Giants*, in which the oversized house/barn structure, intended, like the Ingallses' shanty, as "a temporary shelter," dominates his "Home-Founding" chapter (54). The only gesture Rølvaag makes toward space and house involves Beret's reconciliation with the prospect of sleeping near their livestock. She realizes that Rosie the cow will prove to be "a comfortable companion," since she remembers "how desolate and lonely everything was here" (55). Wilder and Lane, conversely, confront this space/place dichotomy directly, and place-making becomes their central project in the Dakota novels.

The Ingalls family encounters this open space with no familial or community memory attached to it. Lack of memory adds to the difficulty of place-making in Dakota, since, as Stegner claims, memory transforms space into place (205). All that aids the Ingalls family in place-making are memories of and experiences in other, dissimilar locales. Laura, taken aback by "the largeness of the empty [surveyors'] house" when she arrives ahead of her family, senses that it "seemed to know that Laura was there, but it had not made up its mind about her. It would wait and see" (*Shores* 143). The Ingallses must therefore improvise their place-making strategy, and space-claiming rituals begin when the other family members arrive.[1] Pa builds a fire, and Ma, Laura, and Carrie make beds and unpack (145). Eating duck and potatoes on the surveyors' fancy china, they now agree that "it was fine to be eating in such a large house" (146). The tidiness of having unpacked, the fantastic meal they have just eaten, and the warmth now emanating from the stove give the first indications that the surveyors' house will become a place for the Ingalls family to create new collective memories. Moreover, these rituals inspire Pa to play his fiddle when they finish eating, and as Laura fetches the instrument, Pa "looked around contentedly at them all and at the good walls that would keep them comfortable" (147). The song Laura suggests involves bitter wind and isolation, so Pa substitutes a different song about self-reliance that his family knows very well.

Wilder and Lane note that "merrily the fiddle sang and Pa sang with it. Laura and Mary and Carrie sang too, with all their might" (147–48). Their singing is the capstone for warmth and togetherness that first evening in the surveyors' house, highlighting their now-soaring morale in this new place.

Pa's music, merry and solemn tunes alike, not only boosts morale but connects the family to its past and culture, serving as a crucial strand of their place-making project. Wilder and Lane represent this repository in its most complete form in Pa's musical send-off the evening before Laura's wedding in *These Happy Golden Years*. In this bittersweet scene, Pa's fiddle "sang the songs that Laura knew in the Big Woods of Wisconsin, and the tunes that Pa had played by the campfires all across the plains of Kansas. It repeated the nightingale's song in the moonlight on the banks of the Verdigris River, then it remembered the days in the dugout on the banks of Plum Creek, and the winter evenings in the new house that Pa had built there. It sang of the Christmas on Silver Lake, and of springtime after the long, Hard Winter" (277).

While the Ingalls family has firmly established a place by this point, this moment contains a wide range of temporalities, all of which recall and valorize varying degrees of safety if not snugness. Pa's rendition of the nightingale's song even reconnects the family to the night before they moved into the (still roofless) house in Kansas, while their dugout on Plum Creek was, as Quantic notes, "perhaps their most secure refuge" (109). The two Dakota entries in this list are particularly compelling in the context of snugness, since the Ingallses' comfort that Christmas partly comes via the absence of the surveyors, which calls forth the mobility and instabilities roiling in *Silver Lake*. And while Pa's playing springtime sounds immediately following the Hard Winter was surely cheerful, the horrifically unsnug Hard Winter itself is conspicuously absent from this list, even as a prelude to the sounds of spring. Pa knows how to play "the wild, changing melody" of the wind, but he scrupulously avoids it (*Winter* 119–20).

Pa's fiddle playing serves as a form of celebration, but Wilder and Lane more commonly associate it—as on that first night in the surveyors' house and in Pa's send-off serenade to Laura—with the most overarching aspect of the Ingallses' prairie place-making: their obsession with snugness. For the Ingallses, snugness is key, providing moments of comfort when the transient family's motion temporarily ceases. As Wilder wrote to Lane on 25 January 1938, the winter in the surveyors' house and the Hard Winter spent in town were "obstacles to be overcome before the family could have a home again" (*Selected* 149). Creating these fleeting moments of comfort and refuge, a practice we might associate with sticking, thus gestures toward the family's resourcefulness and Pa's boomeresque opportunism. The term *snug* itself boasts five definitions in the *Oxford English Dictionary*, and many of these relate to sailing or husbandry, while others have become obsolete. Two of the adverbial and adjectival definitions, however, help us think about *snug* as Wilder and Lane's response to open space and to the fierce weather in the Dakota texts. Snugness is "a state of ease, comfort, or quiet enjoyment, chiefly pred., freq. with *in* (a place)" (emphasis added). Wilkie Collins's *The Queen of Hearts*, published in 1859, appears in the *OED* as a pertinent example of snugness's warmth and light: "I made a blazing fire ... and sat down to tea, as snug and comfortable as possible." Moreover, in the context of the prairie-as-sea trope, the maritime definition of *snug* helps to illustrate the Ingalls family's vulnerability: "Of a ship or her parts; Trim, neat, compact; adequately or properly prepared for, or protected from, bad weather." The *OED* editors offer a line from the August 1883 issue of *Harper's* to exemplify this definition: "She will be ... snug for any gale." In Dakota Territory's sea of grasses, this maritime definition of *snug*, too, becomes crucial for the Ingalls family.

Wilder and Lane tend to associate snugness in Dakota with comfort and safety in winter, but on their first night in the shanty, Pa declares a state of snugness and refuge: "Now we are all snug ... settled at last on our homestead. Bring me the fiddle, Laura, and we'll have a little music!" (*Shores* 290). This occasion constitutes a significant moment in the family's Dakota place-making project. The family is indoors at this moment, and Pa's definition of *snug* likely involves the impenetrable mosquito netting that protects the family from swarming insects. Yet other forces are at work as well: the family finally has its own refuge from the endless sky and flat land. Wilder and Lane illustrate Quantic's claim that "the tension between eternal horizon-to-horizon space and the need to create some refuge to close off space and time is central in Great Plains fiction" (97). Pa shifts the temporality of snugness by beginning his declaration with "now," suggesting that the family has finally been relieved.

Rølvaag, in marked contrast, complicates Quantic's spatial assertion with his representation of the comically outsized, decidedly unsnug house in *Giants*: "Per Hansa's house certainly looked as if it were intended for a royal mansion" (52), a description Rølvaag rationalizes using the language of settler colonial stickers via Per Hansa's envisioning of future generations. The house-as-refuge motif occurs only once in *Giants*, attributed to Beret rather than Per Hansa, the monstrosity's architect and builder. Once Beret learns of Per Hansa's plan to combine house and barn, she recoils, but "then she thought of how desolate and lonesome everything was here" (55). Rølvaag's resistance to snugness further underscores and distinguishes the Ingallses' devotion to snugness and its role in their project of adaptive sticking.

The family's various houses are vital elements in the Ingallses' place-making. Wilder and Lane relentlessly deploy references to snugness throughout the series, always associating this feeling with a house, usually during the winter, as if they were attempting to reenact the family's comfort in the Big Woods. The success of the house construction in *Little House on the Prairie* (which continues for several chapters) hinges on snugness, and this preoccupation continues into the Dakota texts. And while Slater conflates snugness with expansionist ideology in her excellent reading of *Prairie*, arguing that Pa's desire to live on unpeopled land "drives him to continually uproot his wife and daughters" and therefore shows that he "is also a man who creates confining spaces" (65), I maintain that Pa's colonial project evolves by the time the family arrives in Dakota Territory, particularly in the contexts of sticking and of Pa's burgeoning civic-mindedness, which we do not see in the earlier books. Pa's former ideology, confronted with the De Smet building boom, would surely have prompted another move on the grounds that the area now had too many people and too little game. However, Pa's sense of entitlement diminishes in the Dakota novels, and he regards the prospect of so-called free land more warily. In *Prairie*, Pa tells Laura that "white people ... get the best land because we get here first and take our pick," but by the time the family files a claim in Dakota Territory, Pa has come to see homesteading as a wager against empire (237). The rigors of place-making in Dakota Territory reconfigure Pa's philosophies on nearly every front. In Dakota Territory, the Ingallses' desire to maintain snugness becomes a perpetual struggle, one that first involves taking refuge from unforgiving, open space and seeking protection from potentially lethal Northern Plains winters, and later expands to encompass not only the Ingalls family's temporary comfort but also the well-being of De Smet.

While the Ingallses have encountered subzero temperatures, relentless wind, and treeless space in the earlier books, contending with all three at once amplifies snugness and its absence exponentially. They are not, so to speak, in Kansas—or Wisconsin or Minnesota—anymore. During that first winter in Dakota, the family attempts to come to terms with this barren, frozen landscape, and their borrowed cabin links them to Big Woods memories and other remembered cozy experiences. While the house may be snug, harsh conditions are evident: "On the whole white prairie nothing moved but blowing snow, and the only sound in the vast silence was the sound of the wind. In the *snug* house Laura and Carrie helped Ma with the housework, and Grace played, running about the big room with toddling short steps" (*Shores* 158–59; emphasis added). Outside, everything is cold and white, with no sun, trees, or appreciable topography to provide relief. Inside, there is life.

In contrast, the term *snug* seldom appears in *The Long Winter*: seven months of blizzards force Pa to rethink his place-making strategies. The first mention of snugness appears early in the book and illustrates the insecurity of the

Ingallses' shanty: "Boards and tar-paper were not very snug shelter against a hard winter" (14). Even after the family moves to town, snugness eludes them. The chapters "Three Days' Blizzard" and "We'll Weather the Blast" begin with vivid descriptions of Laura's awakening to bitter cold, with frost feathers visible on every nail in the ceiling, and Wilder opens the chapter "No Trains" with an alarming line: "It was not worth while to get up in the morning" (139). To make matters worse, Pa discovers in the decidedly unsnug chapter "Cold and Dark" that he cannot play his fiddle. Ashamed, he tells Laura, "My fingers are too stiff and thick from being out in the cold so much, [and] I can't play" (239). Making music, one of Pa's crucial contributions to snugness, becomes impossible because of the Hard Winter's inexorable, accretive toll. While Ma does her best to approximate snugness with the button lamp and reserved codfish, the disintegration—and occasionally complete absence—of snugness becomes a trauma that prompts the family's seasonal movements to town for years to come.[2]

At the same time, this disintegration of snugness transforms Pa from isolated hunter to emergent community leader. His investment of time and attention to De Smet indicates that he intends to stick and continue the project of transforming space into place. In particular, he makes two movements in response to the decline of snugness. Both involve going across the street to Fuller's store, which, in good weather, would be unremarkable. Pa prepares for his first outing under the pretense of going to the store "to hear the news"; when Ma second-guesses him, he reveals his true motive: "Somebody may be lost" (127). Ma shares the responsibility of maintaining snugness in this scene, and here we see the return of tensions surrounding her sticker tendencies, since her definition of snugness appears to be more rigidly connected to domesticity and enclosure. After Laura forlornly watches Pa leave, Ma attempts to boost the family's spirits by declaring that "a storm outdoors is no reason for gloom in the house" (127).

We see this tension arise again twenty pages later, when Pa alleges loneliness or cabin fever as an initial excuse for going across the street: "Now I'm going across to Fuller's to find out if anybody but us is alive in this blamed town. Here for three whole days we haven't been able to see a light, nor smoke, nor any sign of a living soul. What's the good of a town if a fellow can't get any good of it?" (147). Ma responds with a brief, pointed remark espousing her domestic definition of snugness: "Supper's almost ready, Charles" (147). When Pa returns, he reveals his true motive for going across the street: "Everything's all right in town" (147). To be sure, Pa goes to the store to be sociable, but he also feels compelled to check on the denizens of De Smet. Moreover, his circuit of house/stable/house/store/house demonstrates that his definition of snugness—even a low, Hard Winter degree of it—has expanded to include the town. This Pa is different from the Pa that Slater addresses, for in *Little House on the Prairie*, as Slater asserts, snugness requires "a good door [that] is not only a door that keeps out the elements but a door that keeps out unwanted persons" (65). Interdependence replaces independence during the Hard Winter, and while Pa continues to associate snugness with warmth, food, light, and music (as we see in *Little Town on the Prairie*'s chapter "Snug for Winter"), his definition now encompasses the well-being of De Smet's townspeople and homesteaders. Pa's redefinition here is radical: other Plains Literature patriarchs, particularly Sandoz's Jules and Rølvaag's Per Hansa, do not make fluid transitions to civic involvement. While Pa initially prefers unpeopled land, Jules concerns himself with "trying to build up the country" from the outset, remaining deeply skeptical of other settlers (Sandoz 270, 120–21). Per Hansa comes closer to approximating Pa's shift from isolationism to civic-mindedness, as we see in Rølvaag's version of the infamous Hard Winter. Hans Olsa, gravely ill after becoming caught in a storm, is in decline, so Per Hansa leaves his so-called kingdom and "drop[s] in to see how they were getting along" (446). He spends the night there, but only after Sörine pleads with him to do so (447). Per Hansa returns home the next day, "looking like a man who has reached the end of his rope," and explains in bewilderment to Beret that Hans Olsa "just lies there and whimpers" (452–53), suggesting that his communal responsibility depletes him and that he, like Jules, cultivates deep pessimism about his fellow settlers.

Pa, in contrast, seems energized by immersion in the community. He becomes an integral element of it in the Dakota novels, whether drafting legitimate-looking legal papers for Mr. Boast or facing down the mob in *Silver Lake*. He threatens to lead a boycott against Mr. Loftus over wheat prices, suggests that townspeople ration the wheat after Mr. Loftus capitulates, and attempts to give advice to inexperienced antelope hunters in *The Long Winter*. His leadership roles become even more varied in *Little Town on the Prairie*, where he serves on the school board, aids in the organization of a church, and participates in the Literaries.

The real Charles Ingalls was throughout his adult life more community-oriented than Wilder and Lane's fictive Pa. The index to *Pioneer Girl* lists instances of his "public offices and positions of responsibility," though Pamela Smith Hill also notes that "the fictional Charles Ingalls, while civic-minded, was always a farmer and not an elected official" (388, 204). While there may be multiple reasons for the fictional Pa Ingalls's evolution, I contend that his evolution comes about because his place, Dakota Territory, continually challenges him: his hunting experiences are unfruitful, blackbirds destroy the oat and corn crops in *Little Town*, and the Hard Winter thwarts his usual methods of creating snugness by depriving the family of light, heat, food, and even his ability to play the fiddle. These discoveries test Pa's already-flexible resourcefulness. It also may be that as one of its first settlers, he feels responsibility to the De Smet community. Pa prides himself on his experience, as we see near the end of *Little House on the Prairie*. There, with only an aborted homesteading attempt to his credit, Pa scoffs at the tenderfeet who refuse to leave their wagon after their horses are stolen. Dakota, conversely, challenges Pa's experience to the point where he is willing not only to accept help but to give it. At the same time, Pa gains satisfaction and occasionally pleasure from his participation: in *The Long Winter*, he learns a new song during the trip to Volga and entertains his family with the story of the clueless eastern railroad superintendent mired in snow (332, 215). His enjoyment of his new community becomes even more evident in *Little Town*, where we see Pa's cheer in his carpentry work on the church and in his role on the school board, particularly the scene in which he appears to sternly question Charley about disrupting class, which Pa does with "twinkling" eyes (27, 180). Furthermore, still reeling from the Hard Winter in *Little Town*, Pa contentedly accepts that wintering in De Smet is a requirement for achieving snugness, stating "with satisfaction" that "we will take our provisions with us when we move to town this time" (138).

In fact, Pa's revised understanding of snugness, evident in his microcirculations between domicile, barn, and store in *The Long Winter*, suggests that he understands the value of motion, deploying mobility when static sticking could be detrimental. We see iterations of these mobile tendencies prior to the onset of the Hard Winter. When a Native American enters Harthorn's store and admonishes the bewildered settlers that they will face seven months of brutal blizzards, Pa takes him seriously and asks questions while the others remain silent (61). Pa's somber exchange inspires communal plans to move to town immediately. Pa does not base this decision to pull stakes and move on economically motivated, Stegner-esque boomerism: instead, at this key moment in the text, Pa becomes a mobile sticker, since he participates in De Smet's collective worry, asserts himself as a community leader, and realizes that the motion of moving to town could help the family reach the requisite level of snugness required to endure seven months of storms. In contrast, Store-Hans, son of Rølvaag's beleaguered Beret, associates her suggestion that "we had better be going back where people live before winter is upon us" with madness (191). The seasonally mobile Ingalls family adapts to the Dakota Territory's vicious weather by electing to circulate between the poles of homestead and town, and other citizens follow their example.

Realizing that the claim shanty is far from snug, Pa responds to the warning about Dakota's fierce weather with, to borrow MacDonald's titular phrasing, an "adaptive strategy," by which I mean his decision to relocate. According to Quantic, "Time and again [in Great Plains fiction], the person who attempts to impose his or her will upon the land is overcome by natural disaster, a blizzard, a prairie fire, or a dust storm, and the person who understands the land's potential reaps bountiful harvests" (4). The Hard Winter's fierce, unrelenting blizzards remain in the settlers' memories for decades and redefine the quotidian. Furthermore, the Native who enters the store insists that the weather pattern is cyclical and that every twenty-first winter means seven months of blizzards (75). The constancy of this cycle calls to mind Stegner's claim that aridity forces creatures to adapt. In Harthorn's store, we see a prairie iteration of the need for such flexibility. Although settlers in De Smet faced neither long-term aridity nor volatile boom-and-bust economies, the prospect of seven months of blizzards certainly gets their attention, and Pa responds by moving his family to town at once.

At the same time, Pa's place-making strategies do not merely involve moving between the poles of homestead and town, and in these moments, he becomes a sticker *in motion*. This seemingly counterintuitive idea is evident in the parallel between Pa Ingalls and MacDonald's interpretation of Bruce Mason (son of Bo the boomer and Elsa the sticker) in *The Big Rock Candy Mountain*: "Bruce surrenders to the relief brought on by his realization that his home is in his movement—that his 'place,' literally, is in motion" (MacDonald 509). Wilder and Lane, in contrast, do not represent Pa as agonizing over such matters. He loves to travel, of course; he "always liked moving" (*Shores* 259). But for Pa, mobility also provides an opportunity for place-making, and in these moments, he fully participates in forging community. The closest Pa comes to having a Mason-like moment of relief—or epiphany—comes in *The Long Winter* when he justifies his wanting to help clear the track to Volga: "I have been in one place for so long, I would like to travel a little" (106). Alleging cabin fever, Pa has bigger aims. Once the men begin pumping and the handcart begins to move, Pa breaks into a popular sea shanty to build community:

> The handcar's wheels began slowly to turn and then to roll rapidly along the track toward Volga. And as they pumped, Pa began to sing and all the others joined in. "We'll ROLL THE O-old CHARiot aLONG, / We'll ROLL THE O-old CHARiot aLONG, / We'll ROLL THE O-old CHARiot aLONG, / And we WON'T drag ON beHIND!" (107)

Bursting into this familiar, maritime work song once the motion begins, Pa transforms the labor of pumping this cart to Volga (thirty-five miles away) in winter into an enjoyable day on the rails. As Anne Phillips puts it, "the 'musicality' of a community serves as a reliable gauge of its spiritual and physical welfare" (146), and here we see that the handcart becomes a mobile place. The men cease singing each time they have to shovel their way out, and they begin again as they resume rolling into the distance (109). Spirits remain high when the rolling community returns home, with its "singing, cheering men" (110), underscoring the increasingly communal importance of music in the Little House series. In this moment, too, the possibilities of snugness for the Ingalls family and for the greater De Smet community prevail because of Pa's communal vision. Here we see Pa as we have never seen him before: the formerly unapologetic, isolationist hunter makes an unexpected shift to community leader, an unprecedented move for a man who once longed to leave settlements behind and uproot his family to so-called virgin land, replete with plentiful game.

Wilder and Lane's Dakota texts, underexamined in the Great Plains canon, offer a significant variation on the project of place-making. In them, Wilder and Lane's motifs of music, snugness, and community become far more complex. Mobility emerges as a crucial strand of the narrative not only in the family's shift from a singular, forward trajectory to more nuanced, seasonal migrations but also in Pa's microcirculations around De Smet to enact communal snugness. In the earlier books, snugness appeared as a singular feeling assigned to a singular home, often in winter and, in the case of *Little House on the Prairie*, as a balm for the disconcerting, open space of Kansas. That volume's title, as Jerry Griswold suggests, pits snugness against this space (27). The titles of the Dakota novels, particularly *By the Shores of Silver Lake* and *Little Town on the Prairie*, convey instead that place-making and sticking have become the family's central projects. Furthermore, via adaptive place-making, we see Pa transition from boomer to sticker-in-motion. The Dakota texts, then, function as a bildungsroman not only for Laura and her sisters but also for Pa, who replies to Laura's wish to go West by explaining, "I'm going to get a homestead, Laura, and you girls are going to school" (*Shores* 126–27). In Dakota and in the culminating novels of the Little House series, Pa employs sticker-in-motion strategies to establish an enduring place.

NOTES

1. Slater connects snugness to imperialist ideologies in *Little House on the Prairie*, while Griswold identifies it as a thematic concern throughout children's literature. Quantic mentions snugness in the context of the Plum Creek dugout's security as well as the Ingallses' need to seek "ever more constricting spaces" in *The Long Winter*. Romines gestures toward snugness in discussing the flimsy claim shanty, while Bosmajian positions the "contracted

space" of the Ingallses' Kansas home in *Little House on the Prairie* against vast landscapes and Louw offers an ecocritical and postcolonial reading of the wild/domestic binary in *Little House in the Big Woods* and *Little House on the Prairie*.

2. Wilder devotes a chapter, "Snug for Winter," to this place-making strategy in *Little Town on the Prairie*.

WORKS CITED

Bosmajian, Hamida. "Vastness and Contraction of Space in *Little House on the Prairie*." *Children's Literature* 11 (1983): 49–63.

Cather, Willa. *O Pioneers*. Houghton Mifflin, 1913.

Collins, Wilkie. *The Queen of Hearts*. Harper and Brothers, 1859.

Griswold, Jerry. *Feeling Like a Kid: Childhood and Children's Literature*. Johns Hopkins University Press, 2006.

Louw, Pat. "Contested Spaces in Laura Ingalls Wilder's *Little House in the Big Woods* and *Little House on the Prairie*." *Mousaion* 29, no. 1 (2011): 166–78.

MacDonald, Bonney. "Ranging over Stegner's Arid West: Mobility as Adaptive Strategy." In *A Companion to the Literature and Culture of the American West*, edited by Nicolas S. Witschi, 499–513. Blackwell, 2011.

Phillips, Anne. "'Home Itself Put into Song': Music as Metaphorical Community." *The Lion and the Unicorn* 16, no. 2 (1992): 145–57.

Quantic, Diane Dufva. *The Nature of the Place: A Study of Great Plains Fiction*. Bison, 1997.

Rølvaag, Ole Edvart. *Giants in the Earth: A Saga of the Prairie*. 1927. Trans. Lincoln Colcord and Ole Edvart Rølvaag. Harper and Row, 1929.

Romines, Ann. *Constructing the Little House: Gender, Culture, and Laura Ingalls Wilder*. University of Massachusetts Press, 1997.

Sandoz, Mari. *Old Jules*. 1935. Bison, 2005.

Slater, Katharine. "'Now We're All Snug!': The Regionalism of *Little House on the Prairie*." *Genre* 47, no.1 (2014): 55–77.

Stegner, Wallace. *The Big Rock Candy Mountain*. 1938. Penguin, 2010.

Stegner, Wallace. *Where the Bluebird Sings to the Lemonade Springs: Living and Writing in the West*. 1992. Modern Library, 2002.

Wilder, Laura Ingalls. *By the Shores of Silver Lake*. 1939. Harper and Row, 1953.

Wilder, Laura Ingalls. *Little House in the Big Woods*. 1932. Harper Trophy, 1971.

Wilder, Laura Ingalls. *Little House on the Prairie*. 1935. Harper Trophy, 1971.

Wilder, Laura Ingalls. *Little Town on the Prairie*. 1941. Harper Trophy, 1971.

Wilder, Laura Ingalls. *The Long Winter*. 1940. Harper Trophy, 1971.

Wilder, Laura Ingalls. *On the Banks of Plum Creek*. 1937. Harper Trophy, 1971.

Wilder, Laura Ingalls. *Pioneer Girl: The Annotated Autobiography*. Edited by Pamela Smith Hill, South Dakota Historical Society Press, 2014.

Wilder, Laura Ingalls. *The Selected Letters of Laura Ingalls Wilder*. Edited by William Anderson. HarperCollins, 2016.

Wilder, Laura Ingalls. *These Happy Golden Years*. 1943. Harper Trophy, 1971.

"MORE THAN GRASSY HILLS"

Land, Space, and Female Identity in the Works of Laura Ingalls Wilder and Willa Cather

Elif S. Armbruster

Laura Ingalls Wilder (1867–1957) and Willa Cather (1873–1947) might be called literary soul sisters. Born just six years apart in the decade after the Civil War, both women went on to become legendary chroniclers of life for white girls and women on the American Great Plains. In their semiautobiographical novels, both authors extol the wonder and possibility of large open spaces, namely the American frontier in the late nineteenth and early twentieth centuries. In their work, girls and women who might have felt dwarfed by the vast landscape instead feel inspired and empowered by it. Wilder and Cather provide their heroines, Laura Ingalls in the Little House books and Alexandra Bergson and Ántonia Shimerda in *O Pioneers!* and *My Ántonia*, respectively, with new ways of being in the world. Rather than confining their female characters to the traditional domestic space of the interior, Cather and Wilder place them out-of-doors, where they resemble pioneer men rather than traditional women. Wilder's Laura is also compared to the "wild men," the indigenous people who, while seldom mentioned by either author, inhabited the land on which Cather's and Wilder's novels unfold. For both writers, "land" is of the utmost importance: it offers the female characters a way out of the house and into realms that they make uniquely theirs.

Both Cather and Wilder write almost exclusively about the experiences of white women and men on the Great Plains. Any positivity and empowerment that their girls and women draw from the landscape comes at the expense of the indigenous people who were displaced by the white settlers. This creates a dilemma for scholars who want to study Wilder as a regional and realist American woman writer, much like her contemporaries Cather and Kate Chopin. As a feminist scholar, I appreciate the way that Wilder actively imagined alternatives to traditional gender roles. Wilder's work also broadens our understanding of pioneering girls in the late nineteenth century. However, her books also remind us of what James Baldwin has called "the price of the ticket" (ix)—that is, Wilder's novels enable readers to buy into the myth of American exceptionalism. In other words, white pioneers were granted the privilege of "settling" at the expense of ethnoracial minorities who were denied the privileges of whiteness. While I emphasize the importance of the land for Wilder's and Cather's heroines, I recognize that others' experiences of the land—specifically, those of Native American peoples—were erased.

To understand the particular characters in terms of the natural world around them, I draw on Edward Soja, a theoretical geographer who argues that people can be understood "spatially" rather than strictly historically or socially. Building on the work of other critics, Soja conceives a new arena through which we can experience the world and which he terms *Thirdspace*.[1] This realm, according to Soja, contains the original and myriad ways that people respond to the environment and moves beyond the typical binary comprising the mental and the physical. In a sense, Soja's Thirdspace contains all that cannot be contained or described in terms of how we experience space and place. As he puts it, "*Everything* comes together in Thirdspace" (56), including "the abstract and the concrete, the real and the imagined, the knowable and the unimaginable ... mind and body, consciousness and unconsciousness" (56–57). While Soja's Thirdspace has specific bearing on geography and urban studies, he makes clear that this concept is "transdisciplinary in scope" (3): Thirdspace "cuts across all perspectives and modes of thought and is not confined solely to geographers, architects, urbanists and others for whom spatial thinking is a primary professional preoccupation" (3). Thus, his salient point of understanding the external world as a realm of possibility is both relevant to and revelatory for my analysis of the ways in which Laura, Alexandra, and Ántonia respond to the Great Plains. Interpreting the out-of-doors for these characters as Thirdspaces makes their experiences therein rich, unique, and promising, particularly for white female readers, even though their experience of freedom comes at the expense of the displaced Natives.

PLACING CATHER AND WILDER TOGETHER

It is not only useful to study Wilder's Laura and Cather's Alexandra and Ántonia in terms of their similar responses to the external world but also important to consider Wilder and Cather as authors of the same import. Bringing them together helps elevate Wilder studies to the level that Cather has long enjoyed. Indeed, in spite of Wilder's and Cather's thematic and stylistic similarities and their success as writers while they were alive, their posthumous careers have taken vastly divergent directions. Cather has enjoyed the privilege of being a canonized author for many decades, while Wilder and her work remain largely marginalized within the academy despite being taught in elementary and college classrooms. In addition, Wilder's work has only very recently begun to be treated as a genre beyond "children's literature."[2] While the work of Ann Romines and Anita Clair Fellman, among others, has helped secure Wilder's reputation in the minds of academics, scholarship on Wilder still lags behind that on Cather and other American women writers who address issues of space, place, and the environment such as Kate Chopin, Ellen Glasgow, and Catharine Maria Sedgwick.

CATHER'S WILD WOMEN

In *O Pioneers!* (1913), her earliest Nebraskan novel, Cather overturns the domestic as a cultural symbol and offers the land as a new world in which women admittedly may resemble men but are nonetheless free. Instead of foregrounding the house and its interior, Cather writes on the first page that the houses in the windy town of Hanover are "set about haphazard" and have no appearance of permanence; the town itself is "trying not to be blown away" (3, 15). Alexandra and her father, John Bergson, prioritize the land, as "[they] had the Old-World belief that land, in itself, is desirable" (15) and are most content out-of-doors. The inside of Alexandra's house is "curiously unfinished and uneven" (56); it is simple and bare, perhaps because of the family's economic circumstances, but it is also unattended to. Unlike the disorganized interior, Alexandra's outdoor world is full of "order" and "fine arrangement" (56). Cather states that "Alexandra's house is the big out of doors" (57) and that "it is in the soil that she expresses herself best" (57). Furthermore, rather than make her feel insignificant, the land fortifies her "to reflect upon the great operations of nature, and when she thought of the law that lay behind them, she felt a sense of personal security" (47). Instead of viewing the home as the expected site of security and comfort, Alexandra feels "secure" in the natural world, with its perfect "operations" and "laws." She "love[s] to watch the [stars], to think of their vastness and distance" (47), and rather than engendering a sense of smallness in her, the enormity of the stellar sky leaves her feeling safe.

Alexandra's response to the land evokes the multiplicity of Soja's Thirdspace. Just as Thirdspace comprises material and mental realms, so, too, does Alexandra's experience of nature. Both conceptions also move beyond these elements to encapsulate something more, something almost indescribable. Cather expresses Alexandra's deep appreciation of the landscape, where the "still, deep-breathing summer night[s], full of the smell of the hay fields" (30) intoxicate her. For Alexandra, "the chirping of the insects down in the long grass [was] like the sweetest music," yet readers do not quite know how that "sweet music" sounds or why it is so "sweet." We do know, however, that this realm "intoxicates" her. Similarly, when outside, Alexandra feels "as if her heart were hiding down there, *somewhere*, with the quail and the plover and all the little wild things that crooned or buzzed in the sun" (47; emphasis added). Alexandra's heart hides "down there, somewhere," with "all the little wild things" that comprise nature, but these words are indefinable and imprecise. While the sensations are vague, they create an effect that sings to Alexandra. The environment offers Alexandra what Soja calls "an-other" alternative "marked by the openness of the both/and also" (7). For Alexandra, the natural world is "rich, strong and glorious" (44) and "frank and joyous and young" (52); it is space that is "open" and in which she feels positive and optimistic. As a woman who works on the land, Alexandra is able to enjoy "the idea of things more than the things themselves" (33), and in this way she differs markedly from her mother, Mrs. Bergson, who is like Laura's mother. Rather than feel intoxicated and enraptured by nature, Mrs. Bergson "still take[s] . . . comfort in the world if she had bacon in the cave, glass jars on the shelves, and sheets in the press" (20). Hers is a material satisfaction.

In *My Ántonia* (1918), the vast landscape again takes center stage and the out-of-doors contains the multiple possibilities of Soja's Thirdspace. Cather considers immigrant women's connection to the land through the character of Ántonia Shimerda. While Cather ignores the indigenous population, she nevertheless pays attention to other oft-forgotten peoples, such as Bohemians and Gypsies, who are typically treated as racial Others. Ántonia's experiences and attachment to the natural world are told through the eyes of a young boy, Jim Burden. Ántonia comes to represent the West for Jim, and like Alexandra, she is remarkably similar to Laura. Fittingly, Ántonia prefers to work outside rather than in a house (110). Indeed, she flees the house, takes off her sunbonnet, and throws it on the ground at every opportunity (108). Ántonia even states, "'I not care that your grandmother say it makes me like a man. I like to be like a man'" (110). Like Alexandra, when immersed in the land, Ántonia is "gay" and "responsive," "strong and independent," "irresponsible," and "like a boy" (110, 140, 158). She loves "rough play and digging in the earth" (140). When she is outside, she feels "a kind of hearty joviality, a relish of life, not over-delicate, but very invigorating" (141). As these words suggest, Ántonia becomes energized and restored in the outdoors far more than she does inside the home.

Once Ántonia marries her first husband and has a child, she remains strong and positive mainly because she has stayed on the land that feels so good to her. When Jim visits and tells her about his life in cities, Ántonia replies, "I'd always be miserable in a city. I'd die of lonesomeness. I like to be where I know every stack and tree, and where all the ground is friendly" (240). As in *O Pioneers!*, the ground in Nebraska is "friendly"; it is where Ántonia belongs. Even though Ántonia has struggled, Jim notes that she is "strong and warm and good" (241). After another twenty years passes, Jim asserts that Ántonia "was there, in the full vigor of her personality, battered but not diminished.... Whatever else was gone, Ántonia had not lost the fire of life" (248, 250). To the end, Ántonia stands firm in her conviction that she belongs on a farm: "I'm never lonesome here like I used to be in town," she affirms (255).

SITUATING LAURA IN SPACE

Delving into Wilder's Little House books after reading Cather's Nebraskan novels is revelatory. Like Alexandra and Ántonia, Laura is from the beginning of the series drawn to the wild and yearns for the out-of-doors. For Laura, the land of the western territories where she roams with her family represents freedom, and she loves it. Readers witness Laura's attachment to the landscape throughout the series, but here I treat primarily *On the Banks of Plum Creek* (set in western Minnesota) and secondarily *By the Shores of Silver Lake* (set in the southeastern Dakota Territory). In these two texts, the land is personified and imbued with beauty and possibility, and it beckons to Laura to travel and explore it, just as it does for Cather's heroines. Like Alexandra and Ántonia, Laura takes note of nature's harmony and majesty from a young age, absorbing its rhythms and whimsies. She has a preternatural love for and attachment to the space and is often preoccupied with the height of the sky and the expansive silence and stillness that surround her. For example, Wilder describes the space beyond the wagon as it makes its way slowly across the plains: "The creek was singing to itself down among the willows, and the soft wind bent the grasses over the top of the bank. The sun was shining and all around the wagon was clean, wide space to be explored" (*Banks* 9). Wilder highlights the prospect of exploration that entices Laura. Further, nature is humanized, recalling Ántonia's sentiment that the ground is "friendly." The creek sings and the wind bends the grass; again, the land offers what Soja deems "an-other" realm of possibility for Laura to discover. The land's effect on Laura is ineffable, as it is for Alexandra and Ántonia. Words and phrases are vague: "down among," "over the top," "clean" and "wide" space. All are imprecise yet suggestive and inviting. Soja describes the domain of Thirdspace as offering "extraordinary openness" (5), just as Wilder's land does. Laura's imagination expands and encompasses Soja's "multiplicity of perspectives" (5). Laura is so contented in the out-of-doors that she yearns to sleep there rather than safely inside (*Banks* 17). Laura seems to find the "so safe" interior of "this house dug under the ground" (*Banks* 17) stultifying compared to the freedom of the outdoors.

Geographer Doreen Massey has argued that space for women can be full of possibility and "open" rather than "closed" and "static" (59), as the domestic interior is often rendered. In Massey's terms, like Soja's, space is "unfinished" and "always becoming" (59). Such is the way the outdoors is conceived for Laura, Alexandra, and Ántonia: space offers a nonstatic realm of possibility where these characters play, dig, and voyage outside rather than remain confined indoors. Cather's women and Wilder's Laura sever themselves from the conventional, feminine, and domestic realms, which they experience as limited. As a result, like the space itself, they are "always becoming," as Massey describes (59): each moment out-of-doors presents them with a new experience in which they can actively participate.

Indeed, there is no greater scolding for the young Laura than to have to spend the day indoors overseen by her mother. As penalty for attempting to go by herself to the swimming hole—a dangerous proposition that is ultimately thwarted by the appearance of a badger—Ma keeps Laura inside, where she can be watched as she does chores. Ma seems to realize that sequestering Laura inside is an awful punishment; she knows how much Laura would prefer to be outside, even if she is doing chores there as well. Laura's outdoor tasks at least allow her mind and body to wander. By keeping Laura inside, Ma reinforces Laura's sentiment that the indoors is stifling. Thus, Laura suffers twofold: she must do indoor chores she dislikes (washing dishes, making beds), and she must be overseen by Ma, something Laura cannot bear: "She thought... that day would never end," Wilder notes of the chagrined Laura (*Banks* 35). Laura concludes that "being good could never be as hard as being watched" (36). While Laura feels constrained indoors, Ma and Mary, her older sister, are much happier inside the house. Outdoors, they seem challenged by heavy tasks or fearful of the unknown. Ma seems to understand and accept that although Laura knows how to do housework, she prefers to run wild outside. Ma allows that Laura is more like her father in this respect and bestows the benefit of youth on her adventurous and independent daughter who consistently breaks the rules.

Laura not only bemoans being kept inside but does not want to be watched, a sign of rebellion against any sort of authority, male or female. Laura's relation to the outdoors—both the way in which she actively craves and fully participates in it and the manner in which it frees her from authority—fulfills the long-held desire for a place of one's own (in this case not a room but space itself) that preoccupies feminist geographers and theorists.[3] Specifically, Laura's desire to be out-of-doors, to feel the embrace of the enormous and powerful silence and stillness encompassed in the Great Plains, recalls bell hooks's concept of "radical openness" (41–50), on which Soja draws extensively (83–105). For hooks, this "openness" means pushing against boundaries set by race or gender (such as girls and women who remain confined within the walls of the house) (203). Indeed, Laura can be seen as "radically open" to the landscape of the western frontier.

Laura's enactment of self in the outdoors is perhaps best illustrated by her behavior during the straw-stack scene in *Plum Creek*. In chapter 8, Laura disobeys her parents and climbs up a large stack of straw gathered and bundled to feed their animals throughout the winter. Laura convinces Mary to join her, and they climb up and slide down the stack so many times that it is reduced to a scatter of grass. While the straw-stack could be construed as a barrier to Laura and her sister—tall and erect as it is—it is an inspiring source of freedom for Laura. Rather than be impeded by the stack, Laura dominates it; in fact, she destroys it. Romines views this scene as an "unaccustomed" opportunity for Laura to "demolish a solid, traditional, phallic structure erected by a patriarch" (*Constructing* 103). I agree with Romines that Laura topples a patriarchal and phallic structure in this scene; however, I argue that doing so is not an "unaccustomed" opportunity for the girl. Rather, playing in nature and using it to her pleasure is a way of life for Laura, no matter how dangerous or frightening it may be, as we witness when Laura plays in the creek.

While Laura knows the creek is dangerous and has been warned by her father never to go near it when it is flooding, she cannot resist the excitement of the rushing water. In her eyes, the water becomes "fearful and fascinating" (*Banks* 98) and "strong and terrible" (99), a mixture of contradictory elements. But rather than scare her, the dangerous water makes her feel "so fine and frisky" (99). Like her defiant act of climbing the straw-stack, Laura cannot resist the lure of the overflowing river—and she almost drowns. Nevertheless, Laura does not feel defeated or fearful: "The creek had not got her. It had not made her scream and it could not make her cry" (106). Rather than show emotion, which might be construed as infantile or overly feminine, Laura remains defiantly bold and brave. By pursuing opportunities that push the boundaries of prescribed roles for white girls at her time, Laura willingly breaks the rules. The contradictory nature of both the river and her emotions in this scene speaks to the landscape's ineffable appeal for Laura.

What, then, lies at the heart of the draw of nature for Laura, Alexandra, and Ántonia, and why is space for these women depicted with what Soja would consider qualities of Otherness that are clearly present yet difficult to pinpoint? If we move for a moment beyond the theoretical Thirdspace and look to scholars who have meditated on the wonders of space and place in literature, we find some answers. Judith Fryer, for example, considers "imaginative structures" in the work of Cather and Edith Wharton and explores the physical and spiritual experiences of "felicitous space," which Fryer contends "frees the imagination" (293). This is precisely the attraction of the frontier for Cather's and Wilder's young women: rather than constricting them as the domestic interior often does, the expanse of the outdoors is a blank canvas on which they can write their own stories. Fryer quotes art critic Eleanor Munro to explain the pull of the Western landscape: "Now, the thing about emptiness is that one can fill it: an empty landscape, an empty paper. One can make one's own mark" (289). Munro maintains, "In a wide, flat, empty landscape, one is centered wherever one is" (Fryer 289). When Laura is outside with her feet on the "friendly" earth, she feels grounded, secure, and happy. These feelings inspire confidence and a sense of freedom, which lead her to explore and push boundaries. Fryer notes that for Alexandra in *O Pioneers!*, the land is a lover (255); for Laura, too, the land feels romantic and welcoming, even if it is also at times threatening.

In contrast, both Ma and Mary see the frontier as risky and dangerous. While Laura shares her father's desire to be outside, Mary yearns to stay indoors and mirrors her mother: both women exemplify domesticity, femininity, and order. Wilder notes, "Mary was cross because she would rather sew or read than pick plums. But Laura hated to sit still; she liked picking plums" (*Banks* 64). This line perfectly illustrates the difference between the sisters. Similarly, Wilder points out that Laura likes "wolves better than cattle" (79) and that Laura would rather play in the creek than with dolls (172). Massey's delineation of space through a feminist lens helps readers understand Laura's preference for wolves over cattle and the creek over dolls. Massey argues that "chance and chaos" (59)—the wildness and danger of the outdoors—offer a new, exciting domain for frontier girls that is preferable to the tame, domesticated interior. Laura would rather be in the exhilarating outdoors because the landscape offers possibility, notwithstanding the dangers embedded in that possibility.

Readers of the Little House books know that Laura ultimately becomes a schoolteacher to earn money to help send Mary to a school for the blind, but Laura often expresses that she does not want to become a teacher. Sitting in the schoolroom, Laura gazes out the window, noting the wind, the grass, and finally the whole "great light of the sky" (*Banks* 150). This broadening view far surpasses the study of books. Even as a teacher, sixteen-year-old Laura struggles to stay inside all day. She wants to work so she can contribute to Mary's school fees, but even more, she yearns to be free.

Laura feels similarly restless in church: once in her pew, she stares out the window, wishing she were outside: "She looked through the open windows at butterflies going where they pleased. She watched the grasses blowing in the wind. . . . [H]er legs ached from dangling still" (*Banks* 186–87). Personified nature beckons to Laura far more strongly than does the minister. In fact, Laura so identifies with the wild that at times she wishes she were an Indian so she would not have to wear clothes (219), reflecting her mistaken assumption that the Native American people are more free than she is.

Soja's Thirdspace also encompasses an Otherness that helps us understand the role of the indigenous population in Wilder's novels. As Donna Campbell has argued, the "wild men" in Wilder's books represent "alternative cultures" (112). Like Laura and Pa, the Indians "contrast with Wilder's notions of gentility," but, as we have seen and as Campbell confirms, "the term 'wild' does not hold for [Laura] the negative connotations that it does for her mother" (112). Comparing Laura to a "wild Indian" (*Shores* 55), Ma means to say that Laura is behaving too rowdily and coming across as too untamed for a white female. As a young child, though, she is nevertheless still a "good" child—her mother loves her—even though she occasionally breaks the rules or seeks the excitement of the outdoors.

Laura's disenchantment with the indoors, specifically with having to sit still in school and church, can also be understood through Jane Tompkins's *West of Everything: The Inner Life of Westerns* (1992). Tompkins equates the West with the loss and distrust of language. Like the men whom Tompkins treats in her work,[4] Laura feels encumbered both by the cultural and traditional fixtures of school and church and by language. In fact, she often resorts to outbursts, questions, or fidgeting when words escape her. (For more on how Laura uses "shameful" tears, unladylike gestures, and questions to communicate what she cannot otherwise express, see Campbell 116.) In this way, Laura again resembles the "wild men" (as Ma calls the Native Americans in the text) and the men of Westerns, such as John Wayne, whom Tompkins equates with "non-language" (52–55). Tompkins contends that the masculine hero of the Western aspires to "nature," to a state of "perfect being-in-itself" (58). When outdoors, Laura, too, embodies this sense of being in the moment, but again, for her, such "wildness" befits her youth; for indigenous people, in contrast, it is a racial judgment.

Laura continuously moves and is propelled by instinct even as she grows older, much like the men of the American West, whom Tompkins describes as "monumentality in motion, propelling themselves forward by instinct" (58). During the Ingalls family's move to Dakota Territory, Wilder writes, "Laura would rather not stop anywhere. She would rather go on and on, to the very end of the road, wherever it was" (*Shores* 35). As much as Laura desires motion, she prefers the covered wagon's slow pace to the train. While the train is "rich and swift . . . , the wagon went slowly, so there was time to see everything" (37). Laura enjoys the wagon because from it she can see "the whole sky . . . overhead and the prairie stretched away on all sides" (37). She has no desire to stop moving, while her mother aches to be settled once and for all.

While Romines and Campbell argue that Laura is gradually domesticated throughout the series, I contend that Laura's desire for motion in particular and for the wilderness in general grows stronger as she matures. In the series' last official book, *These Happy Golden Years*, eighteen-year-old Laura remains frustrated at being housebound and yearns to leave the house and soak up the landscape. After dinner one evening, she wanders restlessly outside, where "the sky was so blue, the floating piles of cloud were so shimmering and pearly, and far and wide the land was green. . . . Laura stood, looking east and south and west at the lovely, empty day" (165). Here again, we encounter Soja's Thirdspace, the seemingly contradictory yet endlessly appealing world of space that is both "lovely" and "empty." This realm is at once open and tantalizing—"so blue" and "so shimmering and pearly"—yet very simple and serene. The "restless" Laura feels immediately calm. Growing older has not diminished her love of the outdoors; like her Pa, she remains drawn to the wild. Wilder explicitly connects Laura to her father and highlights her deep reluctance to be a teacher: Pa "must stay in a settled country for the sake of them all, just as [Laura] must teach school again, though she did so hate to be shut into a schoolroom" (139).

In Wilder's final book, *The First Four Years*, which was posthumously published in 1971 and chronicles Laura and Almanzo's first years of marriage and parenthood, Laura remains attached to the outdoors. Indeed, Almanzo convinces Laura to live on a farm rather than in town because of her connection to nature. As in earlier books, Wilder reaffirms that Laura "liked the horses and enjoyed the freedom and spaciousness of the wide prairie land, with the wind forever waving the tall wild grass . . . and rustling through the short curly buffalo grass. . . . It was all so sweet and fresh" (6). Wilder continues to evoke the "freedom" and "spaciousness" as well as the "wilderness" of the land and its epic draw for Laura. The qualities still beckon to the grown Laura, as evidenced by the words "so sweet and fresh." While pregnant with her first child, Laura resents that she must stay indoors (47). Laura's attachment to the landscape and her desire for the freedom offered by the land remain present until the very end of the Little House books.

Wilder and Cather juxtapose their heroines against women who do not take to prairie life. As Romines argues, Cather often "play[ed] a housekeeper's story against that of a character who is not centrally involved in domestic ritual" (*Home* 139). Cather does so, Romines contends, by contrasting Alexandra with her mother in *O Pioneers!* and positioning Ántonia against Jim in *My Ántonia* (139). Wilder uses a similar strategy by setting Laura against her mother and Mary. Ma is often portrayed as a long-suffering wife who would prefer to live in town, where her daughters can attend school, while her husband wants to move further west. As Holly Blackford writes, "Ma values fashion, beauty, and 'imported' objects like the china shepherdess" (151), while Laura does not. Instead, Laura gallivants in and out of the house, ignoring such domestic upsets as her torn pockets and untied bonnet. Likewise, Alexandra's mother has "never quite forgiven John Bergson for bringing her to the end of the earth" (*Pioneers* 20). Ma feels the same way and often wonders why her husband yearns to keep moving.[5]

Laura's ongoing love of the wild and the independence it provides is made even more clear during her courtship with Almanzo, which occurs during horse-drawn buggy rides across the prairie. Laura is attracted to Almanzo at least in part because his horses provide her with a way to be outside and feel free. Laura eagerly anticipates these Sunday drives but often seems happier to see Almanzo's horses than to see him. Readers sense her discomfort with the idea of becoming a wife and keeping house. Rather than focus on building a home, Laura remains preoccupied with the outdoors: "She wanted to travel on and on, over those miles, and see what lay beyond the hills" (*Happy* 153). The desire to know "what lay beyond" the hills is far more captivating to Laura than what is contained within the house. Even on the verge of marriage, Laura yearns to keep moving, highlighting again how the landscape encapsulates Thirdspace: the draw is more than mental and physical. Nature offers Laura a spiritual experience. Indeed, Laura is so captivated by the "freedom" of the landscape that she tells Almanzo that she will not use the word *obey* in her marriage vows: "I cannot make a promise that I will not keep, and Almanzo, even if I tried, I do not think I could obey anybody against my better judgment" (*Happy* 269–70). In this sense, Laura embodies the land: she seeks the same independence and freedom that is offered by the wind, the sky, and the grass. Almanzo replies that he never knew a decent man who wanted a woman to obey him, and the two marry (269).

Laura Ingalls, like her literary predecessors Alexandra Bergson and Ántonia Shimerda, comes alive in the infinite landscape of the Great Plains. While many people and women especially felt oppressed by the vastness of the space, these female characters feel an affinity with the land that connects them to each other. Cather's women and Laura express a masculine sense of self more than a typically female one. In contrast to Ma and Mary, Laura is akin to her father and offers new ways of understanding late-nineteenth-century women and their relationship to the land. Laura's response to the frontier landscape is intuitive, imaginative, and innovative, filling her with a sense of well-being. For Laura's mother, her sisters, and many of her female peers, the Western hills "would just be hills" (*Happy* 153), but the hills could never be "just hills" to her: "Laura could not say what she meant, but to her the Wessington Hills were more than grassy hills. Their shadowy outlines drew her with the lure of far places" (153). Even at this late juncture in the series' final book, "the lure of far places"—the call of the wild—beckons to the newly married Laura. As far as Laura is concerned, she will forever remain a pioneer girl, dwelling in the poetic space of the eternal now—evoked in Wilder's words "Now is now" (*Woods* 238)—of the western prairie.

NOTES

I thank my colleague and friend Leslie Eckel for providing the spark that reignited my interest in Laura Ingalls Wilder. In December 2015, Leslie gave my daughter a copy of *Little House in the Big Woods* for Christmas. My daughter and I promptly read the book, which led to my rediscovery of the series that had enthralled me as a child and the sharing of that joy with my daughter. A few months later, I responded to the CFP for this collection. I thank the editors, Miranda Green-Barteet and Anne Phillips, both for initiating this important project and for their very helpful comments on my essay. I am indebted to my writing cohort, Lori Harrison-Kahan and Kimberly Davis, for their support, friendship, and feedback on early versions of this work. I also thank Lori Harrison-Kahan and Jennifer Tuttle for organizing a panel on Recovering and Rediscovering Western Women's Writing for the American Literature Association's annual conference in Boston in 2017 and including my paper on Laura Ingalls Wilder that provided the springboard for this essay.

1. For an overview of the meaning of Thirdspace, see Soja, especially 1–17. Soja draws in particular on Foucault, Lefebvre, and hooks to derive Thirdspace. See also Soja 6–12, 25–82, 145–63.

2. While Cather was once relegated to the status of a regional writer, an explosion of academic interest in her and her works has occurred over the past several decades. Biographies and collections have helped secure Cather's now-canonical status. See, for example, Bohlke; Lee; Woodress. In contrast, Wilder has been gaining momentum in scholarly circles only in the past twenty years or so, thanks in part to the work of Romines, Miller, Fellman, Hill, and most recently Ketcham and in part due to interest in the life and career of her daughter, Rose Wilder Lane (see Holtz). Wilder has also begun to appear more regularly in scholarly

journals as a consequence of the growing interest in the value of children's literature, largely pioneered by Rosa Ann Moore in the late 1970s.

3. Here I refer of course to Woolf's masterpiece, *A Room of One's Own*.

4. In addition to John Wayne, Tompkins treats the cowboy at the center of Owen Wister's 1902 novel, *The Virginian*, and the heroes in later works by Zane Grey and Louis L'Amour.

5. The historical Caroline Ingalls was much more of a partner to Charles than is displayed in the Little House books. For example, in *Laura Ingalls Wilder: A Writer's Life*, Hill suggests that Ma and Pa make many decisions together, and Ma was likely key in their decision to move to South Dakota. However, she was also instrumental in the family's decision to stay in De Smet rather than going further west.

WORKS CITED

Baldwin, James. "Introduction: The Price of the Ticket." In *The Price of the Ticket*, iii–xv. New York: St. Martin's, 1985.

Blackford, Holly. "Civilization and Her Discontents: The Unsettling Nature of Ma in *Little House in the Big Woods*." *Frontiers: A Journal of Women's Studies* 29, no. 1 (2008): 147–87.

Bohlke, L. Brent, ed. *Willa Cather in Person: Interviews, Speeches, and Letters*. University of Nebraska Press, 1986.

Campbell, Donna. "'Wild Men' and Dissenting Voices: Narrative Disruption in *Little House on the Prairie*." *Great Plains Quarterly* 20, no. 2 (2000): 111–22.

Cather, Willa. *My Ántonia*. 1918. Penguin, 1994.

Cather, Willa. *O Pioneers!* 1913. Penguin, 1994.

Fellman, Anita Clair. *Little House, Long Shadow: Laura Ingalls Wilder's Impact on American Culture*. University of Missouri Press, 2008.

Foucault, Michel. "Of Other Spaces." 1967. Trans. Jay Miskowiec. *Architecture/Mouvement/Continuité*, October 1984, 2–9.

Fryer, Judith. *Felicitous Space: The Imaginative Structures of Edith Wharton and Willa Cather*. University of North Carolina Press, 1986.

Hill, Pamela Smith. *Laura Ingalls Wilder: A Writer's Life*. South Dakota Historical Society Press, 2007.

Holtz, William. *The Ghost in the Little House: A Life of Rose Wilder Lane*. University of Missouri Press, 1993.

hooks, bell. *Yearning: Race, Gender, and Cultural Politics*. South End, 1990.

Ketcham, Sallie. *Laura Ingalls Wilder: American Writer on the Prairie*. Routledge, 2014.

Lefebvre, Henri. *The Production of Space*. 1974. Blackwell, 1991.

Lee, Hermione. *Willa Cather: Double Lives*. Vintage, 1989.

Massey, Doreen. *For Space*. Sage, 2005.

Miller, John E. *Becoming Laura Ingalls Wilder: The Woman behind the Legend*. University of Missouri Press, 1998.

Moore, Rosa Ann. "The Little House Books: Rose-Colored Classics." *Children's Literature* 7 (1978): 7–16.

Romines, Ann. *Constructing the Little House: Gender, Culture, and Laura Ingalls Wilder*. University of Massachusetts Press, 1997.

Romines, Ann. *The Home Plot: Women, Writing, and Domestic Ritual*. University of Massachusetts Press, 1992.

Smulders, Sharon. "'The Only Good Indian': History, Race, and Representation in Laura Ingalls Wilder's *Little House on the Prairie.*" *Children's Literature Association Quarterly* 27, no. 4 (2002): 191–202.

Soja, Edward W. *Thirdspace: Journeys to Los Angeles and Other Real-and-Imagined Places.* Blackwell, 1996.

Tompkins, Jane. *West of Everything: The Inner Life of Westerns.* Oxford University Press, 1992.

Western Literature Association. *Updating the Literary West.* Texas Christian University Press, 1997.

Wilder, Laura Ingalls. *By the Shores of Silver Lake.* 1939. HarperCollins, 1971.

Wilder, Laura Ingalls. *The First Four Years.* Harper and Row, 1971.

Wilder, Laura Ingalls. *Little House in the Big Woods.* 1932. Harper and Row, 1971.

Wilder, Laura Ingalls. *Little House on the Prairie.* 1935. Harper and Row, 1971.

Wilder, Laura Ingalls. *On the Banks of Plum Creek.* 1937. Harper and Row, 1971.

Wilder, Laura Ingalls. *Pioneer Girl: The Annotated Autobiography.* Edited by Pamela Smith Hill, South Dakota Historical Society Press, 2014.

Wilder, Laura Ingalls. *These Happy Golden Years.* 1943. Harper and Row, 1971.

Woodress, James. *Willa Cather: A Literary Life.* University of Nebraska Press, 1987.

Woolf, Virginia. *A Room of One's Own.* 1929. Harcourt, 2005.

BREATHING LITERARY LIVES FROM THE PRAIRIE

Laura Ingalls Wilder and the Promises of Rural Women's Education in the Little House Series

Jericho Williams

When Laura Ingalls Wilder started writing the Little House series, her principal challenge was transforming moments from her childhood into episodic children's stories after a career spent writing primarily for adults.[1] In her sixties, Wilder began writing the series' first book after a decade as a columnist for the *Missouri Ruralist*, a statewide farming journal. She drew from an unpublished autobiography (released in 2014 as *Pioneer Girl*) and her memories, using deeply personal family vignettes that her daughter, Rose Wilder Lane, already a successful author, helped expand and shape for publication.[2] The resulting original series that focuses on her heroine, Laura, contains seven novels and continues to attract droves of fans. Three of the first four books relate portions of Laura's childhood, while the series' later novels detail Laura's coming of age, as she prepares to leave her family and begin her life with her husband, Almanzo Wilder.

This essay considers *Little Town on the Prairie* (1941) and *These Happy Golden Years* (1943), specifically examining Laura's focus on her education and future as a teacher, as well as the posthumously published *The First Four Years* (1971), which documents the beginning of her marriage.[3] In these works, Laura becomes serious about school, realizing she can become a teacher to help support her family. These novels are less carefree than the earlier ones, as they bemoan Laura's loss of childhood freedoms and maturation and emphasize the changing nature of education in Laura's life.

Through Laura, Wilder argues that education can empower girls who live in rural areas, a fact that distinguishes *Little Town on the Prairie* and *These Happy Golden Years* from writers Hamlin Garland and Willa Cather, both of whom wrote about rural American prairie land and received more critical attention than Wilder. Wilder's books reveal how her school experiences shape her teaching and postteaching career; by extension, they convey the idea that education provided opportunities for rural young women during the late nineteenth century. In arguing that education can benefit young women in rural communities, Wilder offers a notable contrast with two fictional women who also reached adulthood between the early 1880s and 1890s: Rose Dutcher from Garland's *Rose of Dutcher's Coolly* (1895) and Thea Kronborg from Cather's *The Song of the Lark* (1915). Wilder, Garland, and Cather grew up in rural communities, and each wrote about gifted women striving to find themselves while facing difficult circumstances. Although Garland and Cather emphasize Rose's and Thea's vitality, perseverance, and intelligence, both insist that their heroines must leave their hometowns for cities to find fulfillment. Wilder, however, prepares Laura for a community-based life, which enables her to thrive in rural environments like those of her childhood. In considering Wilder's texts alongside *Rose of Dutcher's Coolly* and *The Song of the Lark*, I place Wilder within a wider literary context than solely children's literature. Through Laura, Wilder offers an alternative to Garland's and Cather's perspectives on the lives of rural women, which emphasized the need for talented young women to escape their hometowns.

While Garland's and Cather's books are moving testaments to art's power to inspire young women, they also reflect negatively on education and fulfillment in rural communities. Wilder, however, disrupts the notion that rural women lead inferior lives. Whereas Garland and Cather position school and teaching as a springboard for upward social, intellectual, or material mobility in faraway locales, Wilder insists that women do not have to abandon their roots for a respectable education and personal success. Like her predecessors, Wilder highlights Laura's determination and self-reliance, but not at the expense of others. Offering a more tempered and realistic perspective, Wilder redefines the purpose of rural education. In Wilder's view, rather than just a means for talented women to leave their hometowns, education is a multifaceted process that consists of learning rural arts and skills, living within one's means, adapting to one's environment, and assisting one's family members and community. Each of these responsibilities develops through a combination of learning and a sense of duty toward others as opposed to narrow specialization. In charting

Laura's path toward adulthood, Wilder offers an alternative vision of womanhood, advocating the mastery of traditional and nontraditional literacies and determining how best to support family and community. Through Laura, Wilder suggests that rural women's success depends on a gradual increase in knowledge and skills as well as the understanding that rural responsibilities demand sacrifice, community awareness, and self-reliance.

OF SCHOOL AND CANON: WILDER'S EDUCATIONAL LEGACY

The Little House series garners more attention for its role in contemporary elementary education classrooms than for Laura's own educational experiences. Anita Clair Fellman notes that schoolteachers have long incorporated Wilder's books into the curriculum, primarily because of "the accuracy of their details of everyday life, the tracing of Laura's emotional and ethical development, and the feelings of security conveyed by the stories," and that these attributes foster a "strong emotional commitment and respect for the series" (137). As a result, the novels became classics for children. However, Laura's adolescence and young adulthood are often ignored; given that children are Wilder's primary audience, it is easy to understand why the later books attract less interest. In these novels, Wilder reaffirms formal education as a vital component of women's progress, but she also asserts that for rural women, education must be supplemented by other knowledge that may be less valuable to metropolitan outsiders. Consequently, Wilder's books are at odds with the dominant literary discourse about possibilities for women during the late nineteenth century.

American women living in cities experienced drastic changes between 1880 and 1920. As Jean V. Matthews notes, a "New Woman" appeared: "Many of women's expansive possibilities had to do with the rapid growth of American cities in the post–Civil War era. In 1870, 14 cities could boast a population of more than 100,000; by 1900 there were 38. While most Americans lived on the land until 1920, urban areas were attracting more and more newcomers, both native-born from farms and foreign immigrants seeking a better life" (8). Consequently, novels about women overcoming the odds of their rural upbringings became popular, representing this period as a time of social change. *Rose of Dutcher's Coolly* and *The Song of the Lark* offer moving portraits of women making courageous decisions prior generations of women could not. Garland's Rose and Cather's Thea benefit from new opportunities, escaping their hometowns for a more fulfilling life. In contrast, Wilder offers Laura an alternative: rather than escaping the farm via a rags-to-inner-riches narrative, she stays and is content with her life. Even as Wilder saw family farming decline and experienced financial struggles herself, she understood that many farm women prospered from a combination of traditional literacies such as reading, writing, and mathematics along with nontraditional literacies related to farmwork, and by participating and contributing to the larger farming community.

LEARNING, LABOR, AND LITERACIES: ADOLESCENCE AND SCHOOL IN *LITTLE TOWN ON THE PRAIRIE* AND *ROSE OF DUTCHER'S COOLLY*

Garland and Wilder had remarkably similar childhoods. Born seven years apart in Wisconsin, each lived near Burr Oak, Iowa, during the 1860s and 1870s and moved to various frontier areas as children; both homesteaded in South Dakota; and both worked as teachers, expressing interest in midwestern children's education (Spaeth 96). Eventually, however, they chose different paths. Unable to find teaching positions in Iowa or Minnesota, Garland moved to Boston to study, struggling there before beginning his writing career. Conversely, Wilder earned a teaching certificate and took a job twelve miles from her family's home in De Smet, South Dakota. At eighteen, she married Almanzo Wilder and committed to farming with him. While Garland bitterly rejected midwestern life, Wilder, despite struggling financially, chose to remain in the Midwest.

Despite their different life choices, both writers view education as transformative. Reflecting on his experiences at Cedar Valley Seminary, Garland writes, "I loved school and could hardly be wrested from it even for a day. I bent to my books with eagerness.... I forgot the farm, I forgot the valley of my birth, I lived wholly and with joy in the present" (*Son* 162–63). For Garland, school was far preferable to the drudgery of farmwork. Education provided so great an escape that, in his mid-twenties, he spent hours studying alone in Boston, where he checked out library books so that he could read "fourteen hours a day instead of ten" (262). Devoting time to literary study afforded Garland the knowledge and confidence that laid the groundwork for his writing career. Wilder, however, initially disliked school and studying, especially in comparison to her older sister, Mary, but she gradually became more studious, earned a teaching certificate, and worked as a teacher (*Pioneer* 58). As she began to see formal education as a way to improve communities, she fiercely advocated for rural schools. In 1917, fifteen years before she began publishing her novels, Wilder wrote,

> We think we cannot afford to give children the proper schooling, "besides, their help is needed on the farm," we say. We shall pay for that education which we

do not give them. Oh! We shall pay for it! When we see our children inefficient and handicapped, perhaps thru life, for the lack of knowledge they should have gained in their youth, we shall pay in our hurt pride and our regret that we did not give them a fair chance, if in no other way, tho quite likely we shall pay in money too. The children, more's the pity, must pay also. ("To Buy" 123)

Then fifty years old, Wilder had briefly been a teacher; had witnessed how education fostered the writing career of her daughter, Rose; and had realized the importance of schools and talented teachers in preparing students for rural lifestyles, an idea that she addressed in *Little Town on the Prairie* and *These Happy Golden Years*.

Little Town on the Prairie focuses primarily on Laura's journey toward earning a teacher's certificate, offering Wilder the opportunity to explore Laura's increasing responsibilities. Within the series' trajectory, Laura's teaching preparation represents a transitional phase. In *By the Shores of Silver Lake*, she realizes that she is "not a little girl anymore" (12) and that her mother hopes she will become a schoolteacher (75), but her family's relocation to the developing De Smet area and the focus on survival at the heart of the next novel, *The Long Winter*, prevent her from considering tasks unrelated to her family. *Little Town* shows Laura realizing that working to help support her family is central to adulthood. John E. Miller notes that the novel's central thematic problem is "negotiating adolescence" and "learning how to relate to other people in school and in town" (*Laura* 93). The novel's opening chapter, "Surprise," announces this transition, with Pa asking, "How would you like to work in town, Laura?" (371). In response, everyone remains quiet, "as if they were frozen" (371). Ma breaks the silence by questioning Pa's idea and suggesting that teaching is the only suitable possibility for Laura. The chapter concludes before Pa can reply, but Laura thinks to herself that "they were all so busy and happy now in the springtime, and she did not want anything changed. She did not want to work in town" (371). Here, Pa suggests that she needs to contribute to the household more substantially. Laura is bothered by the implication that her present contributions are no longer sufficient and that growing up means working in town to help support the family.

Similarly, the first chapter of Garland's *Rose of Dutcher's Coolly* begins with a surprise that redirects Rose's life. The narrator "was only five years old when her mother suddenly ... took rest in death" (4). Her mother's passing forces Rose to rely on her father and her widowed aunt, Mrs. Diehl, who cannot fill Rose's mother's place. Unlike Wilder, Garland uses a traumatic family moment to redirect Rose from a potentially bleak way of life. Whereas Wilder's portrayal of Laura drew from the author's realizations of the need to assume greater responsibilities within her family, Garland was motivated by feelings of guilt. Throughout his early adulthood, Garland regretted leaving his mother behind when he pursued a writing career in Boston. In July 1888, after visiting his parents, the twenty-seven-year-old Garland reflected, "It seemed a treachery to say good-bye to my aging parents, leaving them and my untrained sister to this barren, empty, laborious life on the plain, whilst I returned to the music, the drama, the inspiration, the glory of Boston.... I entered the car, and when from its window I looked back upon my grieving mother, my throat filled with a suffocating sense of guilt. I was deserting her, recreant to my blood!" (*Son* 300). Two years later, he created Rose Dutcher to represent the talented women he imagined scattered throughout America, trapped and unable to pursue higher education and the arts (Newlin xv). In separating Rose from her mother at the beginning of the novel, Garland introduces an alternative trajectory of womanhood, one he imagined as infinitely more fulfilling than the lives of his mother and women like Wilder.

Wilder envisions a different outcome for rural women than Garland, as she believed that women could be more fulfilled if they took on various community roles requiring a multitude of skills. She knew firsthand that living in rural communities could be endlessly challenging. In 1898, no longer able to support their family by farming, Wilder and her husband settled in Mansfield, Missouri (*Selected* 7). They remained there until 1910, when supplemental farmwork began to pay off and supported them for more than a decade. During this period, Wilder also shared her expertise, demonstrating her commitment toward helping other farming families. In February 1911, she began writing for the *Missouri Ruralist*, contributing articles regularly through December 1924. She also served as a secretary-treasurer and then as director of the Mansfield Farm Loan Association from 1917 until 1928, "working at home and in office space on the town square, processing loans and recording minutes at meetings" (*Selected* 18). Despite experiencing her own challenges, Wilder stressed the benefits of perseverance. In 1911, she reaffirmed women's contributions by warning them not to lose "time envying their sisters in the city" ("Favors" 16). Wilder appreciated the amenities made possible by urban technological progress, but she also championed "the beauty in everyday things" in the country (Miller, *Becoming* 131). She also knew that women completed many farming duties, so she argued that they were often "overlooked in the march of progress" ("Shorter" 23). This article reflects Wilder's persistent view that farming communities depended on women and that outsiders underestimated the extent of women's contributions.

These thoughts and ideas are woven throughout Laura's multifaceted development in *Little Town on the Prairie*, particularly regarding her work as a seamstress and her preparation to become a teacher. Wilder believed that a fine line existed between hardship and success throughout rural America. As Laura says to her mother, "The prairie looks so beautiful and gentle [but it] seems like we have to fight it all the time" (*Town* 420). Ma immediately replies, "This earthly life is a battle. . . . The sooner you make up your mind to that, the better off you are, and the more thankful for your pleasures" (420). Ma's outlook could easily be the tagline for Laura's struggle throughout *Little Town*, which stresses her trouble rationalizing the great amount of time she spends studying. Laura's main motivation is to help finance Mary's college education, but she finds the countless hours of homework overwhelming. Eventually, her patience increases, and obtaining her first job helps alleviate some of her distress. Pa helps her secure paid work as a part-time seamstress, and she earns nine dollars over the course of several weeks. This job allows her to practice a nonacademic skill and enables her to understand the benefits of earning money. Reflecting on the synthesis of studying and sewing, Laura realizes that teaching pays more, so she concentrates even harder as she becomes more determined to succeed in the classroom.

Like Laura, Rose studies tirelessly, but Garland positions formal learning as a step toward specialization and away from the farm. Garland presents Rose as intellectually superior to her classmates, whose poor progress effectively chains them to the region. In positioning Rose against her peers, Garland depicts rural education as simply school-based. Instead of considering other skills young people may acquire, he focuses on how poor teaching and burgeoning sexuality threaten nearly all of Rose's companions. Garland characterizes rural teachers as "generally farmers' daughters or girls from neighboring towns, who taught for a little extra money to buy dresses with" and as incapable of modeling critical thinking or motivating their students (*Rose* 34). From this deterministic vantage point, he suggests that rural schools ensnare young women and limit their progress. For Rose, the surprise return of Dr. Thatcher, a former resident who has gone on to become a successful doctor, facilitates her escape from the schoolhouse, which is a "squalid little den" (65). After visiting the school and witnessing Rose's potential, Thatcher talks to Rose's father about helping her move to avoid the fates of her companions: "At sixteen they had beaux, at seventeen many of them actually married and at eighteen they might often be seen riding to town with their husbands, covered with dust, clasping wailing babes in their arms; at twenty they were often thin and bent in the shoulders, and flat and stiff in the hips, sallow and querulous wives of slovenly, careless husbands" (83). Rose transcends the fate of all her peers, while Laura navigates schoolhouse culture and home responsibilities as part of a greater process that includes gaining other skills such as sewing and public speaking that impact her potential in similar rural communities. Even as Rose routinely questions her choices after leaving home, she depends on the promise of something elsewhere that demands leaving and increasing specialization, while Laura, like Wilder, looks nearby and strives to become proficient at a variety of paid and unpaid tasks that will enable her to adapt and thrive.[4]

THE TIES THAT BIND: TEACHING AND COMMUNITY IN *THESE HAPPY GOLDEN YEARS*, *THE FIRST FOUR YEARS*, AND *THE SONG OF THE LARK*

Earning her teaching certificate allows Laura to obtain a job that provides more personal freedom, yet in the series' final two novels, Wilder reveals that her heroine's career success depends on skills and qualifications and on her ability to apply them and to adapt and grow within a larger, rural community. This observation—that Laura succeeds after much sacrifice for the sake of other people—is often overlooked, as readers focus on the self-reliance and politicized ideals that characterize the series. In *Libertarians on the Prairie* (2016), Christine Woodside argues that Rose Wilder Lane's anti–New Deal and libertarian-minded politics during the 1930s influenced the series' latter half, as she assisted her mother with revisions. In "the first four novels," Woodside claims, Lane "enlivened and simplified [Wilder's] prose and built structure"; in the final four books, Rose "inserted ideas that she also wrote in her libertarian treatise *The Discovery of Freedom*" (198). Although Lane's alterations may not have been intentional, they nevertheless shape the story when certain scenes become "fables for the power of the individual" (199). In addition, because of the emphasis on Pa as well as his and Almanzo's insistence on the virtue of independence associated with farming, the series undeniably celebrates the individual against cultural, governmental, and natural forces, particularly with regard to masculinity. However, even if Pa's promulgations of self-reliance inform Laura's opinions and decisions, she—and by extension many other women like her—acts in ways that connect her with the well-being of others. From teaching, she learns to act as a guardian and protector, a notion that becomes more transparent when contrasted with Thea Kronborg of Cather's *The Song of the Lark*.

Like Garland, Cather grew up in rural communities, first in Winchester, Virginia, where she was born and lived until she was ten, and then in Red Cloud, Nebraska, where she experienced adolescence. After stints as a teacher, editor, biographer, and writer in Pittsburgh and New York, Cather composed her Prairie Trilogy, which includes *O Pioneers* (1913), *The Song of the Lark* (1915), and *My Ántonia* (1918). Although each novel explores the hardships of living in isolated locales, *The Song of the Lark*, a story about Thea, a talented singer from Moonstone, Colorado, is the only traditional bildungsroman of the three. Like *Rose of Dutcher's Coolly*, *The Song of the Lark* traces an artist's development, but Cather's novel emphasizes Thea's growth, independence, and devotion to art (Schedler 111). The multipart novel's structure is comparable to Wilder's series. The first segments of each seemingly overshadow the final sections about Thea's progress away from Moonstone and the concluding novels about Laura's adolescence and young adulthood. Cather supported this assertion when she admitted that her novel's principal problem was its "descending curve," in which Thea's later artistic achievements are nowhere near as "interesting as the life of a talented young girl 'fighting her way'" toward adulthood (416). Cather employs a pattern that Wilder later followed, highlighting her protagonist's adolescent struggles and her premature abandonment of formal education to work as a teacher. In contrast to Wilder, however, Cather presents Thea's community as socially draining, as it threatens to suffocate Thea and prevent her from pursuing her career.

Cather's opening section also foreshadows the toxicity of tiny rural towns such as Moonstone for talented young adults such as Thea. For example, Professor Wunsch, a community outsider and Thea's treasured music teacher, experiences a drinking binge that embarrasses him and causes him to leave Moonstone. His abrupt departure changes Thea's life. Unable to find a replacement for Wunsch, town members hire her to teach music; at fourteen, she abandons the life of a student to pursue that of a teacher. Second, after a circus tramp appears and is gravely mistreated by townspeople, he climbs a standpipe, vandalizes it, and then drowns himself inside, tainting the water supply and causing a fever that sickens many and kills "several adults and a half a dozen children" (121). If the first incident forces Thea to take on more responsibility as she approaches adulthood, this more horrendous event prompts her to reflect on the town's moblike response before the tramp's death, causing her to question the nature of the local residents. Cather does not link these tragic events with what might happen to Thea if she remains in Moonstone but examines a troubling code of behavior that restricts room for both gifted and impoverished outsiders.

Cather combats Moonstone's stifling social atmosphere by emphasizing individualism at all costs, presenting Thea's efforts to grow and define success in her own way. Thea's family nurtures this attitude. Realizing that Thea possesses musical talent, her mother makes her practice piano four hours a day, acting on the philosophy that "a child with talent must be kept at the piano, just as a child with measles must be kept under blankets" (25). Later, when Thea receives her own room, Cather describes the moment as "one of the most important things that ever happened to her" (53). Thea is removed from the "constant turmoil" of "the family, the day school, and the Sunday-School" (53). In Cather's view, Thea cannot flourish as a creator amid "the clamor about her [that] drowned the voice within herself" (53). On her own, ideas become "older and wiser friends," and thoughts seem "like companions" (54), and Thea begins to prepare for a permanent split from Moonstone. Professor Wunsch also urges Thea to yearn for something different than her neighbors. With deep admiration of Thea's "power of application" and "rugged will," he pushes her to think beyond Moonstone, telling her on her thirteenth birthday that her desire to succeed may define her life (30). Wunsch warns, "The world is little, people are little, human life is little," but desire is the "one big thing" that can lead to a more rewarding place (69). In time, Thea heeds his advice, but not before working as a teacher to help support her family.

Cather presents teaching as a dead end for women like Thea. Teaching demands an immense amount of time and distracts Thea from fulfilling her artistic potential. Thea initially embraces the profession, determined to help her students: "If a pupil did not get on well, she fumed and fretted.... Wunsch had taught only one pupil seriously, but Thea taught twenty" (93). Her dedication pays off when her students improve and she earns money. Teaching also enables Thea to begin her career and prepares her to better understand and trust the demanding teachers who eventually guide her in Chicago. However, teaching is also unfulfilling and tiring. Thea needs a new direction when Dr. Archie, her most ardent supporter after Professor Wunsch, convinces Thea's father that she should move to Chicago, where she can study with other artists.

Dr. Archie is proven correct when Thea succeeds, yet her arduous ascent from a small-town pianist and teacher to a professional singer far away from Moonstone is not without consequence. Cather foreshadows this tension by detailing Thea's father's perspective before she leaves Moonstone. Mr. Kronborg supports his daughter, but he privately considers large cities places where people "lose their identity and [are] wicked" (136). While Cather reserves judgment about urban wickedness, she conveys the risks of significant personal change as Thea becomes a world-renowned artist. For Cather, Thea must either leave Moonstone's restricting confines or risk "get[ting] warped, or wither[ing] up before her time" (132). Cather presents Thea with an ultimatum, which she later recapitulates, reminding readers that the story concerns "how a Moonstone girl found her way out of a vague, easy-going world into a life of disciplined endeavor" (405).

In contrast, Wilder resists identifying women of small towns as domestic failures ensconced within an "easy-going world." In 1930, responding to the beginning of the Great Depression, she composed but did not publish her autobiography, *Pioneer Girl*, which became the basis for much of the Little

House series. Throughout the decade, Wilder kept writing as her farming hopes diminished. She and Almanzo "had not grown fruit, raised cattle, or tended hens for income since the late 1920s," and in 1937, they felt that their lives consisted of "enduring hard luck" (Woodside 87, 99). Wilder realized that difficult times exacerbated some women's suffering from rural isolation, which she details in the *These Happy Golden Years*, with her descriptions of the isolated Brewster settlement, where she takes her first teaching position. While boarding with the Brewsters, she witnesses a distressed Mrs. Brewster threaten her husband with a butcher knife and demand to move closer to her family. Wilder implies that not all women can manage the isolation of farm life, yet she also emphasizes that this incident did not represent most rural women's responses to hardship; she believed that women's unnoticed contributions were central to farms and the communities closest to them. Writing for the *Missouri Ruralist*, she explained that "life on a farm as elsewhere is just what we make of it ... that much ... is being proved every day by women who, like this one, pick up a thread connecting farm life with the whole, great outside world" ("All" 50). Here, as in *These Happy Golden Years* and *The First Four Years*, Wilder stresses the necessity of accepting responsibilities and making commitments to family farms and local communities to feel personal fulfillment.

If *Little Town on the Prairie* details Laura's preparation for work, *These Happy Golden Years* stresses her growth in uncomfortable situations as she moves beyond the safety of her home and into a larger community. For example, she must learn to live with Mrs. Brewster, who seems "to enjoy hurting people" (563). Laura adapts to Mrs. Brewster's bitter negativity by remaining positive, a tactic she employs in the classroom. Laura concentrates on teaching despite wanting to abandon her responsibilities. Rather than focus on her own desires, Laura makes choices after considering what is best for her family and her students. For Wilder, these motivations are valuable and involve difficult situations like those Thea experiences. In *These Happy Golden Years*, for example, Laura teaches three terms at three different schools. At the first school at the Brewster settlement, she undergoes an arduous first term. She has five students—three older than she is, two much younger. As she teaches them, Laura has little support from the Brewsters, and she comes to rely on her weekends away from the settlement to sustain her spirit. She does not give up, however, and improves in the classroom. On the final day of the term, Laura tells her students, "You have made good use of the opportunity you had to come to school," and she emphasizes the importance of continuing to study, whether at school or at home (603). This model, which Laura herself follows as both teacher and student, stems directly from Wilder's conviction that continued learning and education help rural children prepare for opportunities that may appear in good or tough times.

Laura's teaching experience prepares her for the challenges she and Almanzo face when they marry and have a farm of their own. Before beginning her first teaching term, Laura feels "very small" (*Happy* 549) about going to school, but she later relies on the same level of determination she felt while earning her first teaching certificate in an effort to become more effective. Learning how to teach children equips Laura for future difficult circumstances beyond her control. In *The First Four Years*, when Almanzo claims that farming productively depends on their work ethic, Laura is skeptical but nevertheless agrees despite knowing that their life will be full of disappointment (737). Instead of teaching, Laura spends her time "cooking, baking, churning, sweeping, washing, ironing, and mending" as well as plowing and haying (745). All of this work is integral if they are to have a chance to break even, and both know that the unpredictability of the weather can undermine their most earnest efforts. Already struggling financially following three failed harvests and Almanzo's stroke, Laura bluntly asks, "Do you call this farming a success?" (781). Almanzo responds with some uncertainty, but they persevere. At the novel's conclusion, when they consider the same question, Wilder shares Laura's perspective: "It would be a fight to win out in this business of farming, but strangely she felt her spirit rising for the struggle" (795). In both teaching and farming, Laura clings tightly to her belief in hard work, but she realizes that she depends both on her own skills and on the efforts of others.

Part of the lasting beauty of *The Song of the Lark* and the Little House series are Thea's and Laura's responses to their communities. Both characters excel as students and teachers, but Cather aligns Thea with urbanity while Wilder has Laura represent rural America. Whereas Cather commemorates the determination of women committed to farming in *O Pioneers*, she asserts that if they wish to grow, girls like Thea must abandon their hometowns for more sophisticated cities. If memories of Moonstone stifle and torture twenty-year-old Thea, she confesses ten years later that "the old things [there] are in everything I do" (388). After a decade away, Thea assesses the costs of her career, complaining to Dr. Archie that "your work becomes your personal life. You are not much good until it does" (385). Years after leaving Moonstone, Thea can neither escape the career she pursued and obtained nor prevent comforting dreams of her hometown from influencing her art. Laura, conversely, worries about debt and farming failures but stays connected with others who live similar lives. Although she questions Almanzo's belief that "everything evens up in the end" (763), she seeks ways to improve their lives and feels the burden of others more than pressure to succeed at one particular thing. Laura's story, then, represents that of many women in rural America who made the best of difficult circumstances by working hard and relying on community relationships to sustain them and their families in challenging situations.

Like Laura and Almanzo, Wilder and her husband eventually found their place in the country, while Garland and Cather experienced artistic awakenings in eastern cities. Garland moved to Hollywood, and Cather remained in New York City, while the Wilders lived outside of Mansfield, Missouri, until their deaths. Because the Little House series details a life lived on a farm, exploring successes and failures, Wilder's books offer an extended overview of a young girl's growth and maturation as well as a full portrait of the sacrifices many talented women made to live an agrarian lifestyle. If Garland and Cather warn readers of the opportunities impossible in rural areas, Wilder asserts that rural women can adapt their strengths to help shape who they become and how they function within close-knit communities. She reminds readers that women have always played pivotal roles in making America, which needs both agriculture and art, and that women's great efforts as teachers and community stewards merit greater admiration.

NOTES

1. One notable exception is a collection of five poems that Wilder composed for children about fairies, which were later published in *Laura Ingalls Wilder's Fairy Poems* (1998).

2. Scholars continue to debate each writer's contributions to the Little House series. John E. Miller writes, "For some time now, any realistic assessment of the Little House series has had to start from the proposition that the words on the pages of the books got there as a result of a continuing collaborative process that occurred between Wilder and her daughter, Rose Wilder Lane. Any serious study of Wilder's writing in the future will likewise have to be undertaken in the same spirit" (*Laura* 23–24).

3. *The First Four Years* was not rewritten and edited as extensively as the prior novels. The novel has a more adult tone, and one of its dominant themes is the great challenge of farming.

4. Garland's foresight and Wilder's hindsight have differing effects with regard to narrative. Rose ultimately chooses to marry and stay in Chicago, saying, "I realize it all, and I choose it" (403). Here, Garland asserts Rose's independence in her choices both to marry and to pursue a career as an artist in a burgeoning metropolis. In this sense, the progressive vision of Rose as an ideal New Woman is not only important in terms of its publication date but also functions as a hypothetical, forward-looking ideal. In contrast, Laura's strife comes directly from Wilder's reflections about her entire life.

WORKS CITED

Anderson, William. "Laura Ingalls Wilder and Rose Wilder Lane: The Continuing Collaboration." *South Dakota History* 16 (1986): 89–143.

Cather, Willa. *The Song of the Lark*. Edited by Janet Sharistanian. Oxford University Press, 1999.

Fellman, Anita Clair. "Laura Ingalls Wilder and Rose Wilder Lane: The Politics of a Mother-Daughter Relationship." *Signs: Journal of Woman in Culture and Society* 15 (1990): 535–61.

Fellman, Anita Clair. *Little House, Long Shadow: Laura Ingalls Wilder's Impact on American Culture*. University of Missouri Press, 2008.
Garland, Hamlin. *Rose of Dutcher's Coolly*. 2nd ed. University of Nebraska Press, 2005.
Garland, Hamlin. *A Son of the Middle Border*. Penguin, 1995.
Hill, Pamela Smith. *Laura Ingalls Wilder: A Writer's Life*. South Dakota Historical Society Press, 2007.
Jurca, Catherine. "Dreiser, Class, and the Home." In *The Cambridge Companion to Theodore Dreiser*, edited by Leonard Cassuto and Claire Virginia Eby, 100–111. Cambridge University Press, 2004.
Love, Glen. *New Americans: The Westerner and the Modern Experience in the American Novel*. Bucknell University Press, 1982.
Matthews, Jean V. *The Rise of the New Woman: The Woman's Movement in America, 1875–1930*. Dee, 2003.
Miller, John E. *Becoming Laura Ingalls Wilder: The Woman behind the Legend*. University of Missouri Press, 1998.
Miller, John E. *Laura Ingalls Wilder and Rose Wilder Lane*. University of Missouri Press, 2008.
Pizer, Donald. *The Significant Hamlin Garland*. Anthem, 2014.
Newlin, Keith. Introduction to Garland, *Rose*, vii–xxxi.
Schedler, Christopher. "Writing Culture: Willa Cather's Southwest." In *Willa Cather and the American Southwest*, edited by John N. Swift and Joseph R. Urgo, 109–23. University of Nebraska Press, 2002.
Spaeth, Janet. *Laura Ingalls Wilder*. Twayne, 1987.
Romines, Ann. *Constructing the Little House: Gender, Culture, and Laura Ingalls Wilder*. University of Massachusetts Press, 1997.
Romines, Ann. "Preempting the Patriarch: The Problem with Pa's Stories in *Little House in the Big Woods*." *Children's Literature Association Quarterly* 20, no. 1 (1995): 15–18.
Wilder, Laura Ingalls. "All in the Day's Work." *Missouri Ruralist*, 5 February 1916. In Wilder, *Laura Ingalls Wilder, Farm Journalist*, 48–51.
Wilder, Laura Ingalls. *By the Shores of Silver Lake*. In Wilder, *Little House Books* 2:1–168.
Wilder, Laura Ingalls. "'Dear Children': A Letter from Laura Ingalls Wilder." In Wilder, *Little House Books*, 2:801–2.
Wilder, Laura Ingalls. "Favors a Small Farm Home." *Missouri Ruralist*, 18 February 1911. In Wilder, *Laura Ingalls Wilder, Farm Journalist*, 13–16.
Wilder, Laura Ingalls. *The First Four Years*. In Wilder, *Little House Books*, 2:731–96.
Wilder, Laura Ingalls. *Laura Ingalls Wilder, Farm Journalist: Writings from the Ozarks*. Edited by Stephen W. Hines. University of Missouri Press, 2007.
Wilder, Laura Ingalls. *Laura Ingalls Wilder's Fairy Poems*. Doubleday, 1998.
Wilder, Laura Ingalls. *The Little House Books*. Edited by Caroline Fraser. 2 vols. Library of America, 2012.
Wilder, Laura Ingalls. *Little Town on the Prairie*. In Wilder, *Little House Books* 2: 371–544.
Wilder, Laura Ingalls. *Pioneer Girl: The Annotated Autobiography*. Edited by Pamela Smith Hill. South Dakota Historical Society Press, 2014.
Wilder, Laura Ingalls. *The Selected Letters of Laura Ingalls Wilder*. Edited by William Anderson. Harper, 2016.
Wilder, Laura Ingalls. "Shorter Hours for Farm Women." *Missouri Ruralist*, 28 June 1913. In Wilder, *Laura Ingalls Wilder, Farm Journalist*, 22–26.

Wilder, Laura Ingalls. *These Happy Golden Years*. In Wilder, *Little House Books* 2: 549–730.
Wilder, Laura Ingalls. "To Buy or Not to Buy." *Missouri Ruralist*, 20 September 1917. In Wilder, *Laura Ingalls Wilder, Farm Journalist*, 123–24.
Woodside, Christine. *Libertarians on the Prairie: Laura Ingalls Wilder, Rose Wilder Lane, and the Making of the Little House Books*. Arcade, 2016.

THE UNDERGRADUATE AMERICAN STUDIES CLASSROOM

Teaching American Myths and Memories with Laura Ingalls Wilder

Christiane E. Farnan

I regularly teach an American Studies course, The American Dream, that includes undergraduate liberal arts, science, and business students, I assign Laura Ingalls Wilder's first three Little House novels along with Mary Rowlandson's *A True History of the Captivity and Restoration of Mrs. Mary Rowlandson* (1682), Thomas Jefferson's *Notes on Virginia* (1781–83), J. Hector St. John de Crèvecoeur's *Letters from an American Farmer* (1782), Horace Greeley's *What I Know of Farming* (1871), Frederick Jackson Turner's "The Significance of the Frontier in American History" (1893), James Agee and Walker Evans's *Let Us Now Praise Famous Men* (1941), and Henry Nash Smith's *Virgin Land: The American West as Symbol and Myth* (1950), all of which discuss farming. As the course examines the creation and perpetuation of models, memories, and myths of the American Dream through the cultural modification of America's changing landscape, the looming mythic/historic figure of the American farmer is central to our analysis.

Distinguished by Jefferson as the expanding nation's "most valuable citizens ... wedded to [America's] liberty and interests" (217), federally supported white settlers pushed the western frontier across the continent, cutting, clearing, plowing, and planting along the way. Planters and tillers, fused to the interests of the new republic and celebrated by Jefferson as the "most vigorous, the most independent," and "the most virtuous" (217) citizens, were widely seen as natural and spontaneous designers of the agrarian-based American Dream. Nearly two hundred years later, Smith identified the Jefferson-infused agrarian narrative as among the most influential American myths of the nineteenth century: "the promise of American life," otherwise known as the American Dream, was found through "blissful labor in the earth, all centering about the heroic figure of the idealized frontier farmer armed with that supreme agrarian weapon, the sacred plow" (123). Wilder scholars, including Anita Clair Fellman, Katharine Slater, and Susan Larkin, have established the Little House books as "superb examples of the mythology of the American frontier" (Fellman 114) even while addressing their problematic position as "surrogate historical texts ... designed to appeal to urban readers' nostalgia for an imagined bucolic past" (Slater 56). However, I contend that Wilder's representation of the American farmer in her earliest novels, *Little House in the Big Woods* (1932), *Farmer Boy* (1933), and *Little House on the Prairie* (1935), demonstrates a more complicated, multifaceted stance in relation to the American Dream. Wilder's adoption of and challenge to the Jeffersonian-infused mythology underscores the Little House books' value in the undergraduate American Studies classroom.

Wilder's first three novels present conflicting examples of nineteenth-century farmers that both solidify and reject Smith's mid-twentieth-century analysis of the historical/mythological perception of farmers. Charles "Pa" Ingalls is formed from Wilder's childhood memories of her antigovernment, romantic, self-determinist father during the family's pioneer farm days in Pepin, Wisconsin, and on the Osage Indian Reserve in Kansas. James "Father" Wilder is constructed through Almanzo Wilder's memories of growing up in northern New York state that center on his wealthy, agriculturally empowered father, who was also a civic leader. In these three novels, the patriarchs embrace the myth of America as Eden and the notion that self-reliance and hard work guarantee prosperity; however, as critic Ann Romines demonstrates, Wilder's father was not a successful farmer (44–45), and her father-in-law lost his magnificent farm when Almanzo was a teenager. Nevertheless, Wilder's first two novels reinforce the agrarian myth. In contrast, *Little House on the Prairie* disrupts the American farmer's legendary role as the hero of the nation. Wilder's first three Little House novels provide a greater understanding of the American farmer's complex position as the locus of the American Dream shifted from the seventeenth-century wilderness to the eighteenth- and nineteenth-century frontier and farm.

Wilder's complex representations of American farmers prompted me to include the Little House books in my course despite my worry that my students would not read children's books. The first time I taught the course, I had students read Rowlandson, Crèvecoeur, and selections from Jefferson's *Notes on Virginia* and Smith's *Virgin Land* before beginning Wilder. While reading *Little House in the Big Woods*, my students also review Crèvecoeur's letters.

Up to this point, students had shared varying views regarding the representations of farmers in the readings as well as the contemporary farming profession. I teach at a northeastern college that draws regional students, a few of whom were familiar with dairy farming and most of whom had participated in agritourism, the new blend of entertainment and agriculture that includes visitor/farmer interactions such as apple and pumpkin picking. Through these experiences, students identified as customers and saw farmers as business owners rather than recognizing their relationship to the land. My students' historical view of farmers followed the Jeffersonian ideal: their perceptions emphasized nostalgic, masculine images of overall-clad men cheerfully tilling fertile soil. Students' reading of Smith's *Virgin Land* had not affected their romantic view of farmers. I believe this was because they had no concrete image of a historical farmer that contradicted this romanticized viewpoint. Indeed, the students struggled to translate the "amber waves of grain" ideal into the practical terms of agricultural labor. As I asked students about their previous experiences with Wilder's series and popular culture, I wondered if my questions would cause them to remember prior knowledge of historical farming. It did not.

Overall, the sixteen female students knew more about Little House popular culture, primarily from the syndicated television series; while the majority of these women were aware of the series, they recalled nothing of pioneer farming. Instead, they remembered the childhood antagonism rambunctious Laura feels toward her demure sister, Mary. The ten male students had little knowledge of Little House popular culture, although four remembered reading *Farmer Boy* in school. When I asked what they remembered about farming from the book, each recalled the incredible amount of food Almanzo consumes rather than the way the food was produced. After we established everyone's prior knowledge of the novels, we began reading *Little House in the Big Woods*, which confirmed the students' nostalgic expectations for American pioneer farmers.

The students' responses to *Little House in the Big Woods* certainly reflected their beliefs in the agrarian myth. The students were enchanted by Wilder's "creation born of memory, wish fulfillment, artistry and ideology" (Fellman 114). Students commonly expressed such sentiments as, "I actually thought about making cheese! You could do it, all the steps are there in the book!"; "This whole book reads like a Native American origin story, except it leaves out the creation part. The family just *is* in the woods, like they have always been there and will always be there"; "It reminds me of the Old Testament, of the Garden of Eden." Overall, the students easily identified Wilder's representations of an earthly paradise in the Wisconsin woods. Pa is a fiddle-playing, storytelling, and benevolent agrarian patriarch who sends his daughters "laughing to bed" (*Woods* 100) and soothes Laura after disciplining her. Ma, "with her bare arms plump and white, her cheeks so red and her dark hair smooth and shining" (220), is a calm, cheerful, skilled, and self-assured homemaker. Under Pa's direction, the Ingallses raise corn, wheat, pumpkins, carrots, squash, beans, turnips, potatoes, and cabbage as well as cows and pigs. Because of Pa's resourcefulness and determination, the Ingallses' home is "snug and cozy" (20) and "fairly bursting with good food stored away for the long winter" (18). The children bake, churn, and clean while "helping all they could" (188) in food preservation. They also have fun. Wilder writes that "the attic was a lovely place to play" (20), as were the "playhouses under the two big oak trees in front of the house" (157). The family is part of a supportive network of extended family and friends who gather for community events. Aside from one male student's condemnation of Pa's whipping of Laura, the students speak wistfully of "when people lived like this," confirming Slater's declaration that the Little House books reveal an "intense homesickness . . . for a lost way of independent life" (73). *Little House in the Big Woods* discloses the students' nostalgic willingness to accept intertwined American myth and memory as historical fact, but Wilder's text also represents their desire for this imagined past.

As David Russell points out in "The Pastoral Influence on American Children's Literature," Little House readers are "drawn by the pristine quality of rural images, the seductive feeling of comfort and security . . . and they may relish a pastoral world" (123). My young adult students are no exception: they both admire and desire the Ingallses' simple, earnest life, which exists because Pa adheres to the process in which Crèvecoeur's Farmer James exults: "This formerly rude soil has been converted . . . into a pleasant farm, and in return it has established all our rights; on it is founded our rank, our freedom, our power as citizens, our importance as inhabitants of such a district. These images . . . may be called the true and the only philosophy of an American farmer" (20–21). My students, however, recognized the one seemingly disruptive image in Wilder's American pastoral: the "rackety-banging and clanging" threshing machine with "long iron teeth" (*Woods* 224) that Pa hires to thresh his wheat crop in one day. "It's so strange," a student commented, "Pa's cutting oats with a hand blade, and Laura's stewing pumpkin with a wooden paddle, and Ma's hulling corn with her bare hands, and then this huge machine arrives." In response, I suggested that Wilder's carefully scripted contribution to the agrarian myth might include a break from the pastoral but that the "Wonderful Machine" chapter reads as a possible exhortation of the federal government's mid-nineteenth-century promotion of progressive farming methods.

Pa's embrace of new agricultural technology seems less disruptive when examined within the progress-driven renewal of the agrarian myth that prevailed from the late 1840s to the early 1860s. Wilder's family lived in Pepin, Wisconsin, when, as agricultural historian Alexandra Kindell describes, "the more scientifically minded reformers ... feared that the farmer had become a backward thinking ignorant drudge" (348) because of the westward flow away from eastern institutions of education and civility. Favoring progress, Pa rejects farmers who followed the "old-fashioned ways" (*Woods* 228), which were characterized as "backward, superstitious, and unproductive" (Kindell 352). Fearing that an extension of the perceived decadelong drop in agrarian industriousness would negatively affect national economic growth in already tumultuous times, reformers identified George Washington, a scientific farmer of his own era, as the "new icon of agrarianism" and detailed his experimental farming techniques to promote "new implements, plant species, and types of fertilizer" (352). Through this revision of the agrarian myth, the public persona of the American farmer emerged as a more dignified, intelligent figure, and Wilder clearly characterizes Pa as a modern farmer.

Wilder's second example of a nineteenth-century farmer, Father Wilder, follows the "old-fashioned ways" Pa dismisses. Complete with grist and potato starch mills, Malone, New York, boasts a fine coeducational academy, is frequented by urbanites, and receives news from New York City. The Wilder family's exposure to agricultural progressive reform efforts is made clear in the "Threshing" chapter, when Almanzo asks why Father does not use a threshing machine to process his enormous wheat harvest. Cataloging threshers as tools of "a lazy man" who would "rather get ... work done fast than do it himself," Father explains that the thresher "chews up the straw til it's not fit to feed stock" and "scatters grain around and wastes it" (*Farmer* 308). My students quickly pointed out that Father's argument is the opposite of Pa's; Pa exults in the greater amount of "clean" (*Woods* 227) grain the thresher provides as well as the additional "weeks" (227) of time that can be used for other necessary labors.

Pa's and Father's differing views of agricultural technology are not a mere difference between an 1866 New York farmer and an 1872 Wisconsin frontier farmer's probable knowledge of and access to advanced machinery. As Kindell's research demonstrates, agricultural progressivism was widespread beginning in the 1840s. Wilder's portraits of two philosophically opposed mythic American farmers may have been part of her attempt to "preserve ... family stories" (Hill 147); more importantly, however, Wilder's presentation of these differing farmers in books published only one year apart respectively, demonstrates how Wilder wrestles with perpetuating America's mythic origins while describing the technological farming revolution she experienced. Even though Wilder's fictional accounts of Pa's and Father's lives contribute to the overall agrarian myth, their contrasts demonstrate disruptions in the historic position farmers occupy within that narrative.

Pa's view of technological innovations as necessary to achieve the promise of American life and Father's commitment to traditional farming techniques are represented in Greeley's *What I Know of Farming*. I assign my students various chapters, including "Plowing: Good and Bad," "Soils and Fertilizers," "The Farmer's Calling," and "Science in Agriculture." As the students immediately discerned, Greeley argues not only that farmers should pursue scientific farming methods such as soil analysis, crop rotation, and natural and chemical fertilization but also that the farming community should make cooperative investments in innovative machinery, including "a Stump or Rock-Puller, A Clod-Crusher, Thrashing Machine ... and so everyone shall be nearly as well accommodated as though he owned them all" (240). However, the students also noted that Father both refutes the agricultural science advocated by Greeley and embodies the legendary qualities Greeley attributes as inherent to farmers: a superb work ethic, a strong moral sense, and a manliness of character (149–52). As morality is absorbed as part of Greeley's interpretation of "work ethic" and "manliness of character," I asked students to cite specific examples of how Father exemplifies Greeley's legendary farmer.

My students argued that Father's wealth signifies his work ethic and demonstrates that he has surpassed the "modest independence" that Greeley declared "nearly certain" (149) for any man who seeks agricultural success. Father argues that agricultural success is a choice—he has chosen to work hard and is consequently rewarded. As Father tells Almanzo, "If you're a farmer, you raise what you eat, you raise what you wear, and you keep warm with wood out of your own timber. You work hard, but you work as hard as you please" (*Farmer* 371). The students offered evidence of Father's prosperity: livestock, immense harvests, tools, and land. They also declared that Father's never-ending labors have made him one of the most powerful men in town. One student cited a particular passage: "Father was an important man. He had a good farm. He drove the best horses in that country. His word was as good as his bond.... When Father drove into Malone, all the townspeople spoke to him respectfully" (22). Another student noted that Father has "one of the best front seats" during the town's Fourth of July Celebration and that "all the important men stopped to shake hands with Father" (178). By the end of our discussion of *Farmer Boy*, the students recognized that as Father trains Almanzo in the mantra that hard work automatically results in agrarian success, Father also models the other benefits of labor: value and power in the community.

I emphasized that Wilder wrote *Farmer Boy*'s tale of agricultural empowerment in 1932, when 30 percent of American farmers could not pay their taxes and mortgages, resulting in the loss of drought-ridden land at unprecedented rates. She published the novel in 1933, when two hundred thousand farmers experienced foreclosure (Alston 886–88). *Farmer Boy*, however, asserts that agrarian success, along with community and civic power, comes to those who choose to work hard.

Following our discussion of Wilder, I assigned my students portions of Agee and Evans's *Now Let Us Praise Famous Men*, published three years after *Farmer Boy*. After sharing the extensive field research on depression-era southern cotton tenant farmers, I read to them the description of children laboring in the cotton fields:

> Meanwhile ... you are working in ... heat that makes the jointed and muscled and fine-structured body glow.... [T]he head ... is ... roaring, like a private blowtorch.... [T]he bag, which can hold a hundred pounds, is filling as it is dragged ... and the sack still heavier and heavier, so that it pulls you back as a beast might rather than a mere dead weight: but it is not only this: cotton plants are low, so that in this heat and burden of the immanent sun and of the heavying sack you are dragging, you are continuously somewhat stooped over even if you are a child. (339)

Here, Agee and Evans assert that the tenant children's labor is monotonous, miserable, and physically detrimental. Wilder, however, suggests that Almanzo's labors are ever-changing, educational, and joyful. Above all, Almanzo's work is overseen by a wealthy, engaged parent who "steep[s] him in the mythic tradition of the farmer" (Erisman 124). Almanzo milks Wilder cows, weeds Wilder gardens, hoes Wilder crops, sows Wilder vegetables, harvests Wilder foodstuffs, stores Wilder ice, hauls Wilder wood, and cleans the Wilder house. But the tenant farmer's children prepare someone else's cotton fields, set someone else's cotton plants, and finally, tortuously, pick someone else's cotton. Every *Farmer Boy* chapter shows Almanzo learning a new, interesting skill, and when work is physically difficult, it is never tortuous. Even the periods of intense farm labor, such as the spring plowing, when Almanzo is "a little soldier in this great battle" (*Farmer* 124), are balanced by a near-pastoral farm scene. Specifically, Wilder follows the rigors of plowing by depicting the pleasure of sowing: "Planting potatoes was fun. A good smell came from the fresh earth and from the clover fields. Alice was pretty and gay.... Father was jolly, and they all talked while they worked" (126). Almanzo enjoys farm life so much that he is delighted when the local school's spring term ends because that means "he could work all summer" (166). Holding fast to the established narrative Father inculcates in his son and influenced by her staunch anti–New Deal politics (McCabe 85), Wilder ends the novel by rewarding Almanzo's unwavering perseverance and attention to Father's lessons with both money and a powerful symbol.[1] Almanzo has earned an invitation to take his rightful place in the agrarian myth, and this invitation takes the form of the beautiful colt, Starlight, one of the many horses Father breeds, trains, and sells for profit.

The students also noted that Father's patriotism underlies what Greeley refers to as the American farmer's "manliness of character. Nobody expects him to cringe, or smirk, or curry favor" (152), and this manliness is deeply tied to Father's reverence for the revolutionary-era farmers who "took all that country and made it America" (*Farmer* 188). During the Malone Fourth of July celebration, Father is not impressed by the celebratory cannon fire, commenting that even though "it was muskets that won the revolution . . . don't forget it was axes and plows that made this country" (175). The students notice that Father uses *we* to refer to the westward-moving pioneer farmers, incorporating himself and his family as he lectures Almanzo that "we were farmers, son; we wanted the land. It was farmers that went over the mountains, and cleared the land, and settled it, and farmed it. . . . [I]t's the biggest country in the world and it was farmers who took all that country and made it America, son" (188–89). The students pointed out that Father praises farmers for the physical creation of America and connected his words to the ideas of both Smith and Turner. Specifically, the students linked Father to a passage from Smith's *Virgin Land*: "They plowed the virgin land and put in crops, and the great Interior Valley was transformed into a garden: for the imagination, the Garden of the World" (123). They then tied Smith's imagery to Turner's analysis of how "this expansion westward with its new opportunities, its continuous touch with the simplicity of primitive society, furnish[ed] the forces dominating American character" (2). The students thus perceived Father's American manliness of character as inherited and saw him as instilling this manliness in Almanzo. The students also pointed out that Father's use of *we* credits himself with continuing to maintain the "Garden of the World" and categorizes farming as a nationalistic and exclusionary activity. As one student said, "Father sees America as a farm and if you don't farm, you aren't a real American"; another added, "To Father, *farmer* and *American* mean the same thing."

I then directed their attention back to Crèvecoeur, whose third letter, "What Is an American?," defines Americans according to Father's classification and provides examples of those who live outside the agrarian/American way of life. Focusing on men who live in the wilderness rather than on cleared farms, Crèvecoeur warns of the consequences of trading the plow for a rifle. Some frontiersmen, "by living in or near the woods... soon become professed hunters; once hunters, farewell to the plough" as the pursuit of game leads men to "neglect their tillage" and affects "their wives and children" who "live in sloth and inactivity"; the children, lacking education, "grow up a mongrel breed, half civilized, half savage" (47–48). The students immediately connect Crèvecoeur's fringe hunters to French Joe and Lazy John, secondary characters in *Farmer Boy* "who lived in little log houses in the woods. They had no farms. They hunted and trapped and fished, they sang and joked and danced" (67). The men, who do not send their children to school, are rendered non-American not only by the appellations *French* and *Lazy*, but also, and more importantly, by the fact that they have no farms. One student declared this description of the Frenchmen to be opposed to Greeley's overall description of farmers as "temperate, industrious, intelligent, frugal, and energetic" (141). She stated that the text ties the Wilders' wealth to their willingness to work harder than anyone else, an idea that contrasts with the "lazy" French and suggests that a superior work ethic is a suitably rewarded American trait.

While I agreed that Wilder connects wealth and patriotism to Father's (and Almanzo's) work ethic, Father's wealth also authorizes his staunch Jeffersonian view of the farmer's role in American history and privileges his adherence to "old-fashioned" (*Farmer* 228) farming techniques. Father's accumulated herds, fields, orchards, and timber lot privilege his scorn for the use of technology to capture the success he already enjoys. Father tells Almanzo that a thresher saves only "time, son. And what good is time, with nothing to do? You want to sit and twiddle your thumbs, all these stormy days?" (*Farmer* 308). Father implicitly asserts that his affluence provides him with the leisure to employ outdated farming techniques and the authority to present those techniques as more frugal and virtuous and therefore more American than his profligate neighbors. Pa's farming methods in *Little House in the Big Woods* tread a fine line between French John and Lazy Joe's woodsman lifestyles and Father Wilder's established farmer routine. Like the Frenchmen, Pa lives in the woods, and while he clears, plows, plants, and harvests, he does not spend his winters threshing by hand. Rather, Pa hunts and traps, supplementing both his dinner table and his ability to trade for cloth, shoes, lead, and powder.

While Wilder presents two contradictory versions of the mythic American farmer in the series' first two novels, in *Little House on the Prairie*, she fiercely challenges the overall Jeffersonian myth she initially supported. As Pamela Smith Hill writes in *Laura Ingalls Wilder: A Writer's Life*, "*Farmer Boy*, like *Little House in the Big Woods*, focuses on a year in the everyday life of a nineteenth-century American farm family. Like the Ingalls clan in *Little House in the Big Woods*, the Wilders are content with their circumstances; they have no need to dream of a better future" (146). However, in *Little House on the Prairie*, Pa displays a "restless nervous energy" and "dominant individualism" that Turner described in "The Significance of the Frontier in American History" (59). As my students noted, the novel begins with Pa's dissatisfaction with Wisconsin's increasing population. There are "too many people in the Big Woods," he says; "in the West, the land" is ideal for farming (*Prairie* 2). Ma is reluctant to leave, particularly because the "weather was so cold and the snug house was so comfortable," but Pa brushes this aside because he does "not like to stay" (2–3) in settled country. Because he claims a place in the conquest of the western frontier so admired by Father Wilder, Pa might be expected to exemplify those characteristics that Turner credited with shaping the nation: optimism, independence, adaptability, ingenuity, and self-reliance. However, Wilder's third book emphasizes Pa's repeated errors in judgment, lack of resourcefulness, and irresponsible recklessness. Here, Wilder offers more than a variation of the myth; she disrupts it altogether. As one student stated, "There's something wrong with the father of this family": "he doesn't care that his family is scared all the time. He's crazy. They should have stayed in Wisconsin." In short, the Pa of *Little House on the Prairie* is not the American Adam of *Little House in the Big Woods*.

In fact, my students thought *Little House on the Prairie* read like a terrifying sequel to Mary Rowlandson's captivity narrative rather than a book in a nostalgic children's series about settling the frontier. Referring to it as *Little Haunted House on the Prairie*, they highlighted Pa's numerous acts resulting in chaos, injury, and near death. First, Pa miscalculates the temperature and drives across ice-covered Lake Pepin hours before the ice begins cracking, causing five-year-old Laura to imagine that "the ice had cracked under the wagon wheels and they had all gone down into the cold water in the middle of that vast lake" (9). Then Pa almost drowns the family again by deciding to drive their wagon across a "pretty high" creek while Laura trembles "cold and sick" and "Mary crie[s]" (23). Next, Pa illegally settles the family on the Osage Indian Diminished Reserve in Kansas, relying on false information he received from "a man in Washington" (47) and consequently exposing them to continual threat from the vulnerable and land-robbed Osages.[2] Ma is almost crushed by a log helping Pa build the cabin. A prairie fire, with "great flames" (280), endangers the log cabin. Pa and Mr. Scott, a neighbor, are overcome with ground gas while digging a well, nearly dying. Wolves encircle the house. The family contracts malaria, and since Pa refuses to live near other people, it is a miracle when they are found "more dead than alive" (192). Ma, Laura, Mary, and Baby Carrie are removed from their supportive Wisconsin network, utterly without power to stop or challenge Pa's decisions. Students repeatedly commented on Ma and the girls' enforced isolation, connecting their demonstrations of fearful helplessness to those expressed by Mary Rowlandson. Rowlandson, captured by the Narragansett in the Lancaster Raid during the terrible and bloody King Philip's War and compelled to travel 150 miles during the New England winter, was likewise stripped of her family and friends. In particular, students recalled Rowlandson's emphasis on her aloneness, citing her references to the "vast and desolate wilderness" (11) and the "howling wilderness" (24) as well as her statement that she "saw nothing but wilderness, and woods, and a company of barbarous heathens" (39). However, the students also noted that while Rowlandson excoriated the Narragansett, Nipmuc, and Wampanoag as evil-intentioned "black creatures in the night" (9), Wilder gradually places the blame for his family's increasing fear and trauma on Pa's "recklessness" and "radical frontierism" (Heldrich 102) rather than the displacement-threatened Osage.

As the novel unfolds, the Ingalls women's terror of the unknown on the Kansas prairie at first mirrors Rowlandson's terror of the unknown New England forest. Wilder uses Laura to transmit this terror to the reader. Laura discovers the Osage trail, next to which Pa has unwisely built their home, and alerts the reader that something on the prairie is wrong: "Laura went along" the path "a little way. She went slowly, and more slowly, and then she stood still and felt queer.... When she looked over her shoulder, there wasn't anything there. But she hurried" (*Prairie* 55). Laura also cannot identify who or what might be "in the place where the dark mixed with the edge of the firelight. Shadows moved there as if they were alive" (86). Laura does not comprehend the word *massacre* any more than she understands Pa' simplification of it into "bad trouble" (211, 146). The reader, though, knows why "Laura was too scared to make a sound" (95). My students, fresh from reading Rowlandson's report of the captive pregnant colonist, whose Native American captors "stripped ... naked" and murdered her after "they had sung and danced about her (in their hellish manner) as long as they pleased" (20), easily imagine what Laura and Mary cannot as they shiver and shake through chapter 11, "Indians in the House." The girls are playing outside when "two naked, wild men" (*Prairie* 134) walk up the trail and enter the house while Pa is away hunting. Laura does "not know what those Indians were doing to Ma and Baby Carrie" (135) but assumes that they must be "doing" something. Just as my students understood that seventeenth-century European settlers' increasing encroachment on Native American lands in New England precipitated King Philip's War and Rowlandson's captivity, they also understood that Pa's flagrant trespassing on the Osage Indian Reserve has endangered his family. The terror of the girls' experience, my students explained, became anger on Laura, Mary, Ma, and Baby Carrie's behalf.

In "Little Squatter on the Osage Diminished Reserve: Reading Laura Ingalls Wilder's Kansas Indians," Frances W. Kaye argues that Wilder, "writing as honestly as she knew how," created "a book that lulls us into believing that the dispossession of the Osage people from Kansas was sad but necessary and even 'natural,' like all losses of the innocence of childhood and other primitive ways of being" (124). I attempted to provide my students with a different reading. As my students observed, *Little House on the Prairie* creates a mood of terror "reminiscent of tales of Indian attack and entrapment" (Woodard 115), but it firmly holds Pa, the mythic hero farmer, responsible for said terror. Wilder re-creates the captivity narrative, which "directly addressed the fears of colonists who felt threatened by the power of the vast American wilderness and its indigenous population" (Woodard 115) as the narrative of a white woman and her children vulnerably dependent on an irresponsible, imprudent white man.[3] "No one is any better off, no one's life has improved, at the end of this book," said one student. He continued, "We see through Laura that this has all been a waste, all this work and fear hasn't earned them anything." He read from the scene in which the supplanted Osage tribes literally ride West: "Laura could not eat anything, either. She sat a long time on the doorstep, looking into the empty west where the Indians had gone. She seemed still to see waving feathers and black eyes and to hear the sound of ponies' feet" (*Prairie* 311). He concluded, "This isn't the American Dream, and it sure isn't a celebration of the farmer's role in the American Dream, because no one gets to better themselves off this land. The Indians have to leave and then the Ingallses have to leave. Everyone's life is worse. They should have stayed in Wisconsin." The students did not experience the lull Kaye describes and saw through Laura's horror and sorrow more than a nostalgic glimpse of childhood's natural end via displaced Native Americans. Wilder's marked shift in her presentation of the agrarian myth sees Laura wrenched from the pastoral tranquility of *Little House in the Big Woods*, terrified on the Kansas prairie, and witnessing Pa's final unmasking as a false American hero in the novel's conclusion.

Wilder ends *Little House on the Prairie* with as striking an image as she does *Farmer Boy*. The conclusion of *Farmer Boy* is full of pleasurable tension until the moment Father Wilder rewards Almanzo's choice of the farming profession with the beloved colt he so badly desires. The tension turns to joy as Almanzo hears this news, and "suddenly, the whole world was a great, shining, expanding glow of warm light" (371). *Farmer Boy*'s "warm light" is replaced with the "scents of earth and of growing things" in *Little House on the Prairie*'s conclusion: "After the Indians had gone, a great peace settled on the prairie. And one morning, the whole land was green" (312). The novel's sad, frightening tone suddenly changes to cheer and optimism. The students immediately realized that Wilder is returning to the "Garden of the World" symbolism, presenting the possibility for a blissful Kansas Eden after all. In the end, Ma, Mary, and Laura spend their days planting an enormous vegetable garden, while Pa plows acres of rich earth to sow wheat, corn, and oats. The family works with a unity they have not known since leaving Wisconsin: "Pa hurried with his plowing, and Mary and Laura helped Ma plant the early garden seeds. With the hoe Ma dug small holes in the matted grass roots that the plow had turned up, and Laura and Mary carefully dropped the seeds. Then Ma covered them snugly with earth. They planted onions and carrots and peas and beans and turnips. And they were all so happy because spring had come.... [S]oon they would have vegetables to eat" (313–14). Wilder seemingly returns to the agrarian myth of her first two books. Pa has his hard-earned plow, the fertile garden is growing, and peace returns now that the Native Americans have been displaced by the white settlers, who are busy plowing, planting, and eventually harvesting and consuming. Fear has vanished, along with the threat of violence, and the children and parents are "all so happy."

Unlike the "warm light" in *Farmer Boy*, however, this ill-won paradise proves an illusion. Pa again reacts impetuously to an unconfirmed news report, this one claiming that "the government is sending soldiers to take all us settlers out of Indian Territory" (317). Without waiting to learn if the federal government really will hold him accountable for breaking a treaty with the Osage, Pa gives away his livestock, dumps his plow in the prairie grass, and tells Ma "We're going now!" (*Prairie* 316). After a brief respite, Laura is again struck with fear, but this time it is her father who frightens her: "His face was very red and his eyes were like blue fire. Laura was frightened; she had never seen Pa look like that" (317). Pa's face signifies to the reader who the real source of fear has always been: not the wolves or the fire or the unseen howling Native Americans but reckless, heedless Pa. Self-assured Ma, who slapped a bear in Wisconsin, "didn't say anything" (319). At Pa's mercy on the prairie, with three small, frightened children relying on her, she simply packs the wagon.

Presenting Pa as angry and irrational, Wilder challenges the legendary role of the American farmer as the nation's hero and proves herself so valuable to the undergraduate classroom. After perpetuating the mythic American farmer in her first two novels, Wilder challenges the American agrarian patriarch and provides a more complicated and critical lens through which to analyze displaced Native peoples and Jefferson's imagined virtuous tillers. *Little House on the Prairie* can be read and taught as Wilder's contradictory response not only to Jefferson, Crèvecoeur, and Turner but also, most importantly, to her own contributions to the mythic origins of westward expansion in *Little House in the Big Woods* and *Farmer Boy*. History's path is not always a straight furrow, Wilder suggests, and the historic idealized figure whistling behind the plow is just as likely to be misguided and dangerous as not.

NOTES

1. For Wilder's criticism of New Deal policies and her belief that the federal government's increasing presence in the lives of private citizens transformed the American character from one of self-reliance and independence into one of trained helplessness, see Woodside.

2. The 1868–70 legislative battle over the sale of Osage Diminished Indian Reserve acreage through the Sturges Treaty was highly publicized. According to Burns, "Without a doubt, the controversy over the Osage Ceded Lands . . . by 1868 had reached every corner of the nation" (293). Charles Ingalls may have expected Congress to ratify the treaty, but he trespassed on Osage lands during a time of widespread national debate over the issue.

3. Wilder's awareness of white women's complicity in the displacement of Native Americans is made clearer through her inclusion of fellow squatter Mrs. Scott in *Little House on the Prairie*. While Ma's fearful determination to "live like civilized folks" (129) illustrates Amy Kaplan's argument that pioneer domesticity "create[s] a home by rendering prior inhabitants alien and undomesticated" (591), Mrs. Scott's brutal words, "The only good Indian is a dead Indian" (*Prairie* 211), underscore Wilder's assessment.

WORKS CITED

Agee, James, and Walker Evans. *Let Us Now Praise Famous Men*. Mariner, 2007.

Alston, Lee J. "Farm Foreclosures in the United States during the Interwar Period." *Journal of Economic History* 43, no. 4 (1983): 885–903.

Burns, Louis F. *A History of the Osage People*. University of Alabama Press, 2004.

Crevecoeur, J. Hector St. John de. *Letters from an American Farmer*. Oxford University Press, 2009.

Erisman, Fred. "'Farmer Boy': The Forgotten 'Little House' Book." *Western American Literature* 28, no. 2 (1993): 123–30.

Fellman, Anita Clair. "'Don't Expect to Depend on Anybody Else': The Frontier as Portrayed in the Little House Books." *Children's Literature* 24 (1996): 101–16.

Fellman, Anita Clair. *Little House, Long Shadow: Laura Ingalls Wilder's Impact on American Culture*. University of Missouri Press, 2008.

Greeley, Horace. *What I Know of Farming: A Series of Brief and Plain Expositions of Practical Agriculture as an Art Based upon Science*. Palala, 2015.

Heldrich, Philip. "'Going to Indian Territory': Attitudes toward Native Americans in *Little House on the Prairie*." *Great Plains Quarterly* 20, no. 2 (2000): 99–109.

Hill, Pamela Smith. *Laura Ingalls Wilder: A Writer's Life*. South Dakota Historical Society Press, 2007.

Jefferson, Thomas. *Notes on Virginia*. In *The Life and Selected Writings of Thomas Jefferson: Including the Autobiography, the Declaration of Independence, and His Public and Private Letters*, edited by Adrienne Koch and William Peden, 177–267. Modern Library, 1998.

Kaplan, Amy. "Manifest Domesticity." *American Literature* 70, no. 3 (1998): 581–606.

Kaye, Frances W. "Little Squatter on the Osage Diminished Reserve: Reading Laura Ingalls Wilder's Kansas Indians." *Great Plains Quarterly* 20, no. 2 (2000): 123–40.

Kindell, Alexandra. "Washingtonian Agrarianism: Antebellum Reformers and the Agrarian Image of George Washington." *American Nineteenth Century History* 13, no. 3 (2012): 347–70.

Larkin, Susan. "Life Writing/Writing a Culture: Laura Ingalls Wilder." *Midamerica: The Yearbook of the Society for the Study of Midwestern Literature* 34 (2007): 118–25.

McCabe, Nancy. *From Little Houses to Little Women*. University of Missouri Press, 2014.

Miller, John E. "Freedom and Control in Laura Ingalls Wilder's De Smet." *Great Plains Quarterly* 9, no. 1 (1989): 27–35.

Romines, Ann. *Constructing the Little House: Gender, Culture, and Laura Ingalls Wilder*. University of Massachusetts Press, 1997.

Rowlandson, Mary White. "A True History of the Captivity and Restoration of Mrs. Mary Rowlandson." In *The Sovereignty and Goodness of God: Together with the Faithfulness of His Promises Displayed: Being a Narrative of the Captivity and Restoration of Mrs. Mary Rowlandson and Related Documents*. Bedford, 1997.

Russell, David L. "The Pastoral Influence on American Children's Literature." *The Lion and the Unicorn* 18, no. 2 (1994): 121–29.

Slater, Katharine. "'Now We're All Snug!': The Regionalism of *Little House on the Prairie*." *Genre* 47, no.1 (2014): 55–77.

Smith, Henry Nash. *Virgin Land: The American West as Symbol and Myth*. Harvard University Press, 2007.

Turner, Frederick Jackson. *Rereading Frederick Jackson Turner: "The Significance of the Frontier in American History" and Other Essays*. Commentary by John Mack Faragher. Yale University Press, 1994.

Wilder, Laura Ingalls. *Farmer Boy*. Scholastic, 1961.

Wilder, Laura Ingalls. *Little House in the Big Woods*. Scholastic, 1960.

Wilder, Laura Ingalls. *Little House on the Prairie*. Scholastic, 1963.

Woodard, Maureen L. "Female Captivity and the Deployment of Race in Three Early American Texts." *Papers on Language and Literature* 32, no. 2 (1996): 115–46.

Part 4

CULTURAL AND INTERCULTURAL WILDER

THE WILDER MYSTIQUE

Antimodernism, Tourism, and Authenticity in Laura Ingalls Wilder Country

Anna Thompson Hajdik

From Pepin, Wisconsin; Independence, Kansas; and Walnut Grove, Minnesota, through Burr Oak, Iowa; and finally De Smet, South Dakota; Laura Ingalls Wilder documented her family's migrations in her iconic Little House series. Today, the homesites and their communities trade on their association with Wilder, from a simple wayside marker near Pepin to festivals held each year in Walnut Grove, De Smet, and at Wilder's adult home in Mansfield, Missouri. Examining the phenomenon of Laura Ingalls Wilder–related tourism demonstrates that her enduring cultural currency is connected to the still salient role of frontier nostalgia in popular culture, involving conservative interpretations of American history, the complex relationship between heritage and tourism, and the search for authenticity on the American landscape.

The little girl in the little house is long gone, yet a complex set of cultural meanings connected to Wilder's youth and literary works continues to circulate. These cultural meanings, which I term the Wilder mystique, are tied in part to an ever-present antimodern impulse in American culture. As literary scholar Chilton Williamson Jr. observes, "While Mrs. Wilder, as a former hardscrabble pioneer girl, was certainly not opposed to 'progress' and 'modern conveniences,' ... an implicit criticism of dependency on modern technology is perceptible throughout her books, and so is the (also implicit) suggestion that the old ways were somehow better, not just because they were simpler but because they helped develop character and moral stamina" (21). Indeed, Wilder's treatment of technology and innovation is frequently portrayed in a positive light, whether it concerns the coming of the railroad to De Smet or the increased availability of mass-produced goods. However, antimodern attitudes pervade the books and deeply influence how fans relate to Laura and the world Wilder fashions in these stories. Rooted in the early twentieth century, antimodernism remains a significant force in the twenty-first. Furthermore, Wilder's fans are motivated not only to seek out the childhood homesites that are so vividly described in Wilder's books but also to engage in various forms of consumption predicated on a heady combination of frontier nostalgia, literary fandom, and heritage tourism.

FRONTIER NOSTALGIA AND ANTIMODERNISM: THE WILDER MYSTIQUE AND INTERPRETING THE PAST

At its core, the Wilder mystique relies on an antimodernist sensibility that relates to deeply held beliefs about the place of the nineteenth-century American frontier in popular culture. Popular culture, according to Patricia Nelson Limerick, has effectively imbued *frontier* with quaint, nostalgic notions that effectively remove more negative aspects of nineteenth-century pioneer life. Under these conditions, "the word 'frontier' uses historians before historians can use it" (75). Crafting stories for a children's audience, Wilder participated in this cultural process and therefore aided in the development of a powerful form of frontier nostalgia, glossing over the violence and brutality of "winning" the West and the human cost of "civilizing" the prairies. Indeed, Wilder's portrayal of Native Americans as "savages" or as mere impediments to white settlement in the Little House series has come under particular scrutiny in recent decades as scholars began to champion a more inclusive New Western history (see, for example, Kaye; Reese; Smulders; W. A. C. Wilson).

While Wilder's Little House books certainly touch on the struggles her family and other settlers faced, these events are secondary to the values emphasized in the stories: perseverance, self-reliance, domesticity, faith, and community solidarity. In particular, the priority placed on the nuclear family is one of the most compelling themes of the books. As Anita Clair Fellman has observed, "The values and relationships described in Wilder's stories have in fact served as benchmarks against which Americans have measured their own families" ("Laura" 537). The appeal of the Wilder mystique hinges on those values as well as a nostalgia fostered by commercialism, represented by a seeming inexhaustible supply of "old-timey" merchandise.

Nostalgia itself has often been associated with conservative strains of intellectual thought, and the frontier nostalgia present in Wilder's books has led to her identification with conservative values and the paradigm of American exceptionalism. Wilder and her daughter, Rose Wilder Lane, held highly critical views of President Franklin Roosevelt's New Deal policies. Indeed, Lane is frequently credited as the founder of the modern-day Libertarian Party. The broader themes within the Little House series can be linked back to the frontier nostalgia embedded in the books and what Limerick identifies as "a presumption of innocence and exceptionalism [that] is interwoven with the roots of frontier history" (74). For example, *Little House on the Prairie* culminates with a conflict between the Ingalls family and the federal government after it determines that their home lies in "Indian Territory." Wilder paints an unsympathetic portrayal of the government, prioritizing the perseverance of her father and family. In reality, the Ingallses returned to Wisconsin to reclaim their property after the man to whom they sold it could no longer make payments. Given the growing scholarly consensus that Wilder and Lane collaborated on the writing of the Little House series, it would seem that the women worked together to amplify the perceived heroism and indomitable pioneer spirit of their forbears.[1]

Fellmann, in fact, identifies two types of political conservatism that converge in the Little House series. One is wrapped up with Lane's anti–New Deal philosophy, which eventually contributed to her involvement with the Libertarian Party. The second holds up Wilder as the poster child for the nuclear family and by association Republican "values voters." Through her books, she romanticized the strong, heroic father figure, the genteel mother who did her best to civilize despite the perils of pioneer life, and children who found amusement in simple pleasures. As Fellman observes, "The popularity of the Little House books ... helped create a constituency for politicians like [Ronald] Reagan who sought to unsettle the so-called liberal consensus established by New Deal politics" (*Little* 234–35). The fact that Wilder's books and her literary persona continued to wield such significant cultural power during the Reagan administration and beyond illustrates her lasting appeal and affiliation with a more conservative approach to American history.

Ultimately, Wilder's books and literary persona, infused as they are with frontier nostalgia, endure because her own mythic origin story parallels Frederick Jackson Turner's pivotal "frontier thesis." Like the formation of American democracy, which, as Turner suggests, was formed by overcoming obstacles in the wilderness, Wilder's representation of hardship and deprivation on the frontier forms an integral piece of her timeless appeal in the American popular imagination. This appeal carries over to the realm of tourism, where the Wilder mystique has merged with what Michael Kammen terms the "heritage phenomenon," defined in part as a highly selective, nostalgic, and sanitized version of American history (214). Kammen's scholarship demonstrates that "heritage nostalgia" freezes history into a "vague golden time" devoid of complexity (214). For better or worse, the enduring cultural power of the Wilder mystique depends on Kammen's concept of the heritage phenomenon, whether it manifests itself through celebrations such as festivals or pageants or through commodification of Wilder-themed merchandise from prairie dresses to corncob dolls.

TOURISM AND THE WILDER MYSTIQUE

In the twenty-first century, tourists continue to seek out heritage experiences that sentimentalize the distant past. Edward M. Bruner, in his study of the "authentic reproduction" of New Salem, Illinois (home to a young Abraham Lincoln), posits three major reasons that this form of tourism holds appeal: to consume nostalgia that is linked to a yearning for a simpler time and place in opposition to today's perceived machine age; to embrace the idea of American progress; and to participate in the commemoration of a traditional America closely associated with values such as neighborliness and wholesomeness—in other words, an idyllic time warp of an invented small-town America (411). The tourist sites associated with Laura Ingalls Wilder fit squarely into the category of heritage tourism, but they also cross over into agricultural, literary, and popular culture tourism. However, much like Wilder in her authorship of the Little House books, the tourist sites blend the history, heritage, and nostalgia of the stories. Some sites unabashedly incorporate more recent popular conceptions of Wilder's books into their exhibitions to appeal to visitors who are perhaps more strongly influenced by popular culture than by history or literature.

Although eight different Wilder-related tourist sites exist around the country, this essay focuses primarily on Walnut Grove and De Smet. Geographic proximity allowed me to spend a sustained amount of time in each community, conducting fieldwork and archival research. While Walnut Grove is the setting of only one book, it is home to the Ingalls family on *Little House on the Prairie*, the imaginative but influential 1970s television version of Wilder's stories. De Smet serves as the setting of four of the Little House books, and Wilder spent much of her young adulthood there.

In their museums, these communities present narratives of Wilder's life, literary legacy, lasting impact on American culture, and personal connection to the town. The height of tourist season occurs in July, when each town stages an outdoor pageant retelling one of Wilder's stories. The two pageants attract roughly the same number of visitors—more than twenty thousand annually—and each generates well over three hundred thousand dollars a year in revenue, helping to support local businesses (Palmud; Leckey). In addition, Walnut Grove and De Smet share similar histories as communities united by the ascendance of the railroad in the late-nineteenth-century Midwest.

In some ways, however, the two towns are a study in contrasts. The museum in Walnut Grove, which offers more of a pop-culture-inflected approach, originated in 1974 as a response to an influx of visitors to the town after the premiere of the television version of *Little House on the Prairie*. De Smet's Laura Ingalls Wilder Society, in contrast, was founded in 1957, just a few months after Wilder's death, and is more focused on her literary legacy. The different orientations of the museums stand as good indicators of the various types of Wilder tourists they attract. Many are curious road-trippers who read one or two of Wilder's books as children and have foggy memories of the TV series. For others, visits are carefully planned family vacations that coincide with their children's first encounter with the Little House book series. Still others equate their trip to Laura Ingalls Wilder country with a kind of pilgrimage, a long-held dream to visit a mythic landscape far removed from the realities of everyday life.

Whatever expectations or preconceptions visitors bring to their Wilder-related sightseeing, there is no doubt that a curious blend of history, heritage, literature, and commerce informs their tourist experiences. The vague boundaries between these various elements of Wilder tourism work together to facilitate sustained economic viability for these small towns.

THE WILDER MYSTIQUE: WHERE LITERARY AND HERITAGE TOURISM MEET

In 2006, the Miller family from West Creek, New Jersey, set out on a cross-country Laura Ingalls Wilder–themed road trip. Bethany Miller read Wilder's books as a child, and she and her husband, Chuck, were reading them to their children. Beginning in Pepin, Wisconsin, they sought out every museum and tourist site associated with the Little House books and attended multiple Wilder pageants. The Millers even stayed in a stationary covered wagon at the Ingalls Homestead, a living history attraction on the outskirts of De Smet. The Millers' expedition resulted from Bethany's childhood memories, but as adults, they were drawn to the stories because of their historical significance, Wilder's still-vivid writing, and Chuck and Bethany's desire to instill in their children a love of reading. For the Millers and many others, including those who read the Little House books in school, literary tourism is foremost. While Wilder's books are taught in schools less frequently in the twenty-first century for diverse reasons, including greater reliance on textbooks, standardized elementary school curricula, and increased sensitivity regarding portrayals of Native Americans, the books continue to appeal to young audiences.

More recently, Wilder's Little House series has found a more frequent place in the college classroom as English and English education faculty, among others, seek to contextualize Wilder's writings by providing more nuanced pictures of American frontier experience. In the wake of *Pioneer Girl*'s success, editor Pamela Smith Hill taught a massive open online course through Missouri State University that proved exceedingly popular, and enrolled nearly seven thousand students in its inaugural semester ("MSU"). Other universities have followed suit. The University of Minnesota, for example, recently offered a one-day summer immersion course through its continuing education program ("Little Classroom").

Wilder's twenty-first-century popularity can also be viewed through the additional lens of online blogs that are not necessarily focused on the Little House books per se but that demonstrate a sustained interest in rural and farm life. Author Wendy McClure, for example, has parlayed her fandom of Wilder from a popular blog into the 2011 travel memoir *The Wilder Life*, which chronicled her journey to the various Wilder homesites across the Midwest.

Tourism-related fandom associated with Wilder's stories began soon after *Little House in the Big Woods* was published in 1932. Throughout the ensuing decades, thousands of fans, chiefly but not solely children, wrote to Wilder, emphasizing their identification with the stories, asking for additional details regarding her childhood, and telling her about their lives. Wilder often responded with handwritten notes. While Wilder still lived, many fans also took the additional step of visiting her at home in Missouri. She and her husband, Almanzo, usually obliged these literary tourists with pictures and lively conversation. On one occasion, a group of visitors arrived at the Wilders' doorstep around seven in the morning, causing Wilder to remark that "summer tourists beat even farmers for getting up early!" (*Dear Laura* 51).

Despite the lack of commercialized Wilder tourism sites throughout the 1940s and 1950s, these early Little House fans participated in a combination of literary and heritage tourism that became extremely popular in the immediate postwar period. Growth in civic-minded heritage tourism combined with a fascination about the West also laid groundwork for the development of the Laura Ingalls Wilder Pilgrimage Trail, which today runs west from Pepin, Wisconsin, down to Independence, Kansas, and then back up to Highway 14, which links Walnut Grove to De Smet. The trail also includes additional sites in Burr Oak, Iowa; Spring Valley, Minnesota; the Wilders' adult home in Mansfield, Missouri; and Almanzo Wilder's boyhood home in Malone, New York.

Within weeks of Wilder's death in 1957, community leaders in De Smet founded the Laura Ingalls Wilder Memorial Society. Rocky Ridge Farm, Wilder's adult home outside of Mansfield, Missouri, opened to tourists soon thereafter. The De Smet Society worked throughout the next decade to erect memorials and plaques to commemorate anything with Little House literary significance or that related to the Ingalls family, culminating in the acquisition of the surveyors' house (home to the Ingalls family during *By the Shores of Silver Lake*) in 1968 and the Ingalls family home in 1972. Aubrey Sherwood, the editor of the *De Smet News*, was a key figure in the formation of the Memorial Society. Sherwood corresponded with both Wilder and Lane and became one of the most prominent tourism boosters in the community. Over the years, the Wilder Memorial Society also benefited from the financial contributions of Lane's unofficially adopted grandson, Roger MacBride (Pechan).[2] In De Smet, the Wilder Memorial Society continues to maintain the structures associated with Wilder and to provide tours. In addition, the Society preserves Ingalls-Wilder artifacts, including family photographs, quilts, and furniture.

Walnut Grove's recognition of Wilder's link to the community began with a 1948 visit from Garth Williams, who had been commissioned to illustrate a new edition of the Little House series. Charles Lantz, a lawyer and columnist for the *Walnut Grove Tribune*, along with his wife, Doris, perhaps did more than anyone to promote Walnut Grove's link with Wilder in these early years. His brother, Everett Lantz, published the *Tribune*, and Charles often used his column as a tool for community boosterism. The Lantz trio also printed the first informational brochures about Wilder's connection to Walnut Grove and distributed them to the handfuls of tourists who stopped by during the 1950s and 1960s (Anderson 26–28).

THE WILDER MYSTIQUE AND THE SEARCH FOR AUTHENTICITY

Whether a reader first encounters the Little House series as a teacher, parent, or child, a major component of the books' enduring appeal lies in the stories' perceived authenticity. As writer Jon May observes, the search for authenticity is linked to the rise of modernity (713). In this vein, the antimodern appeals to a certain segment of the population because it is thought to be authentic and somehow more closely linked to a perfected past. The appeal of authenticity in the books easily extends to the tourism associated with Wilder's life.

Again, because Wilder's writing often obscures the boundaries between history, heritage, and literature, for many tourists, seeing the places associated with the Little House stories not only authenticates Wilder's narratives but also represents a kind of living history.

In her analysis of Massachusetts's living history attraction, Plimoth Plantation, Barbara Kirshenblatt-Gimblett writes of a "shifting locus of authenticity" (195) that informs the tourist experience as visitors learn about colonial history through interactions with costumed performers. At this site, it is perpetually 1627, and the theatricality of living history stands side by side with a museum of artifacts gathered from excavation of sites lived in by those actual Pilgrims who descended on Plymouth Rock so long ago. Similar shifts underlying the meaning of authenticity take place at the different Wilder tourism sites, especially in De Smet, where the Laura Ingalls Wilder Memorial Society firmly lays claim to the author's legacy. The Society holds many artifacts once owned by the Ingalls family, and MacBride's philanthropic contributions provide an air of legitimacy. However, the presence of another popular Wilder-related attraction on the outskirts of town demonstrates the complexity of authenticity's definition and illustrates Kirshenblatt-Gimblett's point that a tension between "an aura of actuality and virtuality" informs the tourist experience (195).

The Ingalls Homestead, the original 160 acres claimed by Charles Ingalls in 1880, is located just east of De Smet. The small cluster of cottonwood trees planted by the Ingalls family and described in *By the Shores of Silver Lake* still stands, with a marker placed nearby by the Laura Ingalls Wilder Memorial Society. Promoted as Laura's Living Prairie, the site provides tourists with opportunities to roam the farm site, take in immense country vistas, speak with costumed interpreters, ride in a covered wagon, sit in a one-room schoolhouse, and engage in a variety of hands-on activities inspired by Wilder's books. The Ingalls Homestead also offers overnight or weekend stays in stationary covered wagons or the larger bunkhouse.

The owners of the attraction, Tim and Joan Sullivan, are embodiments of the turn toward postproductivist agriculture, defined as the involvement of farmers in diversified enterprises (in this case, agricultural and heritage tourism), not simply traditional agriculture (G. A. Wilson). The Sullivans were once small-scale family farmers in Earling, Iowa, but fell victim to the farm crisis of the 1980s. They purchased the Ingalls Homestead in 1997. While the Sullivans independently run the Ingalls Homestead, they compete locally for tourist dollars with the Laura Ingalls Wilder Memorial Society. Vona Leckey, a Society board member and resident of De Smet since 1953, believes that the Society's appeal to prospective tourists rests on the authenticity of its buildings and artifacts. Leckey privileges the Society's holdings over the Ingalls

Homestead, noting, "They don't have anything authentic out there except the land. Nothing is real."

Leckey's comments get to the root of the debate in tourism studies and popular culture that has long compared the authentic reproduction to the original. Umberto Eco observed that "the past must be preserved and celebrated in full-scale authentic copy; a philosophy of immortality as duplication" (6), while Jean Baudrillard wrote that "Americans constantly construct imitations of themselves" and that the perfect definition of the simulacra is when the reproduction is "more real" than the original (41). The Society arguably has a greater claim to the term *authenticity* than the Ingalls Homestead because actual Ingalls family artifacts are on display in homes the Ingalls family actually lived in. Yet the appeal of the Ingalls Homestead rests on the complex definition of *authenticity* and closely mirrors scholarly discussions about such sites as Plimoth Plantation and New Salem.

The Sullivans emphasize that at the Ingalls Homestead, the "authentic tourist experience" comes not from the artifacts themselves (all of which are replicas) but from the ways tourists are encouraged to interact with the artifacts. Children and adults can try their hand at running laundry through a wringer, twisting hay into sticks, or grinding flour—all tasks that Wilder describes in her books. These opportunities to participate in forgotten country skills are central to the tourist experience and work to authenticate Wilder's experiences for both children and adults. Another level of authenticity comes from the land itself. Most of the attractions at the Ingalls Homestead are outdoors and blend into the prairie landscape. Because this part of South Dakota has experienced relatively little commercial and residential development, tourists can easily imagine how the land might have looked during Wilder's childhood.

The types of tourist experiences available to visitors at the Wilder sites reflect the kinds of authenticity available to Wilder fans. The Ingalls Homestead offers that "shifting locus of authenticity" (Kirshenblatt-Gimblett 195) commonly found at living history sites. The Wilder Society, by contrast, engages in artifact-based authenticity tied closely to objects and relics. Walking through the cozy surveyors' house where the Ingallses spent their first winter in Dakota and seeing needlework delicately handcrafted by Mary Ingalls or handwritten manuscripts completed by Laura holds powerful meaning for some fans that simply cannot be replicated at the Ingalls Homestead. The significance of these artifacts reaches far beyond their original use or intent. Rocky Ridge Farm is home to perhaps the most powerful Ingalls-Wilder artifact of all, Pa's fiddle. Wilder wrote often of this instrument in the Little House series, often associating it with happy, festive occasions. The curators of the museum in Mansfield realize the symbolic power of the fiddle. Displayed prominently near the museum entrance, it commands the attention of visitors. The gift shop also offers an album comprised of songs recorded by a local artist. The evocative instrument is played every fall during the annual Fiddle Off, held on Wilder Day at Rocky Ridge Farm.

Such debates and discussions over authenticity are less overt in Walnut Grove, although residents have their own set of challenges. The most significant issue for the area was how quickly fame and the resulting tourist influx hit the community after *Little House on the Prairie* began airing on television in 1974. Harold and Della Gordon bought the property near Walnut Grove that contains the Ingallses' dugout homesite in 1947, and the family's experience before and after the television show illustrates the effect of a more popularized representation on their property and daily lives. For many years, only a few hundred fans per year stopped by the Gordons' farm. Redwood County erected a small marker near their home in the early 1960s, during the county centennial celebration. The Gordons could handle the small crowd, even treating visitors to lemonade and cookies in their kitchen. Their son, Stan, recalled, "My parents loved meeting all the different people. My dad especially really enjoyed it."

However, the pleasure Harold Gordon derived from his encounters with tourists took a sharp turn in 1974, when the Gordons suddenly found themselves deluged with visitors. One day they came home and met strangers coming down their staircase. The tourists had just walked right in, thinking that the Gordons' home was part of the attraction. The Gordons called an emergency town meeting and spoke to the community about the pressing need for somewhere else to corral the influx of visitors. Why had the tourists felt so compelled to cross the line? As David Herbert notes, "Former homes, in which a writer lived and worked, may create a sense of nostalgia and inspire awe or reverence" (312–13). Furthermore, some tourists feel such a deep connection to a writer that seemingly obvious boundaries become invisible, demonstrating the profound emotional power of literature and popular culture.

Yet the experience of the Gordon family also illustrates how the production of place impacts the social, economic, and cultural identity of a real community. The dramatic reenvisioning of *Little House on the Prairie* indelibly reshaped how millions of people discovered Wilder's stories and strongly influenced how tourists imagined the places associated with her life.

MERCHANDISING THE WILDER MYSTIQUE

At each Wilder homesite, shopping is a major part of the tourist experience. To business owners in Walnut Grove and De Smet as well as the other communities that claim some aspect of Wilder's childhood, selling souvenirs is a key component of the economy. In Walnut Grove, visitors can shop at Oleson's Mercantile or eat lunch at Nellie's Cafe. In De Smet, visitors can choose between two Wilder-themed bed-and-breakfasts, Prairie House Manor or Heritage House, a historic red-brick structure that previously served as the community's bank. De Smet is also home to the Loftus Store, a combination souvenir shop, florist, and community gathering spot that evokes a setting prominently featured in Wilder's De Smet books.

De Smet certainly claims places mentioned within the literary world of the books, while Walnut Grove's place-making has been more improvised in response to the television program. Enterprising business owners in Walnut Grove borrowed liberally from the books in naming their retail shops and cafés. Wilder herself had only dim memories of the community and her time there. De Smet's business landscape is much more authentically connected to the Ingalls family.

However, items available for purchase at both town's museums and gift shops now extend far beyond the Little House book series, although special boxed sets and commemorative editions are prominently displayed. Cookbooks, educational curriculums, travel guides, compact discs of fiddle music, locally made prairie dresses, jams, jellies, and old-fashioned candy are just a few of the twenty-first-century commodities offered for sale. The members of the Ingalls family would surely stare in wonder at the healthy exchange of commerce predicated on their austere way of life.

But Walnut Grove's and De Smet's lack of commercialization contributes to their perceived authenticity, although the communities' historic links with the Little House series still pave the way for a novel consumption experience. Business owners and town residents are expected to have a deep knowledge of Wilder's life and the history and heritage of their towns and generally to greet tourists with enthusiasm, thus performing a form of emotional labor often associated with tourism. In De Smet, for example, most businesses allow their employees to take time during the summer months, with no reduction in pay, to attend training sessions conducted by local experts on the Ingalls family, Wilder's life, and the books.

Perhaps the most explicit examples of the active effort to create Wilder-driven consumer experiences are Walnut Grove's and De Smet's community pageants. Unlike other community pageants, these events occur not solely to celebrate the community's heritage but in large part to serve the needs and expectations of visitors. In that regard, the festivals form an integral piece of a commercialized Wilder mystique and add economic value to the tourist experience.

In the twenty-first century, community heritage pageants seem like quaint, almost throwback forms of entertainment. In many ways, they are. In the United States, the heyday of heritage or "historic" pageants came at the turn of the twentieth century, products of Progressive reform movements that sought to uplift the public by cultivating regional and national pride. According to Steven Hoelscher, pageants have historically served as theatrical forms that effectively made use of "abstract virtues of a state or nation" (89). Community pageants also venerate local legends, myths, or notable residents. The Wilder pageants engage in both practices. The De Smet pageant predates Walnut Grove's by ten years and was first performed on an annual basis in 1968. De Smet's pageants rotate through the different novels that are set in the community, while Walnut Grove has consistently adapted *On the Banks of Plum Creek* as its pageant, with some additional local history occasionally thrown in. Throughout the years, the productions have become more elaborate and have gone from being staged at local high schools to outdoor amphitheaters that seamlessly blend into the prairie landscape.

Beyond simply providing tourists with something more to consume on their Wilder-themed vacations, the pageants are truly vernacular folkloric events that unite much of the community in bringing Wilder's vision of that place to life. From actors to parking lot attendants to ticket takers and prop masters, both pageants require volunteers drawn from throughout the region. However, once again, these events are produced primarily for the benefit of tourists, require a great deal of emotional labor, and represent yet another integral part of the commercialized Wilder mystique.

Christianity and faith more generally are important aspects of Wilder's appeal for some tourists and contribute directly to her marketability as an icon of family values. The Christian homeschooling movement in fact provides Laura Ingalls Wilder–related tourism a small financial boost during the school year, when many families are unable to travel for long periods of time. Several residents in De Smet and Walnut Grove remarked on the homeschoolers' importance from an economic perspective. Larry Cheney, owner of De Smet's Prairie House Bed and Breakfast, estimated that homeschoolers represent about 10 percent of his overall business.

Lavonne Garry, a tour guide for the Laura Ingalls Wilder Society in De Smet, has also noticed the increasing presence of homeschoolers on her tours. "Homeschooling is getting to be a bigger business than it has been before, and many of those families buy the educational plan that we sell." She also noted that "in the wintertime, we have Amish almost every week. We have Amish all winter long." Several other tour guides also speculated on the popularity of the Little House series among the Amish, noting that this religious group, often romanticized for its rejection of the technologies associated with modern life, perhaps sees its world and lifestyle reflected in Wilder's stories (Cramer).

In multiple ways, the commodification of Laura Ingalls Wilder reflects the range of meanings ascribed to the Wilder mystique, from the frontier nostalgia associated with the souvenirs and knickknacks sold in gift shops to the theatrical commemoration of the various Little House pageants performed across the Upper Midwest. The merchandising of Wilder extends into more intimate realms as well, with a plethora of products linked to Christianity, political conservatism, and traditional views of family and gender.

CONCLUSION

The stories of Laura Ingalls Wilder continue to fascinate scores of readers in the United States and abroad. Wilder's timeless appeal was again on display in 2014, when the South Dakota Historical Press published the manuscript autobiography that provided Wilder with the basis for the Little House books. This annotated edition of *Pioneer Girl* was so popular with Wilder's legions of fans that the press quickly ran out of its initial run of fifteen thousand copies. Demand was so high that for a time, as Judith Thurman notes, copies of the book were selling for as much as four hundred dollars. The enduring popularity of the Little House books and related tourist sites illustrates that the cultivation and consumption of nostalgia tied closely to America's frontier heritage continues unabated in modern America. The array of cultural meanings ascribed to Wilder's life and books illuminate the ways the public continues to search for authenticity.

The small tourism industries in Walnut Grove, De Smet, and other Wilder-related communities are also indicative of a postindustrial economy that prioritizes experience, recreation, and commodification over the industrial capitalism of an earlier age. They symbolize a postproductivist shift from the small-scale agriculture that brought idealistic settlers to southwestern Minnesota and eastern South Dakota at the dawn of the twentieth century to an economy largely dependent on tourism. Residents in Wilder-associated towns work to provide a nostalgic vision of the nation's heritage tied closely to the Little House books and adhere to Wilder's version of their own communities' histories, perhaps at the expense of a more multifaceted history. And yet, as one business owner stated, "Laura is our niche. And we don't have to manufacture our niche, like some other towns" (C. Cheney). Wilder's role in sustaining the economies of Walnut Grove and De Smet becomes even clearer when viewed against the surrounding region filled with ghost towns and deserted homesteads. Many of these communities faded away as their populations migrated to regional centers or cities. For better or worse, tourism keeps Walnut Grove, De Smet, and other towns associated with the Wilder mystique alive and thriving.

NOTES

1. Most Wilder scholars agree that Lane played a significant role in editing and writing the Little House series. See Holtz; Woodside. Fellman and William Anderson, among others, regard Wilder and Lane's relationship as a tense collaboration. Lane herself adamantly claimed that her mother wrote the books alone.

2. MacBride seems to have had a much better relationship with the De Smet community than that of Mansfield. After Lane's death in 1968, he waged a legal battle with the library in Mansfield to which Wilder had willed the copyrights of her books. In 1999, the library settled for $875,000, a paltry sum in light of the fact that a recent estimate valued the Little House "empire" at more than one hundred million dollars. For more on MacBride's financial entanglements with the Mansfield Public Library, see Russo; Levitt.

ARCHIVAL COLLECTIONS AND UNPUBLISHED MATERIALS

Collection of Stan Gordon, Walnut Grove, Minnesota
De Smet Historical Society, De Smet, South Dakota
Laura Ingalls Wilder Museum, Walnut Grove, Minnesota

WORKS CITED

Anderson, William. *The Walnut Grove Story of Laura Ingalls Wilder*. Laura Ingalls Wilder Museum, 1987.
Baudrillard, Jean. *America*. Verso, 1988.
Bruner, Edward M. "Abraham Lincoln as Authentic Reproduction: A Critique of Postmodernism." *American Anthropologist* 96, no. 2 (1994): 397–415.
Cheney, Connie. Personal Interview. De Smet, South Dakota, 21 September 2006.
Cheney, Larry. Personal Interview. De Smet, South Dakota, 11 July 2006.
Cramer, Marian. Personal Interview. De Smet, South Dakota, 10 July 2006.
Dear Laura: Letters from Children to Laura Ingalls Wilder. HarperCollins, 1996.
Eco, Umberto. *Travels in Hyperreality: Essays*. Harcourt Brace Jovanovich, 1986.
Fellman, Anita Clair. "Laura Ingalls Wilder and Rose Wilder Lane: The Politics of a Mother-Daughter Relationship." *Signs: Journal of Women in Culture and Society* 15 (1990): 535–61.
Fellman, Anita Clair. *Little House, Long Shadow: Laura Ingalls Wilder's Impact on American Culture*. University of Missouri Press, 2008.
Garry, Lavonne. Personal Interview. De Smet, South Dakota, 19 September 2006.
Gordon, Stan, and Hazelle Gordon. Personal Interview. Walnut Grove, Minnesota, 14 September 2006.
Herbert, David. "Literary Places, Tourism, and the Heritage Experience." *Annals of Tourism Research* 28, no. 2 (2001): 312–33.

Hoelscher, Steven. *Heritage on Stage: The Invention of Ethnic Place in America's Little Switzerland*. University of Wisconsin Press, 1998.

Holtz, William. *The Ghost in the Little House: A Life of Rose Wilder Lane*. University of Missouri Press, 1993.

Kammen, Michael. *In the Past Lane: Historical Perspectives on American Culture*. Oxford University Press, 1997.

Kaye, Frances W. "Little Squatter on the Osage Diminished Reserve: Reading Laura Ingalls Wilder's Kansas Indians." *Great Plains Quarterly* 20, no. 2 (2000): 123–40.

Kirshenblatt-Gimblett, Barbara. *Destination Culture: Tourism, Museums, and Heritage*. University of California Press, 1998.

Leckey, Vona. Personal Interview. De Smet, South Dakota, 22 September 2006.

Levitt, Aimee. "Little House in the Present: America's Economic Downturns Run through Laura Ingalls Wilder's Books Like a Big Three-Hearted River." *Riverfront Times*, 24 November 2011.

Limerick, Patricia Nelson. "The Frontier in the Twentieth Century." In *The Frontier in American Culture: Essays by Richard White and Patricia Nelson Limerick*, 67–102. University of California Press, 1994.

"Little Classroom on the Prairie: Upcoming Immersion Focuses on the Life and Times of Quintessential Prairie Girl Laura Ingalls Wilder." University of Minnesota College of Continuing Education, 20 January 2011. https://cce.umn.edu/news/little-classroom-on-the-prairie.

May, Jon. "In Search of Authenticity on and off the Beaten Track." *Environment and Planning D: Society and Space* 14, no. 6 (1996): 709–36.

McClure, Wendy. *The Wilder Life: My Adventures in the Lost World of Little House on the Prairie*. Riverhead/Penguin, 2011.

Miller, Bethany, and Chuck Miller. Personal Interview. Walnut Grove, Minnesota, and De Smet, South Dakota, 8–10 July 2006.

"MSU Offers Free Online Course on Laura Ingalls Wilder." *Springfield News-Leader*, 28 July 2014.

Palmud, Cheryl. Personal Interview. De Smet, South Dakota, 22 September 2006.

Pechan, Beverly. "What Happened Next? Bill's Scholarly Journey into the Life and Writings of Laura Ingalls Wilder." *Rapid City Journal*, 1999.

Reese, Debbie. *Teaching Young Children about Native Americans*. ERIC Clearinghouse, 1996.

Russo, Maria. "Finding America, Both Red and Blue, in the 'Little House Books.'" *New York Times*, 7 February 2017.

Smulders, Sharon. "'The Only Good Indian': History, Race, and Representation in Laura Ingalls Wilder's *Little House on the Prairie*." *Children's Literature Association Quarterly* 27, no. 4 (2002): 191–202.

Sullivan, Tim, and Joan Sullivan. Personal Interview. De Smet, South Dakota, 11 July, 19 September 2006.

Thurman, Judith. "The 'Little House' Memoir." *The New Yorker*, 18 February 2015. https://www.newyorker.com/culture/cultural-comment/pioneer-girl-memoir-little-house-prairie.

Turner, Frederick Jackson. *The Significance of the Frontier in American History*. State Historical Society of Wisconsin, 1894.

Wilder, Laura Ingalls. *Pioneer Girl: The Annotated Autobiography*. Edited by Pamela Smith Hill. South Dakota Historical Society Press, 2014.

Williamson, Chilton, Jr. "Big Little House in American Literature." *Chronicles* 15, no. 11 (1991): 20–25.

Wilson, Geoff A. "From Productivism to Post-Productivism and Back Again? Exploring the (Un)Changed Natural and Mental Landscapes of European Agriculture." *Transactions of the Institute of British Geographers* 26, no. 1 (2001): 77–102.

Wilson, Waziyatawin Angela Cavender. "Burning Down the House: Laura Ingalls Wilder and American Colonialism." In *Unlearning the Language of Conquest*, edited by Wahinkpe Topa AKA Don Trent Jacobs, 66–80. University of Texas Press, 2006.

Woodside, Christine. *Libertarians on the Prairie: Laura Ingalls Wilder, Rose Wilder Lane, and the Making of the Little House Books*. Arcade, 2016.

A LITTLE PLACE IN THE UNIVERSE

An Ojibwe, Osage, and Dakota View of Laura Ingalls
Margaret Noodin

> But Laura did not feel that she had told a lie. What she had said was true too. Somehow that moment when the beautiful, free pony and the wild man rode into the sun would last forever.
> —Laura Ingalls Wilder, *By the Shores of Silver Lake*

> *Hekta ehanna ded untipi.* Long ago we lived here.
> *Heun he ohinni unkiksuyapi kte.* We will always remember that.
> *Anpetu dena ded untipi.* Today we live here.
> *Heca ohinni undowanpi kte.* We will always sing.
> —Gwen Westerman, "Genetic Code" (22)

Laura Ingalls Wilder created the Little House series of books from memory, myth, and history. She grew up as western North America was becoming the United States and wrote her autobiographical fiction as the period of pioneer expansion was ending. She won the hearts of generations, but much has been said about how her stereotypes and allusions sometimes obscure important facts of history. Yet her imperfect literary offerings are still useful for readers who wish to examine America's literary identity and the ways young adults might continue to shape their own identities against a national landscape.

Wilder's series remains significant because it is still in print, used in classrooms, and part of the American literary tradition. Critics who argue that her work must be read in the context of the time in which it is set are right.

Critics who argue that her work should be read from an informed postcolonial perspective are also right. This essay unravels the ways that these two threads of influence may be reconciled. With the advantage of hindsight, we can reread and review the series from the perspective of the cultures Wilder was shaped by yet never fully explored. The Ingalls family moved from the territory of the Massachusetts people to the woods and Great Lakes populated by the Three Fires Confederacy, then briefly lived on Osage land before eventually settling permanently near the Seven Council Fires on the Great Plains. Each of these multinational diasporas had well-developed oral traditions and belief systems, but their cultures remained largely unknown to settlers because at the time Wilder and her family were making a home in various western locations, indigenous people were literally battling to preserve their way of life. It is easy to associate Wilder with some of the ignorance and drive for Manifest Destiny of the times. It is more challenging to note instead the relevant history that surrounds her novels and imagine how Ojibwe, Osage, and Dakota beliefs might offer young readers a way to better understand the stories of the woods, the prairie, and the riverbanks that had been populated for thousands of years by a diverse range of complex, creative societies. Rendering these parallel historical viewpoints visible can offer today's young Native and non-Native readers a new view of Wilder and her place in a specific regional and mythic national American landscape. In this way, the next generation of American readers can move forward without denial and confusion to shape the future.

LITTLE HOUSE WITH A BIG INFLUENCE

Wilder's Little House series has sold more than sixty million copies and has been translated into nearly three dozen languages (Fellman 5). A website, LittleHouseonthePrairie.com, has been created to "serve as a home for fans," and since 2009, Wilder's life and legend have been celebrated at Laurapalooza, a conference for academics and fans hosted by the Laura Ingalls Wilder Legacy and Research Association. Many voices are clearly dedicated to ensuring that Wilder's stories continue to be read. Yet as Anita Clair Fellman, Philip Heldrich, Frances W. Kaye, Pat Louw, and other scholars acknowledge, the books present only one side of history. Teachers who choose to use these books today should address complex issues of how the west was "won." This essay offers one way to reread the series as a partial and parallel narrative that can benefit from cross-cultural comparison. Although it is generally agreed that the Little

House series consists of nine books, this essay focuses only on the books about Laura as a child and adolescent. *Farmer Boy*, which is about the childhood of her husband, Almanzo Wilder, is not included here, nor is *The First Four Years*, which focuses on her early married life. Most of Wilder's stories focused on her memories of childhood and adolescence and were written for readers of similar ages. This is significant because young readers tend to form a bond with fictional characters, a process communication theorists describe as a parasocial relationship. This relationship often leads readers to take on the views and social perspectives they find in the narrative (Burnett and Beto 30). In many instances, readers trust the protagonist's perspective and consider it authentic (Green and Brock 719). Wilder's view is, of course, her authentic recollection; however, because the Little House books offer only one side of the pioneer story, young readers are exposed to the racism of settlement without an opportunity to understand the diversity that surrounded her. Adults who treasure Wilder's stories and keep the series in circulation should consider ways to help young citizens today understand the American landscape they inherit, one that contains more than five hundred sovereign nations, some of them not mentioned but clearly described by Wilder.

Louise Erdrich's *Birchbark House* series can counter the narrative of the *Little House in the Big Woods* in introducing the language, stories and complex social relationships of the Anishinaabe people to young readers (Noodin). But the Little House series continues beyond the woods of what is now Wisconsin, and no comparable works are yet available to introduce the Osage and Dakota to young readers.

Each of the books in the Little House series exists within intersecting planes of time and space. Each story begins and ends with dates that the author either remembers or has researched. Some larger historical events of the late 1800s are unmentioned but clearly affect the plots. Events that happened long after the time of the series also impacted Wilder's views as she wrote in the 1930s and 1940s. All of the series takes place on either federal or tribal land, in places that are in transition through battle or negotiation. In these spaces, Laura shows either fear or familiarity toward the sound of wolves, the arrival of locusts, the rotation of seasons, and ancient concepts of survival. In several books, Laura has a subtle awareness of the land as connected to indigenous culture, but she never fully explores the specific cultures that surround her. Because Native nations are legally embedded in our federal landscape, adults of today must help young readers understand some of the history that shaped Wilder's life and introduce the complex cultures to which she alludes but that she never fully encountered.

IN THE WOODS, ON THE PRAIRIE, ALONG THE BANKS

As Americans continue to develop and understand their collective identity, it is important to circle back to history as it is rewritten by each generation. Looking at editorial choices made as Wilder's memories filtered forward, readers can see how both foreground and background are necessary for a full perspective on the events she witnessed. The narrative arc across the series is one of American independence and expansion, which dominated the pioneer years and still shapes the way many US citizens view immigration. Like the nation itself, Laura and her sisters move through turbulent times, seeking a way to make sense of the events that contribute to their personal and shared identities.

Laura Ingalls Wilder's great-great-grandfather, Edmund Rice, emigrated from England in 1638, settling in the Massachusetts Bay Colony (Gormley). She was also connected to the Delano family, whose ancestors emigrated to the Plymouth Colony in the early 1620s and which also includes US President Franklin Delano Roosevelt ("Eunice Sleeman"). One paternal ancestor, Edmund Ingalls, was born on 27 June 1586 in Skirbeck, Lincolnshire, England, and in 1629 emigrated to America, where he lived in a place the colonists called Lynn. Those colonists displaced rather than lived together with the Naumkeag of the Massachusetts Confederacy (Gormley). In *Little House in the Big Woods*, Pa remembers playing games where nameless Indians, presumably the Naumkeag, were merely prey: "I began to play I was a mighty hunter, stalking the wild animals and the Indians. I played I was fighting the Indians, until the woods seemed full of wild men, and then all at once I heard the birds twittering good night" (24). His story ends with no human encounter, no cultural exchange, only the haunting sound of a screech owl chasing him home.

By the time Laura Ingalls headed west, both sides of her family had been in America for several generations. Yet the centuries had done little to help descendants of Europeans understand and appreciate the cultures of North America. Born in 1867, Laura knew that her life story was part of a larger story, which she addressed in her Detroit Book Week speech in 1937: "I began to think of what a wonderful childhood I had had. How I had seen the whole frontier, the woods, the Indian country of the great plains, the frontier towns, the building of railroads in the wild, unsettled country, homesteading and farmers coming in to take possession" ("Laura's" 217). At age seventy, she wrote of "Indian country" and the "unsettled country" as part of the past that was changed, like the landscape, in ways that were believed to be for the good. The term *Indian Country* represents all of the people, animals, and resources associated with it. This homogenous stereotype allows Wilder and subsequently her readers to continually miss the perspective of the places and the people alongside whom she lives. Each book in the series is set against a backdrop of indigenous and settler history, and as Laura matures, her awareness of the uneasy imbalance between cultures increases; however, it never reaches the level of actual engagement with a specific nation.

The first book in the series, *Little House in the Big Woods*, begins in winter and follows the cycle of one year. In it, Laura turns five. Although a date is not specified, it is likely that the story begins after the Civil War had ended, slavery had been abolished, and President Abraham Lincoln had been assassinated. Although the Dakota War is never mentioned, adults in the household would certainly have known of it. The conflict took place in 1862 and ended with the US Army taking 1,500 Dakota as prisoners, with 392 of them put on trial and condemned to execution. Although Lincoln pardoned many of them, he approved the largest mass execution ever held in the United States, ordering the hangings of 38 Dakota warriors (Berg 191). Local memory would also have included the recently established Ojibwe reservations and the Sandy Lake Tragedy of 1850, during which 3,000 Ojibwe from Wisconsin were required to leave home to pick up annuity payments and supplies; they did not receive the payments and materials, and as they made their way back to their communities, 400 perished (US Bureau of Indian Affairs). All of these events were well known to settlers traveling in the Midwest, yet the series begins with false information: "As far as a man could go to the north in a day, or a week, or a whole month, there was nothing but woods. There were no houses. There were no roads. There were no people. There were only trees and the wild animals who had their homes among them" (*Woods* 5). Despite clear evidence of their presence on contemporary maps, in the day's newspapers, and in government documents of the time, citizens of Native nations and the large confederacies of the region are not present in Laura's Big Woods. "Indians" are mentioned only once—in Pa's memory of the East. This knowledge can help students understand that they live in places that have been inhabited and managed by people for centuries longer than the United States has existed.

Wilder's views of the landscape and her place in it are consistent with a child's, but fear often overrides curiosity. Her description of the lake can easily be connected to Ojibwe ontology, which is supported by a lexicon with only one word, *ozhaawashkwaa*, for the full spectrum of all blue between *michigaming* (the great sea) and *giizhig* (the heavens): "It was as blue as the sky, and it went to the edge of the world. As far as she could see, there was nothing but flat, blue water. Very far away, the sky and the water met, and there was a darker blue line. . . . Laura had never known that the sky was so big. There was so much empty space all around her that she felt small and frightened, and glad that Pa and Ma were there" (*Woods* 66). But Wilder gives Laura a particularly patriotic reference for this experience: "She knew how Yankee Doodle felt, when he could not see the town because there were so many houses" (66).

A contrasting view of the land and sky would be one based in Anishinaabe culture, which includes members of the Three Fires Confederacy—the Ojibwe, Odawa, and Potawatomi. If she had been introduced to their beliefs, Laura might have been comforted by stories of the moon as a relative of the earth and sun. In Ojibwe, the sun is *giizis* and the moon is literally *dibiki-giizis*, the night sun: they are just two of many important nonhuman parts of the world. It is not likely that Laura would have attended Ojibwe ceremonies or changed the priorities of her family by learning Ojibwe language and stories, but it is possible that she would have seen the Ojibwe people as equal to herself and come to understand that in the space labeled "wild" by the United States, people living beside her had found powerful connections that sustained and informed them. As Ojibwe scholar Roger Roulette points out, in Ojibwe tradition, the universe is the greatest guide for those who understand the lessons it holds: "If Ojibwe people recognize a spiritual entity in the concept of a storm or a wind or anything, it is truly, then, a gift to recognize it like that. If one doesn't recognize it, ponder. Ask and see what can be learned from it" (qtd. in Matthews 11).

The fictional Ingalls family eventually leaves the Big Woods to live on the Osage Indian Reservation, portrayed in *Little House on the Prairie*, which features a six-year-old Laura. The Homestead Act of 1862 led Pa west and caused many whites to view Indians as a monolithic group of enemies in the way of settlement. The act specified that any citizen or intended citizen who had not taken up arms against the United States could claim 160 acres. Women were eligible. African Americans became eligible after they became citizens in 1868. But American Indians were displaced.

In contrast to the 2 instances of *Indian* in *Big Woods*, the word appears 242 times in *Little House on the Prairie*. Most often, it is used in a negative or disparaging way. The "Minnesota Massacre," meaning the Dakota War of 1862, is specifically mentioned as an explanation for Mrs. Scott's hatred for all "Indians": she says, "Land knows, they'd never do anything with this country themselves. All they do is roam around over it like wild animals. Treaties or no treaties, the land belongs to folks that'll farm it. That's only common sense and justice" (356). Pa agrees: "An Indian ought to have sense enough to know when he was licked" (387). Mr. Edwards says that there are too many Indians, and Mr. Scott says he "didn't know why so many of those savages were coming together if they didn't mean devilment" (386). Pa does say that Indians are "perfectly friendly" and "perfectly quiet and peaceable" (363, 375). But this book also includes the line "The only good Indian was a dead Indian" not once but three times (356, 386, 394).[1] Adults in the novel offer only good or evil versions of "Indians," never thinking of them as Dakota or Osage, never using their chosen names. Even Soldat du Chêne, whom Pa calls the "one good Indian" (394), is pure fiction (Kaye 138). The imagined martyrdom of Soldat du Chêne made a better story than realities of land negotiations and trespassing settlers.

The land is described throughout *Little House on the Prairie* almost as if it were a character itself, but Laura and her sister, Mary, are mostly confused and exhausted by it. One particularly interesting passage shows a reverence for rotation and the celebration of sunrise and sunset that is common in many indigenous cultures. Osage, Dakota, and Ojibwe people all have celebrations to mark the passing of day into night as well as one season into another when solstice and equinox occur. Wilder wrote, "Day after day they traveled in Kansas, and saw nothing but the rippling grass and enormous sky. In a perfect circle the sky curved down the level land, and the wagon was in the circle's exact middle (*Prairie* 273). The prairie and the wonder of planetary rotation is not portrayed as a lesson in science and spirituality, as it would by an indigenous narrator/writer; instead, the girls view the prairie as a tiring and lonely place where the wind "mourns": "That prairie looked as if no human eye had ever seen it before. Only the tall wild grass covered the endless empty land and a great empty sky arched over it" (279). In contrast, according to teachings still shared today by the Osage nation, "Everything in the universe is part of Wah-kon-tah, the all-controlling force. There is a visible living world and the invisible spiritual world of Wah-kon-tah. These worlds are connected; everything in the world of the living is also part of Wah-kon-tah.... Osage cosmology divides the universe into sky and earth, and day and night. Every living creature in this system has a specific meaning and role" (Osage Nation). As the Ingalls family and other settlers sought to find peace after the Civil War and during continual migration and immigration, the Osage worldview might have been a helpful framework for healing and reconciliation. These were not the goals of the time, but if the story is read alongside Osage narratives, young readers should realize that it is not too late—and in fact it may be imperative—for reconciliation between settler and indigenous cultures.

On the Banks of Plum Creek, published in 1937, covers the years when the Ingalls family lived near Walnut Grove, in southwestern Minnesota, after moving "all the way from the little log house in Indian Territory, across Kansas, across Missouri, across Iowa, and a long way into Minnesota" (415). Laura is seven, and the family leaves the land of the Osage to cross through spaces where Potawatomi, Kickapoo, Sauk and Fox, Omaha, Pawnee, Iowa, Ponca, Ho-Chunk, and Dakota people lived. Despite their proximity to so many diverse communities, Pa states, "It does beat all. In Wisconsin we lived among Swedes and Germans. In Indian Territory we lived among the Indians. Now here in

Minnesota all the neighbors are Norwegians. They're good neighbors, too. But I guess our kind of folks is pretty scarce" (435–36). As the Ingallses traveled, they thought of "Indians" not as stewards of the land but as a threat. Early in the novel, Ma says, "It is all so tame and peaceful. There will be no wolves or Indians howling tonight. I haven't felt so safe and at rest since I don't know when" (423). There is reference during Thanksgiving dinner to the Indians bringing turkeys to the Pilgrims (453), and Laura says, "I wish I was an Indian and didn't have to wear clothes" (521). Despite living only forty miles south of the Lower Sioux Reservation in what is now Redwood County, the Ingalls family does not mention the Mdewakanton, Wahpekute, Sisseton, or Wahpeton Dakota people who represent the Great Sioux Nation along the Minnesota River.

The year the Ingalls family settled in a dugout on the banks of Plum Creek, General George Armstrong Custer led a military expedition into the Black Hills of Dakota Territory and discovered gold in a region that had been granted to the Sioux. Gold is everywhere in the novel. It is mentioned more than forty times—an average of once every eight pages. Wilder uses the word to describe dust in the road, the bloom of goldenrod, the center of blue flag, the petals of black-eyed Susans, the backs of bees, wheat in the field, hay gathered and baled, a pan of cornbread, the hair of dolls and Mary's coveted curls, bright buttons, satin ribbons, fur collars, gilded saucers, picture frames, Ma's fancy pin, the raw timber of their frame house going up, and the clouds—the clouds, the sky, and the sun. Gold was clearly important to the family and represented beauty and security in a culture where tangible wealth and property were important. Ann Romines has pointed out the materialism of frontier life as it is displayed in *On the Banks of Plum Creek*, and her discussion of ownership reminds us of the chasm between indigenous and industrial cultures (see, for example, chapter 3, "Getting and Spending: Materialism and the Little House"). The gold rush, government aggression, and the Dakota response to encroachment are not topics included in the book, but readers who learn about the way gold led people west will understand some of the behaviors of the adults in Laura's life.

The fifth book, *By the Shores of Silver Lake*, centers on the year the Ingalls family recovers from scarlet fever, Mary goes blind, and the family moves from Minnesota to Dakota Territory. Laura is depicted as slightly older than her real age of eleven at the time, and this book, more than others, marks her transition from childhood to adulthood, as she is asked to help more with the homestead and her siblings.

During the winter, Laura and her sisters are left alone with Ma while Pa goes west to "take a homestead." As he explains, "We can get a hundred and sixty acres out west, just by living on it, and the land's as good as this is, or better. If Uncle Sam's willing to give us a farm in place of the one he drove us off of, in Indian

Territory, I say let's take it" (*Shores* 7). To confirm the impression that the land is theirs for the taking, Pa points out "old Indian trails and buffalo paths worn deep in the ground and now grassed over" (38). Wilder adds, "Only a little while before the vast herds of thousands of buffaloes had grazed over this country. They had been the Indians' cattle, and white men had slaughtered them all" (39). Pa alludes to but does not tell the full story of Uncle Sam and the treaties made with the Dakota and Lakota, which continue to impact resource development in the region today. The adults discuss family decisions with the children but do so in ways that make a simplistic game of their adventures. Pa tells his daughters, "I've bet Uncle Sam fourteen dollars against a hundred and sixty acres of land, that we can make out to live on the claim for five years. Going to help me win the bet?" The girls all answer *yes*, but Ma chides, "I don't like to think of it as gambling," to which Pa replies "Everything's more or less a gamble.... Nothing is certain but death and taxes" (139). His remark reveals a colonial perspective that reaches back to *The Cobbler of Preston*, written by British playwright Christopher Bullock in 1716. The pervasive focus on ownership, payment, and exchange imported from Europe slowly eroded the natural resources of North America. Wilder wrote as if capitalism was ever present and buffalo long extinct, but she and her sisters witnessed immense changes to land, animals, and people. *By the Shores of Silver Lake* recalls the family's life in De Smet in 1879, only one year after the largest southern herd of buffalo was eliminated and four years before the northern herd was completely slaughtered. Regarding what is certain, Dakota tradition would say that more than death and taxes can be counted on. While Pa may only be joking, it is unfortunate that his daughter did not learn the Dakota oral traditions describing how *unktehi*, the powerful water spirit, battles with *wakinyan*, the thunder beings, to create storms until the sun restores peace and balance (Westerman and White 17). Young readers who encounter Laura's story alongside the story of the buffalo can think differently about life in the Dakota. These young readers will one day become the citizens who vote on water, oil, and mineral rights. Perhaps they will work to balance indigenous and nonindigenous geoscientific knowledge with shared economic priorities.

In Wilder's novels, Dakota elders are not invited to teach their language and stories. Too much fear lingered from the 1862 war. Perhaps to acknowledge the continued presence of the Dakota, *By the Shores of Silver Lake* introduces Big Jerry, a "half-breed" with only an English first name. Wilder offers Laura's view of the debate between Ma and Pa about "half-breeds" and whether they can be trusted:

> "I always heard you can't trust a half-breed," Ma said. Ma did not like Indians; she did not like even half-Indians. "We'd all have been scalped down on the Verdigris

> River, if it hadn't been for a full-blood," said Pa. "We wouldn't have been in any danger of scalping if it hadn't been for those howling savages," said Ma, "with fresh skunk skins around their middles." And she made a sound that came from remembering how those skunk skins smelled. "I don't think Jerry steals horses," Pa said. But Laura thought he said it as if he hoped that saying it would make it so. (50)

The argument is framed as a paradigm based on race-based binaries: Indians are either good or bad, and white adults can either appreciate or fear them. The presence of a "half-Indian" supports white notions of blood quantum and enrollment according to the Dawes Act of 1887 rather than Native kinship systems defined by centuries of community use. By speaking of "breeds" and partial ethnicity, Ma and Pa use language that dispossesses Native people, who were not allowed to retain parcels of land if they could not prove they had a high enough quantum. Young readers who learn that Pa and his generation thought of the "half-breeds" as less than human can understand this as a human rights issue. Because American Indians were not US citizens until 1924, the Osage, Ojibwe, and Dakota of the 1880s lacked the same rights as blacks and whites and were treated as enemies of the United States although they were living on land their people had protected for thousands of years. Many college students ask why they do not learn this history when they learn about America's tradition of slavery and involvement in the Holocaust. Reading Wilder's texts in context offers an opportunity to teach about pasts that should not be repeated and continuing issues related to immigration and human rights.

In *The Long Winter*, the family still lives in Dakota Territory, and Laura is between childhood and womanhood. The novel begins when Pa tells Laura that he knows the winter is going to be hard because muskrats always build houses with thick walls before a hard winter. This is verified by a nameless "old Indian" whose dialect appears to be a racist representation until one considers that only the Dakota elder is bilingual.

> "Heap big snow, big wind," he said.
> "How long?" Pa asked him.
> "Many moons," the Indian said. He held up seven fingers. . . .
> "You white men," he said. "I tell-um you." (208)

In keeping with American western semiotics, which regularly depict nameless Indians as disappearing into the sunset, "he walked out of the store to his waiting pony and rode away toward the west" (208), leaving Pa to explain climate oscillation and the nuances of the landscape that predict blizzards.

Often more willing to listen to Indians than other characters are, Pa decides to move the family into town for the winter and mentions to Ma that the family should hurry because he has been warned by an Indian. "'What Indian?' Ma asked him. Without naming the elder he replied, 'There's some good Indians,' Pa always insisted. 'And they know some things that we don't. I'll tell you all about it at supper, Caroline'" (209). But suppertime never comes in the novel, so the Ingallses never hear Pa's promised story of Muskrat, which would offer an opportunity for young readers to find the story and explore what it teaches about living in winter.

Pa, Almanzo, and Laura notice the stars throughout the winter and are occasionally guided by their positions and light, but they do not know that the Dakota are Wicanhpi Oyate, the Star People, whose spirits travel the Canku Wanagi, or Spirit Road—the Milky Way. How much they might have had in common if they had taken time to get to know one another. When Laura notices in spring how "all over the softly green prairie the sloughs were a broken network of water, reflecting the warm, blue sky" (*Winter* 353), she is seeing what the Dakota have known since life began in that place: water is the greatest treasure and source of life on earth. The water, *mni*, is medicine (Westerman and White 19).

Little Town on the Prairie, published in 1941, begins in 1881, just after the long winter. Set in the town of De Smet, Dakota Territory, the story is the twilight of Laura's childhood. Almanzo Wilder begins escorting Laura home from church, and she earns her teaching certificate, solidifying her transition into the world of independent adults. Indians are rarely mentioned, but they are given credit for Ma's idea to preserve the remaining corn: "The hot sun would dry the corn, and next winter, soaked and boiled, it would be good eating. 'That's an Indian idea,' Pa remarked. . . . 'You'll admit yet, Caroline, there's something to be said for Indians.' 'If there is,' Ma replied, 'you've already said it, many's the time, so I needn't'" (427–28).

Published in 1943, as the US government was moving toward terminating treaties and Native nations, *These Happy Golden Years* takes place in the early 1880s, before South Dakota became a state and before the massacre at Wounded Knee. The eighth book in the series, it is perhaps the most explicit about the gold rush and land claim process, represented by the appearance of Uncle Tom Quiner, who confesses to having stayed in the Black Hills illegally until he was escorted out by the US Army (614–17).

For part of the year Laura boards with the Brewsters so that she can take her first teaching assignment. Completing her teaching term, she returns to her family, but the end of childhood is marked by Almanzo's proposal. After he builds a house on his tree claim, the newlyweds settle contentedly into their new home. The bond Laura shares with her family and Wilder's focus on Laura's creation of a family of her own echo the Dakotas' emphasis on kinship. As Dakota anthropologist Ella Deloria wrote, "One must obey kinship rules; one must be a good relative.... Without that aim and constant struggle to attain it, the people would no longer be Dakota in truth. They would no longer be human. To be a good Dakota, then was to be humanized, civilized. And to be civilized was to keep the rules imposed by kinship" (29). If the definition of civilization is to be responsible across generations, then Laura is certainly striving to meet this expectation, but she is unaware that some of the most civilized people on earth, who expanded notions of kinship to the land and water, are living beside her.

LESSONS OF MEMORY AND HISTORY

Laura Ingalls Wilder was shaped by her family's journeys. Her identity was connected to the land that Pa, Almanzo, and other American settlers claimed in Indian Territory. But two terrible mistakes prevented her from knowing the full history of the spaces she inhabited. First, she never allowed Indians to be viewed on their own terms, as part of a shared world. Second, although she clearly noticed and appreciated it, she did not afford any authority to the abundant nonhuman world around her. Every book in the series contains dehumanization and disconnection, and they prevent Laura from moving beyond youthful assertions of justice and a visceral awe of the complex ecosystem around her.

Many readers today wish to excuse little Laura for the sins of her father, but the books were written by a woman who was not uneducated or unaware of American politics. As John E. Miller writes, Wilder and her daughter/collaborator, Rose Wilder Lane, accepted and perpetuated ideas that permeated all aspects of American culture, including the belief that Indians were enemies until they were endangered and believed to be on a path of extinction (154–66).[2] Other authors of the period also accepted and perpetuated these ideas. After the massacre at Wounded Knee in 1890, children's author L. Frank Baum wrote, "The Pioneer has before declared that our only safety depends upon the total extermination of the Indians. Having wronged them for centuries, we had better, in order to protect our civilization, follow it up by one more wrong and wipe these untamed and untamable creatures from the face of the earth." The misunderstanding between European and Native cultures was and remains considerable. At the heart of settler misunderstanding is the concept of property. At the heart of Indian misunderstanding is the concept of connection.

Pioneers saw the land only as property and found only pleasure or fear in new landscapes. The Ojibwe, Osage, and Dakota see in land a connection and have struggled to engender this same respect in others. In *Pioneer Girl*, Wilder writes of "a pair of Indian babies with "bright black eyes" that her younger self "wanted for her very own" (xvi). Laura did not know that the chasm between her world and those Osage children would be the pain inherited by future generations.

At the 1893 Chicago World's Fair, Simon Pokagon distributed a little pamphlet, printed carefully on birch bark and offered as a counterpoint to the official ceremonies. In it he wrote, "On behalf of my people, the American Indians, I hereby declare to you, the pale faced race that has usurped our lands and homes, that we have no spirit to celebrate with you the great Columbian Fair now being held in this Chicago city, the wonder of the world. No; sooner would we hold high joy-day over the grave of our departed fathers, than to celebrate our own funeral, the discovery of America." Both Wilder and Pokagon saw the dawn of the twentieth century as the end of an era, and they knew that the only way to preserve a record of the time was to create history through memories. Wilder's memories became the Little House series. As readers, we can attempt to look between the storms and starlight to glimpse how she was shaped by her location. And we can seek out more of the voices of those who were there before the little house was built and say, *Anpetu dena ded untipi*: "Today we live here." *Heca ohinni undowanpi kte*: "We will always sing." Laura Ingalls Wilder simply did not hear that song. For some, that may be reason to forgo reading her books. For others, it is a challenge to contextualize and include more memories in what is classified as history. What we cannot do is ignore the voices Wilder heard but did not understand as she wrote of the woods, the water, the way the sun rose. The knowledge contained in these places and phenomena is key for the continued survival of the humans, both indigenous and settler descendants, who now share this space on earth.

NOTES

This chapter has benefited from generations of teachers and my memories of reading the Little House books as a child. Searching for quotations, confirmations, and forgotten contradictions, I pulled from the shelves the copies of the book that my grandmother used as a teacher in St. Cloud, Minnesota. Each has a carefully placed bookplate with the image of Laura at age seventy gently smiling across the years, and my grandmother's name, Margaret Orr, written below. Most have a small gold sticker from the Laura Ingalls Wilder Home in Mansfield, Missouri, and an inscription from curators L. D. and Irene V. Lichty. Tucked between the covers are some of the teaching aids, pictures, maps, and clippings my grandmother shared with students. I remember talking about the books with her. I also recall talking about the books with my parents, Terry and Alice O'Donnell, both of whom taught elementary school and in the 1970s and 1980s watched *Little House on the Prairie* with me in Chaska, Minnesota. They taught me to keep asking questions, look harder at history, and learn all versions of any story. Their many innovations included a jingle apron my mother helped create for my father's classroom so that when he taught Ojibwe history and culture, students could take a close look at the curled snuff lids and ponder how they become cones of prayer and hope in a diverse, complex world.

1. Caroline Fraser contextualizes her biography of Wilder through the events of the Dakota War, specifically detailing the events leading up to the conflict, its battles, and its aftermath. Arguing that "the U.S.-Dakota War of 1862 was among the most pivotal in American history," Fraser asserts, "it was not policy or legislation that opened the far west. It was not reasoned debate. It was wrath and righteous retribution that did it, forever changing the contour and condition of the land" (24).

2. This pervasive attitude is evident in the 1836 Great Seal of the Territory of Wisconsin, which includes farmers in the foreground and a Native person in the background with the inscription "Civilitas successitt barbarum" and in the 1849 Great Seal of Minnesota Territory, in which Seth Eastman drew a barefoot farmer and an Indian riding into the setting sun. When Minnesota became a state in 1858, the image was updated but retained the same essential elements. For many years, this image captured the sentiment of the settlers as evidenced by Gertrude Anderson's poem, "The Great Seal of Minnesota" (1944):

> An Indian, mounted on his pony,
> Rides full speed toward the setting sun;
> Behind him, the white man, bending, plowing,
> Visions the glory of work to be done.
> His ax, sunk deep in a near-by tree stump,
> His heavy rifle, lying low. . . .
> Galloping, galloping goes the pony. . . .
> "White man here now; Indian must go."
> Fainter, fainter, the pony's hoofbeats. . . .
> Almost vanished, the Indian horde. . . .
> Freedom! Freedom! The white man's struggle
> Still goes on. L'Etoile du Nord!

WORKS CITED

Anderson, Gary Clayton. *Through Dakota Eyes: Narrative Accounts of the Minnesota Indian War of 1862*. Minnesota Historical Society Press, 1988.

Anderson, Gertrude. "The Great Seal of Minnesota." 1944. League of Minnesota Poets Records, Historical Scrapbook, vol. 1, Minnesota Historical Society.

Baum, L. Frank. "Wounded Knee Editorial." *Saturday Pioneer*, 20 December 1891.

Berg, Scott W. *38 Nooses: Lincoln, Little Crow, and the Beginning of the Frontier's End*. Pantheon, 2013.

Burnett, Ann, and Rhea Rheinhardt Beto. "Reading Romance Novels: An Application of Parasocial Relationship Theory." *North Dakota Journal of Speech and Theatre* 13 (2000): 28–39.

Deloria, Ella. *Speaking of Indians*. Friendship Press, 1944.

"Eunice Sleeman." Edmund Rice (1638) Association, edmund-rice.org. 2002.

Fellman, Anita Clair. *Little House, Long Shadow: Laura Ingalls Wilder's Impact on American Culture*. University of Missouri Press, 2008.

Fraser, Caroline. *Prairie Fires: The American Dreams of Laura Ingalls Wilder*. Metropolitan/Henry Holt, 2017.

Gormley, Myra Vanderpool, and Rhonda R. McClure. "A Genealogical Look at Laura Ingalls Wilder." GenealogyMagazine.com.

Green, Melanie C., and Timothy C. Brock. "The Role of Transportation in the Persuasiveness of Public Narratives." *Journal of Personality and Social Psychology* 79, no. 5 (2000): 701–21.

Heldrich, Philip. "'Going to Indian Territory': Attitudes toward Native Americans in *Little House on the Prairie*." *Great Plains Quarterly* 20, no. 2 (2000): 99–109.

Kaye, Frances W. "Little Squatter on the Osage Diminished Reserve: Reading Laura Ingalls Wilder's Kansas Indians." *Great Plains Quarterly* 20, no. 2 (2000): 123–40.

Little House on the Prairie.com.

Louw, Pat. "Contested Spaces in Laura Ingalls Wilder's *Little House in the Big Woods* and *Little House on the Prairie*." *Mousaion* 29, no. 3 (2011): 166–78.

Matthews, Maureen, with Larry Aitken, Dan Jones, Roger Roulette, and Margaret Simmons. "Thunderbirds." *Ideas*. Canadian Broadcasting Company, 16 May 1995.

Miller, John E. *Laura Ingalls Wilder and Rose Wilder Lane: Authorship, Place, Time, and Culture*. University of Missouri Press, 2008.

Noodin, Margaret. "Language Revitalization, Anishinaabemowin, and Erdrich's *The Birchbark House* Series." In *Frontiers in American Children's Literature*, edited by Dorothy Clark and Linda Salem, 123–32. Cambridge Scholars, 2016.

Osage Nation. *Osage Traveling Trunk Curriculum*. http://osageculturetravelingtrunk.weebly.com.

Pokagon, Simon. *The Red Man's Rebuke*. Engle, 1893.

Romines, Ann. *Constructing the Little House: Gender, Culture, and Laura Ingalls Wilder*. University of Massachusetts Press, 1997.

US Bureau of Indian Affairs. Photostats of documents in the records of the Bureau of Indian Affairs, made by Wisconsin Historical Society, early twentieth century (US Mss BN).

Westerman, Gwen. *Follow the Blackbirds*. Michigan State University Press, 2010.

Westerman, Gwen, and Bruce White. *Mni Sota Makoce: The Land of the Dakota*. Minnesota Historical Society Press, 2012.

Wilder, Laura Ingalls. *By the Shores of Silver Lake*. In Wilder, *Little House Books* 2:1–168.

Wilder, Laura Ingalls. "Laura's Book Fair Speech." In Laura Ingalls Wilder and Rose Wilder Lane, *A Little House Sampler*, edited by William Anderson, 215–24. University of Nebraska Press, 1988.

Wilder, Laura Ingalls. *The Little House Books*. Edited by Caroline Fraser. 2 vols. Library of America, 2012.

Wilder, Laura Ingalls. *Little House in the Big Woods*. In Wilder, *Little House Books* 1:5–95.

Wilder, Laura Ingalls. *Little House on the Prairie*. In Wilder, *Little House Books* 1:269–409.

Wilder, Laura Ingalls. *Little Town on the Prairie*. In Wilder, *Little House Books* 2:371–544.

Wilder, Laura Ingalls. *The Long Winter*. In Wilder, *Little House Books* 2:173–366.

Wilder, Laura Ingalls. *On the Banks of Plum Creek*. In Wilder, *Little House Books* 1:415–578.

Wilder, Laura Ingalls. *These Happy Golden Years*. In Wilder, *Little House Books* 2:549–730.

KAWAII WILDER

Little House in Japan
Emily Anderson and Shosuke Kinugawa

Laura Ingalls Wilder's Little House series is often regarded as quintessentially American. Wilder herself saw her life story as representative of America's story.[1] In her groundbreaking study of Little House's role in American culture, Anita Clair Fellman describes the novels' use in a variety of public and private contexts, including schools, libraries, and homes. "More and more," she concludes, "in a variety of settings, Wilder's books serve as the means by which Americans reconstruct their own history" (216). Despite the fact that much of the novels' appeal is the aura of national history they transmit, the Little House series is also popular internationally. Wilder's novels have been translated into forty languages and were used in postwar Japan and Germany to teach democracy (Suzuki 67). The 1974–82 NBC television adaptation has been broadcast globally, and its actors have received Spain's TP de Oro (a major television award) and continue to appear on talk shows in France (Arngrim "Chapter 18"). Alison Arngrim, who played Nellie Oleson on the show, has received fan letters from "every country" and maintains that Saddam Hussein watched the show ("Introduction").

Assuming that the sense of participating in an American legacy diminishes outside of the United States, why does the Little House series appeal to international audiences? This essay studies the books' reception in Japan, where the franchise has become deeply ingrained in popular culture. As John E. Miller observes, "One of the most intriguing aspects of the Wilder phenomenon is the popularity she enjoys in many foreign countries, especially Japan" (1). The

Japanese translation of *The Long Winter* (1943), the sixth novel in the series and the first to be translated, was published in 1949 (Suzuki 65). On its title page, Wilder included a special message of hope (and her home address) for her readers in a nation devastated by World War II (68). Japanese readers have subsequently embraced the rest of the series. For example, William Anderson's *Laura Ingalls Wilder Country* (1988), a photo essay about Wilder's homesites, was quickly available in Japanese for fans who were unable to travel to the United States (Taniguchi). More recently, the South Dakota Historical Society Press announced that the first offer for the rights to translate the bestselling *Pioneer Girl: The Annotated Autobiography of Laura Ingalls Wilder* (2014) came from Japan. Nancy Tystad Koupal, the press's director, stated that this "does not strike anybody in the Wilder world as odd" because "the Japanese are avid fans of the Little House books and they have all been translated into Japanese" (Lee).

In spite of Wilder's widespread popularity, however, scholarship on Wilder's reception in Japan has remained focused primarily on the books' initial introduction during the aftermath of World War II. Hence, apart from Hisayo Ogushi's work, Wilder's reception beyond the early 1950s has rarely been addressed. Moreover, the study of Wilder's reception in Japan has focused on translations rather than adaptations. Drawing from scholarship in both English and Japanese, this essay examines Wilder's cultural impact in Japan from 1949 through the present across neglected modes of reception, including dollhouses, homeware, interior design, and quilting practices. Although Wilder's novels may not have had the aura of national history that helps endear the books to US readers, the books benefited from a different affective conduit to the hearts and minds of the Japanese audience. The novels are successful in Japan because they are congruent with the Japanese aesthetic category of *kawaii*, which roughly translates as "cute," "endearing," and "adorable."[2] In other words, Wilder's works depict American characters in a distinctively American landscape but resonate with an existing Japanese aesthetic tradition.

Two traits of that aesthetic have remained consistent: littleness and the figure of the young girl, or *shojo* (*sho* literally translates as "little," *jo* as "girl"). Katharine Slater demonstrates that for US readers, Wilder's careful descriptions of little cakes and cozy houses evoke longing for both childhood and a vanished national history. In Japan, however, these elements take on a different significance. One of the signature traits of Japanese adaptations is that they magnify and exaggerate the cozy, cute, and little elements of Wilder's novels, an alteration that reflects *kawaii* culture.

The adaptations, however, also contribute to the evolution of *kawaii* culture by expanding its scope. Specifically, the Little House series became an essential text for the Japanese version of the home decor and lifestyle concept commonly referred to as American Country, a subset of the *kawaii* aesthetic. Noting Wilder's meticulous depiction of the home in *Prairie*, Slater argues that Wilder's "aesthetics of homemaking" allow the little and the cozy to work together with the epic and the political, ultimately evoking nostalgia for a national history that "embodies the quintessential and ideal American spirit" (68). However, some Japanese women fans modify these images of the home and homemaking to satisfy a more personal motive—that is, to reflect the desire to physically re-create the Little House world within their homes.

Thus, these adaptations satisfy nostalgia by allowing adult women to relive their childhoods through domestic labor. The adaptations, however, also constitute female fans' attempts to conceive of domestic labor as a means of expressing creative autonomy while maintaining their place in traditional domestic roles. While contemporary *kawaii* culture is typically regarded as the province of the *shojo*, some of its key participants are mature, adult women engaging in domestic work. Ultimately, understanding Wilder's reception in Japan in the context of *kawaii* culture contributes to both Wilder studies and the study of *kawaii* by shedding light on the reasons for Wilder's ongoing popular appeal outside of the United States as well as by revealing a novel point of intersection between American literature and Japanese culture.

Kawaii commonly describes things that seem vulnerable, imperfect, innocent, or immature. *Kawaii* objects and figures evoke tenderness, affection, and pity. They are often small and roundish and soft and plastic and convey familiarity. Hello Kitty, the global ambassador of *kawaii*, embodies all these features. Similarly, a baby is quintessentially *kawaii*, as are stuffed animals and puppies.

While common in contemporary Japanese vocabulary, *kawaii* has ancient roots. The word's etymological predecessor is said to be *kawayushi*, meaning "shameful" or "pitiful" (*kawaisou*), and later "cute" ("Kawayui"). The term is found in Japanese literature as early as the *Konjaku Monogatarishū*, a twelfth-century anthology of myths, folktales, and legends. Prior to *kawayushi*, however, *utsukushi* was used to describe qualities that we now refer to as *kawaii* ("Utsukushi"). One of its earliest usages appears in *Taketori Monogatari*, a classic Japanese prose narrative likely created around the late ninth century, during the early Heian era ("Utsukushi"). The word describes the diminutive size of the tale's protagonist, Kaguya-hime, a princess roughly ten centimeters tall who is sent to Earth from the moon. Here already, two enduring characteristics of *kawaii* are foregrounded: littleness and the *shojo* (young girl) figure. While *kawaii* is an ancient aesthetic, its contemporary iteration retains the emphasis on the *shojo* figure. *Shojo* frequently appears in contemporary discourses about *kawaii* in phrases such as *shojo shumi* (girlish taste) and *shojo manga* (a subgenre of manga centered around *shojo* characters).

The discussion of the history of *kawaii* aesthetic often begins with the work of Sei Shōnagon, an eleventh-century Japanese writer and lady of the court. Theorists of *kawaii* such as Inuhiko Yomota point to Sei's *Makura no Soushi*, a classic explaining Sei's daily thoughts and observations, as providing a detailed subdivision of *kawaii* things and actions that are iconic expressions of early *kawaii* sensibility (29–33). For Sei, littleness is the essence of *kawaii*: "Absolutely anything that is tiny is endearing [*utsukushi*]" (149). Sei also suggests that the *kawaisa* of physical littleness is magnified when little people and animals perform little tasks with little things, such as a baby picking up "tiny worthless things" (149). Sei's *kawaii*, then, can be defined as the feeling that arises when one observes a physically small being engaging in minor tasks involving little objects. Little is *kawaii* by default. Little in action is more *kawaii*.

This ancient penchant for *kawaii* remains enmeshed in contemporary Japanese life. In *"Kawaii" Ron* (2006), one of the few book-length studies on the theme of *kawaii*, Yomota argues that Sei's description shows how the "sense of intimacy that the Japanese extend toward small, *kawaii* things has not changed at all for more than a thousand years" (33).[3] In 2014, the popular Japanese lifestyle magazine *Pen* published an issue on "'Kawaii' Japan" that examined *kawaii*'s increasing global ubiquity as an aesthetic category. "Today, 'Kawaii' is sweeping the world," claims *Pen*, yet the term also remains deeply Japanese, used by "the young and the old" and therefore "appropriate to call the motto of Japanese culture" (36).

Readers familiar with the Little House series will recognize clear parallels between the *kawaii* aesthetic and the emphasis on the little and the cute within the home present in Wilder's work. For example, both Sei and Wilder highlight domestic details. Just as Sei provides emotionally resonant descriptions of children handling trifling objects, Wilder describes two little girls dividing a cookie and a handful of beads to share with their infant sister. While Japanese readers may interpret the Little House works differently than US readers, Wilder's emphasis on girls, littleness, and details of domestic life provide a basis for cross-cultural comparison.

The Little House series' initial introduction into Japan, however, was motivated not by aesthetics but by politics. General Douglas MacArthur, head of the US military occupation of Japan after World War II, may have decided (on his wife's advice) that *The Long Winter* would be useful to helping establish Japanese democracy (Suzuki 66–67). The occupying Allied forces established the emancipation of women as a cornerstone of democratization in Japan's new constitution and apparently saw *The Long Winter* as befitting this objective despite the fact that it depicted "separate spheres" gender ideology (73–75).

Noriko Suzuki argues that for Japanese readers, *The Long Winter* simultaneously elevates and constricts women. On the one hand, *The Long Winter* "rationaliz[es] the patriarchal gender relationship between the sexes in which women belong to the domestic sphere and men to the public" (72). On the other hand, readers likely admired how Ma "actively exercises her creativity within the domestic sphere," interpreting her creativity as representing how American women enjoyed "autonomy in their sphere as wives and mothers" (76). "In short," Suzuki concludes, "the patriarchal family system in *The Long Winter* showed the Japanese readers a hope for reclaiming women's status within the very patriarchal family system" (76).

As the Little House series became increasingly popular, Japanese women moved from admiring the Ingalls women's domestic creativity to incorporating similar acts of creativity into the material of their own symbolic exercise of autonomy within the patriarchal household. Japanese female fans both read about and idealized the domestic space and labor of the Ingalls women and attempted to physically re-create it within their households. From cooking and quilting like Ma to mimicking the Ingallses' furnishings, fans began to literally bring Little House into their homes.

Understanding this process, however, requires considering the *kawaii* culture of the 1970s, when it rose to the foreground of Japanese popular culture. *Kawaii* culture continued to emphasize the *shojo* but also absorbed influences from American culture, enabling the Little House series to play a unique role in the development of *kawaii* culture.

In his ethnography of *shojo* culture, *Shojo Minzokugaku* (1989), Eiji Ōtsuka designates the 1970s as the "Big Bang of Shojo Culture" and points to the phenomenon as the primary agent through which contemporary "'kawaii culture'" developed (49).[4] While recognizing that *shojo* culture is "too heterogeneous" to be monolithic, Ōtsuka focuses on the relationship between young girls and the market targeting them with *shojo* products that places a premium on *kawaii* such as *shojo manga*, magazines, accessories, dolls, clothes, and homeware (52–60).

An important feature of 1970s *kawaii* aesthetic is the impact of Western culture. Shinji Miyadai, Hideki Ishihara, and Akiko Ōtsuka argue that one element of contemporary *kawaii* aesthetic is young girls' *roman-ka* ("romanticization" or, more prosaically, "to make romantic") of the world (43). Here, *romanticization* means the act of imagining "rooms, cityscapes, trees, small objects" as part of a fictional world set in the historical past of a vaguely Anglo-American or European place (43). For example, romanticization could involve pretending to be living an "early American lifestyle" (43). Here, "early American" refers not necessarily to the colonial era or a specific historical period but instead to the preindustrial era generally. Fiction depicting nineteenth-century North American frontier life was evoked as settings for romanticization, like *Anne of Green Gables* (1908), as Miyadai, Ishihara, and Ōtsuka suggest, or the Little House series.

Marketers of *kawaii* goods provided products that satisfied the need for romanticization. In *Shojo Minzokugaku*, Ōtsuka introduces a Tokyo-based homeware store, Life Shop Many, as the "nearly perfect realization" of a *shojo*'s room imagined as a "cosmos of *kawaii* things" (76). According to *Nostalgic na Zakka no Mise yori* (2005), a chronicle of the store's history, the shop opened in 1978 (74) and developed into an import retail franchise promoting a lifestyle revolving around antique or antique-themed homeware and furniture of mainly French, British, and North American origin or designed to resemble such items. To this day, the store sells "kawaii toys and zakka" (62) ready for use as props to re-create the atmosphere of an idealized, old-fashioned Western household with a *kawaii* emphasis.

While Ōtsuka claims that Life Shop Many's products are used strictly for decorating young girls' rooms because they are "almost too *kawaii*" (76) for the kitchen, *Nostalgic* reveals that these items were marketed toward adult women for both aesthetic and practical purposes. *Nostalgic* repeatedly emphasizes that the store's *kawaii* products are not just props but real tools to be used in daily domestic work. In fact, their use as tools enhances their emotional appeal: "It is through use that *zakka* become increasingly endearing" (20).

Along with their value as usable homeware, Life Shop Many's *kawaii* home goods are marketed as devices for reliving personal memories (*Nostalgic* 12, 18, 80). Childhood recollections of mothers performing domestic chores are particularly emphasized: "There is a time when girls watch very enviously as mothers cook. For that reason, miniature tea sets and stores were ideal toys. And even after becoming adults, they are still in love with playing house. Women are forever in love with the 'little and the kawaii'" (64; see also 5, 38, 68). By purchasing the proper "tools" for the job, women connect with and even become their childhood selves, presenting their continued love for the domestic, the little, and the *kawaii* as a sign that they remain *shojo*.

The *Little House on the Prairie* television series plays a crucial role at this junction between desire for childhood nostalgia and romanticization. The series' arrival coincided with *kawaii* culture's move into the forefront of Japanese popular culture as well as with the development of children of the 1950s into independent cultural consumers and producers, enabling the show to capitalize on audiences' childhood nostalgia for Wilder instilled through the introduction of her novels in the 1950s. But the television series also became a part of the childhood memories of girls who grew up watching it in reruns.[5] Together with their forerunners of the 1970s, these girls went on to create a subgenre of *kawaii* culture in which adult women seek to revive their Little House experiences in their homes.

Kawaii culture, childhood nostalgia, early American decor, and the Little House series fused into the American Country aesthetic, which re-creates the home environment of American frontier life in contemporary Japanese households. This aesthetic favors quaint, antique, or antique-style homeware and furniture made of natural material but with a distinctly *kawaii* bent, as represented by Life Shop Many's products. The American Country aesthetic can be observed holistically in the Japanese lifestyle magazine *Watashi no Kantorii* [*My Country*], which started in 1991 as a quarterly specializing in country-style home decor. Adult women—not girls—are the publication's primary audience. With a recent circulation of twenty thousand, the magazine continues to promote country aesthetics to a large Japanese audience ("Insatsubusuu Kohyo") and explicitly identifies the Little House television series as the "origin" of American Country.

Watashi often reminds its readers of the ties between the Little House series and American Country. Their magazine's tenth anniversary issue, for example, was a travelogue, "American Kantorii no Genryu ga Shiritakute: Daisougen no Chiisana Ie, sono kiseki wo tadoru [In Search of the Origin of American Country/*Little House on the Prairie*, Tracing Its Tracks]," and includes a map of Wilder homesites in Pepin, Wisconsin; Walnut Grove, Minnesota; and De Smet, South Dakota, including directions to nearby antique stores. In 2011, *Watashi* celebrated its twentieth anniversary by again honoring the Little House series, publishing the first installment of an eight-part photonarrative with the purpose of "reflecting once again on this story, which can be said to be the origin of country life" ("Mo ichido" 11).

Watashi's readers frequently mention that the Little House novels and television series provided inspiration for decorating homes in American Country style. Yoko Arai, whose home was featured in the magazine, became aware of American Country style through the television series and a spice rack she bought at Life Shop Many ("Yokoso" 27). Keiko Abe, whose home received *Watashi*'s "Good Old Country Award," has loved the television version since she was a *shojo* and was particularly enthralled with the "lifestyle of the western frontier era and the simple interior" ("Abe Keiko" 23). Another woman's apartment is likened to the show's houses, with the woman describing her home as a "small house of the frontier age" ("Chiisana" 67). A 2014 interior decor handbook published by *Watashi* features a woman who paneled her apartment with wooden boards because she wanted it to "resemble closely as possible Laura's house in *Little House on the Prairie*" (*Sweet Home* 72).

Such an environment allows occupants to immerse themselves in their nostalgia for the Little House novels and television show, enveloped in the *kawaii* prairie narratives they loved as children. Occupants of an American Country home romanticize their environment with *kawaii* homeware to stand in the place of *shojo* Laura and thus become *kawaii*. Such homes help women connect emotionally with Laura as well as their *shojo* selves. If the past US readers seek in Little House is a public past—the history of the nation—Japanese fans look to a past that is exclusively private.

History, however, is valuable not just for nostalgia but also for making things more *kawaii*. *Watashi* readers share the sentiment of Life Shop Many's owners: the longer tools are used, the more endearing they become because usage brings about wear, and wear creates the need for care. The store's owners repeatedly emphasize that the products they cherish are those that show signs of wear and fragility and therefore require careful maintenance. Antique furniture may be "chipped or rusted" but nevertheless has a purpose "in daily life" (*Nostalgic* 20). In selling European toy homeware made of real porcelain, the store sends a message that "'one must take care of things'" (61) so that they last. Life Shop Many's products depend on their owners for survival, thereby increasing the items' *kawaisa* for those owners. Likewise, American Country aficionados repeatedly express their penchant for used and for reusing old (or old-looking) things that require care and attention. Fragility marks these items as objects in need of protection and in turn marks the owners as guardians, generating the tenderness and affection that are the hallmark of *kawaii* sensibility.

Echoing preindustrial times, the American Country aesthetic prefers handmade things over mass-produced products, and fans replicate the make-do mentality of frontier life that the Little House series depicts. While Wilder may have represented handcraft as an expression of ingenuity born out of material necessity, the emphasis on the handmade is important for the American Country aesthetic because it connects domestic labor with creativity. The things that women who pursue the American Country aesthetic design and make are not only work tools but art. For example, the spring 2001 issue of *Watashi* instructs readers how to make American Country–style home furnishing goods such as welcome plates, baskets, curtains, and bread holders (36–44). Most issues of *Watashi* include similar sections along with other home furnishing tips, complemented by books like *Sweet Home* specifically devoted to satisfying the impulse to make things by hand. Through their efforts to create a more *kawaii* version of Little House homes, the women affirm the creativity of housework in a way that parallels Wilder's validation of women, whose domestic work transforms a cabin into a "real" home.

The American Country style, then, is an aesthetic that can be a creative platform for Japanese women even as it relies on the traditional patriarchal gendering of the domestic sphere. The combination of *kawaii* and Little House materializes into a home furnishing art in which the home becomes a canvas that allows women to express their creativity via handcrafts and renovations that mimic *kawaii* frontier homes. Daniel Harris calls the television version of *Little House on the Prairie* "a manifesto of quaintness" (25) and argues that the making-do (or ad hoc) feeling of quaint objects converts domestic work into creative, poetic acts. Therefore, many twentieth-century homes become "massive, site-specific art installation projects" that serve as a stage for "play-acting" in "the theater of quaintness" (41). In crafting their homes in the image of the Ingalls household, many Japanese women not only re-create Ma's domestic space but also reenact her making-do ethos. In so doing, they develop a subculture that allows them to assert their agency as artists, consumers, and aesthetic connoisseurs even within the confines of daily domestic labors.

While *Watashi* attempts to present a holistic view of American Country and its link to Little House, other adaptations focus on specific aspects of the domestic sphere, emphasizing the *kawaisa* of Laura, the *shojo* protagonist.[6] For example, Little House fans and devotees of American Country who want to cook like Ma can turn to *Laura no Oryouri Nouto* [*Laura's Cookbook*] (1991) (Homma and Homma). The *kawaisa* of this book is emphasized by its focus on the little *shojo*, Laura, which is emphasized from the opening pages through a quote (translated into Japanese) from the first sentence of *Little House in the Big Woods*: "Once upon a time, a hundred years ago, a little girl lived in the Big Woods of Wisconsin, in a little gray house made of logs" (3). The cover illustration features Laura holding a butter churn with a handle taller than she is, a visual contrast that highlights Laura's littleness. The emphasis on Laura continues throughout the book: *Laura's* family, *Laura's* mother, *Laura's* father, *Laura's* era (26, 27, 48, 60, 106). The same foregrounding of Laura as a *kawaii* figure is evident in *Dōru Hausu: Laura no Chiisana Ie* [*Doll House: Laura's Little House*] (1998) (Murakami), a photodocumentary of dollhouse replicas of the Ingallses' homes. Again, it is *Laura's* little house. The dollhouse replica points to an analogical relationship between the book's (presumed) *shojo* reader and its starring prairie *shojo*. Magnifying Laura's already conspicuous role in the stories adds *kawaisa* to the adaptations by packaging the book as the experiences of a little girl rather than a family.

The use of a *kawaii* little girl as the focal point of these books is part of an overarching pattern of Wilder's Japanese reception: the fixation on the *Little House*. The titles of the original works foreground littleness by describing the house as "little," in contrast to threatening, expansive spaces (prairie, big woods). The Ingallses and their homes feel little and vulnerable by default. *Little House on the Prairie* offers readers dollhouse-like scenes: as the Ingallses await a roof on their newly erected cabin, sunlight flows through the open window holes and makes "every crack in the four walls glow a little" (299). The holes in the walls and thin canvas roof enable readers, who literally tower over the text, to inspect the little house, holding in their hands the book as they imagines the little diorama Wilder stages: "The beds [are] neatly made on the floor. The wagon-seat and two ends of logs [are used] for chairs. Pa's gun [lies] on its pegs above the doorway" (299). With such scenes placed inside the already compact space of a book, the smallness of the virtual Little House world is made twofold. Wilder's cultivation of littleness and the dollhouse-like presentation of spaces in the novels make Little House ripe for incorporation into *kawaii* culture.

Dōru Hausu makes the Little House houses little. The book consists of photographs of miniature replicas of "Laura's house" and includes a replica of the Little Town of Walnut Grove (16). Dioramas embedded in small, enclosed spaces further emphasize the littleness of the original Little House world: a one-room house built inside a basket; a miniature classroom nestled inside a desk drawer; a "collection box" filled with tiny replicas of the everyday items used by the Ingalls family. If readers miss the entire book's puns on the *Little House*, a section on "Decorating the 'Little World'" features a picture of a Christmas wreath with "little wreaths" and "little tableware" snuggled inside (36, 37). The miniature world of *Dōru Hausu* materializes readers' appreciation of littleness in the original series, giving physical shape to the original works' littleness.

The adaptations not only present readers with visual representations of miniature Little House homes and homeware but also encourage readers to participate in its materialization. The "Komono Catalog" (*ko* meaning "little" and *mono* meaning "things") that concludes *Dōru Hausu* is a two-page spread filled with miniature replicas of homeware used in the Little House stories. The catalog is followed by instructions for manufacturing the homeware, furniture, and houses that appear in the book. In *Daisogen no Chiisana Ie no Kiruto no aru Kurashi* [*Life with Quilts in "Little House on the Prairie"*] (2004), Japanese quilt artist Emiko Furusawa catalogs her Wilder-themed blankets, bags, pouches, clothes, and other accessories and provides patterns so that readers can make their own quilts.[7]

These adaptations allow fans to participate in the Little House world by giving it physical shape, mimicking what the characters do, making what they make, collecting what they have, living where they live, all the while emphasizing their littleness and Laura's *shojo* perspective. The home becomes a theater that doubles as a portal to childhood and a creative conduit that allows women to participate in a variety of cultural communities revolving around the Little House series and the aesthetic of homemaking.

The fixation on *kawaii*, despite its connotations of innocence and childhood, does not constitute a refusal to grow up. Rather, it allows contemporary Japanese women working in domestic spheres to view housework as an artistic endeavor and avoiding having their efforts overlooked as anonymous labor. Sharon Kinsella emphasizes that *kawaii* is almost unique among global youth and pop culture movements because, unlike punk or hip-hop, it is led by women, not young men (243). She argues that *kawaii* aesthetic "is a passive-aggressive (aka, aggressive) refusal to grow up and assume work, family and social responsibilities ... and that it places the value of the single, fun-having woman against the value of the dutiful, hard-working husband" (242, 243). While Kinsella, like many theorists, focuses on young girls' role in *kawaii* culture, the relationship between the American Country lifestyle and *kawaii* culture shows that participants in *kawaii* included and in fact was developed by mature, adult women.

While these activities afford new means of social participation for women, they also do not directly challenge sociopolitical structures limiting women's political or economic agency and often reinforce and aestheticize women's roles in the domestic sphere. These *kawaii* adaptations do not take us very far from Wilder's initial Japanese reception, where women's status was simultaneously elevated and constricted. The gender contradictions inherent in both Wilder's novels and *kawaii* culture continue to play out on the little, private stages of American Country–style Japanese homes.

For centuries, *kawaii* has motivated Japanese people to actively seek out and examine littleness as a source of aesthetic pleasure. The Little House adaptations magnify and appreciate domestic things and tasks. The aesthetic of housework becomes the root of a lifestyle culture popularized by shops and magazines and materialized within domestic spaces across Japan. The adaptations provide an inventory of Little House littleness that satisfies the desire for the small and the detailed. In finding and adapting Wilder's *kawaisa*, Japanese Little House fans draw Wilder and her national tradition into an aesthetic tradition that is both ancient and keenly relevant for contemporary global pop culture. As the critical conversation around Wilder examines her social meaning, an awareness of how the littleness and femininity expressed in Wilder's works manifests in the imagination and daily lives of Japanese readers (particularly women) provides a broader view of how Little House has survived—and thrived—like the Ingalls family, in an unfamiliar environment.

NOTES

1. In a 1937 speech at book fair in Detroit, Wilder defined her frontier experiences as inspiring her writing: "In my own life I represented a whole period in American history" (qtd. in Wilder and Lane 217).
2. Unless otherwise indicated, all translations from Japanese to English are by the authors.
3. Scholarship on Japanese visual arts from the seventeenth-century Edo era to the twentieth century supports Yomota's claim. In *Kawaii Rinpa* (2014), Nobue Mito examines the representation of *kawaii* aesthetic in paintings of the Rinpa school (94–101). In the introduction to *Kawaii Edo Kaiga* (2013), Nobuhisa Kaneko outlines the history of *kawaii* sensibility in Japanese visual arts from the late Heian era through the early nineteenth century, pointing to *Makura* as among the earliest manifestations of the sensibility. Kaneko shows, for example, that the "sense of endearment towards 'small things'" shared among people "produced various kinds of miniatures during the Edo era," such as exquisitely detailed miniature *emakis* (illustrated scrolls) (80–81). However, Masahiko Abe cautions against seeing *kawaii* as a universal Japanese aesthetic (90–93).
4. Kazuma Yamane's *Hentaishojomoji no Kenkyu* (1986) is often cited as initiating scholarship on contemporary *kawaii* culture. The book studies *hentaishojomoji* (girlish characters), a term invented by Yamane for Japanese characters written in roundish, *kawaii* manner that enjoyed popularity among girls in the late 1970s. Ōtsuka claims that *hentaishojomoji* is a manifestation of shifts in *shojo* culture that occurred in the 1970s. According to Ōtsuka, *shojo* culture rapidly increased its *kawaisa* as the result of two expansions in aspects of the market targeting young girls. First, "fancy business"—commercial enterprises involving products anchored around *kawaii* merchandise, particularly *kawaii* characters—grew (53). Sanrio led the trend, opening a Fancy Shop in 1973 and introducing Hello Kitty the following year. These years coincided with the golden age of *shojo manga*. The works of Moto Hagio, Keiko Takemiya, and Yumiko Oshima, whose *kawaii* themes and techniques became cornerstones for subsequent *shojo manga*, rapidly expanded the market during the 1970s. This expansion of the *shojo* market, Ōtsuka argues, pushed *kawaii* into the forefront of Japanese youth culture.
5. The initial show was broadcast for eight years, with a new series beginning in April 1991 ("Daisougen" 2011). NHK bought broadcasting rights for all nine seasons of the HD version of the TV drama and began airing season 1 on 2 May 2016 ("Daisougen" 2016).
6. Although a 1975–76 anime adaptation of Wilder, *Sougen no Shojo Laura* [*Laura the Prairie Girl*] falls outside the scope of this essay, the title explicitly positions Laura as a *shojo*.
7. Furusawa is not the only quilter inspired by Little House. Teresa Duryea Wong describes Japanese quilters' appreciation of the quilting scenes in the television version of Little House and points out that the show was honored with a special exhibition at the Tokyo Dome's 2014 annual quilting festival, which 250,000 people attended.

WORKS CITED

"Abe Keiko san no 'American *Kantorii* wo Aisuru Kurashi' [Abe Keiko's 'Life Cherishing American Country']." *Watashi no Kantorii* 79 (Winter 2011): 22–27.

Abe, Masahiko. *Osanasa to iu Senryaku: "Kawaii" to Seijyuku no Monogatari-saho [Tactic of Immaturity: The Narrative Methodology of "Kawaii" and Maturity]*. Asahi Shimbun, 2015.

"Akage no shitei, Kokki wo Mochifu ni Shita Pureto." *Watashi no Kantorii* 36 (Spring 2001): 24–25.

"American Kantorii no Genryu ga Shiritakute: Daisougen no Chiisana Ie, sono kiseki wo tadoru [In Search of the Origin of American Country: *Little House on the Prairie*, Tracing Its Tracks]." *Watashi no Kantorii* 36 (Spring 2001): 51–72.

Anderson, William. *Laura Ingalls Wilder Country*. Harper Perennial, 1988.

Arngrim, Alison. *Confessions of a Prairie Bitch: How I Survived Nellie Oleson and Learned to Love Being Hated*. Kindle ed. IT Books, 2011.

"Chiisana Ie ni koso Shiawase wa Yadorimasu [It Is in Little Houses That Happiness Presides]." *Watashi no Kantorii* 81 (Summer 2012): 66–75.

"Daisougen No Chiisana Ie." NHK Archives. 24 June 2011. https://www.nhk.or.jp/archives/search/special/detail/?d=drama016.

"'Daisougen No Chiisana Ie' Zen 9 Shizun no Hosouken—Haishinken wo Shutoku." NHK Enterprise. 20 March 2016. https://www.nhk-ep.co.jp/topics/release-little-house-160330/.

Fellman, Anita Clair. *Little House, Long Shadow: Laura Ingalls Wilder's Impact on American Culture*. University of Missouri Press, 2008.

Furusawa, Emiko. *Daisogen no Chiisana Ie no Kiruto no aru Kurashi [Life with Quilts in "Little House on the Prairie"]*. Shufu to Seikatsu-sha, 2004.

Harris, Daniel. *Cute, Quaint, Hungry, and Romantic: The Aesthetics of Consumerism*. Da Capo, 2000.

Homma, Chieko, and Nagayo Homma. *Laura no Oryouri Nouto [Laura's Cooking Notebook]*. 1981. Bunka Shuppan Kyoku, 1991.

"Insatsubusu Kohyo." *Japan Magazine Publishers Association*. 2018. https://www.j-magazine.or.jp/user/printed/index.

Kaneko, Nobuhisa. "Kawaii e no Ronri to Rekishi [The Logic and History of Kawaii Painting]." In *Kawaii Edo Kaiga [Cute Edo Paintings]*, ed. Fuchu-shi Art Museum, 7–20. Kyuryudo, 2013.

"'Kawaii' Japan." *Pen: With New Attitude* 568 (October 2014).

"Kawayui." In *Nihongodaijiten*, 374. Tokyo: Shogakukan, 2005.

Kinsella, Sharon. "Cuties in Japan." In *Women, Media, and Consumption in Japan*, ed. Lise Skov and Brian Moeran, 220–54. University of Hawaii Press, 1996.

Lee, Stephen. "SD Historical Society Press Ready to Sell Rights for First Translation of 'Pioneer Girl.'" *Capital Journal*, 28 April 2016.

Miller, John E. *Becoming Laura Ingalls Wilder: The Woman behind the Legend*. University of Missouri Press, 1998.

Mito, Nobue. *Kawaii Rimpa [Rimpa-Kawaii! Engaging Japanese Art]*. 2014. Tokyo Bijyutsu, 2015.

Miyadai, Shinji, Hideki Ishihara, and Akiko Ōtsuka. *Subculture Shinwa Kaitai: Shojo-Ongaku-Manga—Sei no 30 nen to Communication no Genzai [Analysis of the Myth of Subculture: 30 Years of Shojo-Music-Sex and Communication Today]*. Parco Shuppan Kyoku, 1993.

"Mo ichido yomitai Daisougen no Chiisana Ie [*Little House on the Prairie*: A Tale We Want to Reread]." *Watashi no Kantorii* 76 (Spring 2001): 10–13.

Murakami, Kazuaki. *Dōru Hausu: Laura no Chiisana Ie [Doll House: Laura's Little House]*. Nihon Hoso Shuppan Kyokai, 1998.

Nostalgic na Zakka no Mise yori: maison de many no Monogatari [*From a Nostalgic Zakka Store: The Story of Maison de Many*]. Shufu to Seikatsu-Sha, 2005.

Ogushi, Hisayo. "Little House in the Far East: The American Frontier Spirit and Japanese Girls' Comics." *Japanese Journal of American Studies* 27 (2016): 21–44.

Ōtsuka, Eiji. *Shojo Minzokugaku: Seikimatsu no Shinwa wo Tsumugu "Miko no Matsuei"* [*Shojo Ethnology: The "Descendent of the Miko" Who Creates the Myth of the Century's End*]. 1989. Kobunsha, 1991.

Romines, Ann. *Constructing the Little House: Gender, Culture, and Laura Ingalls Wilder.* University of Massachusetts Press, 1997.

Sei Shōnagon. *The Pillow Book.* Trans. Meredith McKinney. Penguin, 2006.

Slater, Katharine. "'Now We're All Snug!': The Regionalism of *Little House on the Prairie.*" *Genre* 47, no. 1 (2014): 55–77.

"Sougen No Shojo Laura." *Nippon Animation Official Site.* http://www.nippon-animation.co.jp/work/937/.

Suzuki, Noriko. "Japanese Democratization and the Little House Books: The Relation between General Headquarters and *The Long Winter* in Japan after World War II." *Children's Literature Association Quarterly* 31, no.1 (2006): 65–86.

Sweet Home: Furui—Semai—Chintaijyutaku no heyazukuri aidea 180. Shu to Seikatsu-Sha, 2014.

Taniguchi, Yumiko. "Translations of Laura's Books into Japanese." Paper presented at Laurapalooza, South Dakota State University, Brookings, 17 July 2015.

"Utsukushi." In *Kogodaijiten*, 424–25. Kadokawa, 1982.

Wilder, Laura Ingalls. *The Little House Books.* Edited by Caroline Fraser. Vol. 1. Library of America, 2012.

Wilder, Laura Ingalls, and Rose Wilder Lane. *A Little House Sampler.* Edited by William Anderson. Harper and Row, 1988.

Wong, Teresa Duryea. "Learning to Quilt in Japan: *Little House on the Prairie* Influenced a Whole Generation." Little House on the Prairie.com. http://littlehouseontheprairie.com/learning-to-quilt-in-japan-little-house-on-the-prairie-influenced-a-whole-generation/.

Yamane, Kazuma. *Hentaishojomoji no Kenkyu* [*A Study of Hentaishojo Characters*]. Kodansha, 1986.

"Yokoso! Waga itoshi no American kantorii libing e [Welcome! To My Endearing American Country Life]." *Watashi no Kantorii* 36 (Spring 2001): 14–27.

Yomota, Inuhiko. *"Kawaii" Ron* [*Theory of "Kawaii"*]. 2006. Chikumashobo, 2012.

CONTRIBUTORS

Emily Anderson holds a doctorate from the University of Buffalo. Her writing has appeared in a variety of publications, including *Harper's*, *The Atlantic*, and *The Kenyon Review*. She is the author of *Little: Novels* (BlazeVOX, 2015), which reimagines Wilder's Little House novels. She was recently elected to public office and serves as a member of the city council in Eau Claire, Wisconsin.

Elif S. Armbruster is an associate professor of English at Suffolk University and researches and teaches nineteenth- and early twentieth-century American literature, women's writing, and immigrant literature. She is the author of *Domestic Biographies: Stowe, Howells, James, and Wharton at Home* (Lang, 2011) and wrote the introductions for and edited the Barnes and Noble editions of Wharton's *Summer* (2006) and Stowe's *Uncle Tom's Cabin* (2012). Most recently she published two pieces in *Critical Insights: Edith Wharton* (Salem Press, 2017) and has an essay forthcoming in the *Oxford Handbook of American Literary Realism*.

Jenna Brack teaches English at Metropolitan Community College–Penn Valley in Kansas City, Missouri. She holds a master's degree in English with an emphasis in composition, rhetoric, and literature from Kansas State University. Her research interests include teaching and learning, composition studies, and first-year student success.

Christine Cooper-Rompato is an associate professor of English at Utah State University, where she directs the graduate program in English. A medievalist who works primarily in the areas of religious studies and medieval England, she is also interested in the nineteenth-century United States and has published on western women's inventions.

Christiane E. Farnan is an associate professor at Siena College in Loudonville, New York, where she teaches American literature, serves as codirector of the American Studies Program, and is a member of the advisory board of the McCormack Center for the Study of the American Revolution. Her research and teaching interests involve nineteenth-century women writers, children's literature, mapping technology, and digital humanities.

Melanie J. Fishbane holds an MFA from the Vermont College of Fine Arts and an MA from Concordia University. She lectures internationally on children's literature, Laura Ingalls Wilder, and L. M. Montgomery and teaches English at Humber College. Her YA novel *Maud: A Novel Inspired by the Life of L. M. Montgomery* was published in 2017 and was shortlisted for the 2018 Vine Awards for Canadian Jewish Literature.

Vera R. Foley holds a doctorate from the University of North Carolina at Chapel Hill and currently serves as a visiting assistant professor of early American literature at Gustavus Adolphus College. She specializes in American literature by women, with a particular focus on women's influences on social institutions such as marriage and domestic hierarchy.

Sonya Sawyer Fritz is an associate professor of English at the University of Central Arkansas, where she teaches courses in children's and adolescent literature. Her recent publications include an essay on literary representations of child mobility in *Children's Literature and New York City* and an article in *Girlhood Studies* on representations of domestic space in Victorian girls' literature. She had coedited an essay collection with Sara K. Day on depictions of the Victorian period in twenty-first-century children's and adolescent literature.

Miranda A. Green-Barteet is an associate professor in the Department of Women's Studies and Feminist Research and the Department of English and Writing Studies at the University of Western Ontario. She has published on Harriet Jacobs, Harriet Wilson, and Sarah Pogson as well as on race and gender in *The Hunger Games*. She is the coeditor (with Sara K. Day and Amy L. Montz) of *Female Rebellion in Young Adult Dystopian Fiction* (Ashgate, 2014).

Anna Thompson Hajdik holds a doctorate in American Studies from the University of Texas at Austin. A lecturer in the English and Film Studies Department at the University of Wisconsin–Whitewater, she teaches courses on visual culture, film history, and literature of American Midwest. With the support of the State Historical Society of Iowa, she is currently working on a book-length project examining the national significance of the state's visual culture.

Keri Holt is an associate professor of English and American Studies at Utah State University. Her research focuses on eighteenth- and nineteenth-century regional American writing and print culture, and she has published on this topic in *Western American Literature*, *Studies in American Fiction*, and *Early American Literature*. She is the author of *Reading These United States: Federal Literacy in the Early Republic, 1776–1830* (University of Georgia Press, 2019) and coeditor (with Edward Watts and John Funchion) of *Mapping Region in Early American Writing* (University of Georgia Press, 2015).

Shosuke Kinugawa is an associate professor in the English Department at the Kobe City University of Foreign Studies. His research interests include nineteenth-century American literature, Mark Twain, and detective fiction. His most recent publication is an article on the use of wordplay in Agatha Christie's detective stories. He is working on a book examining the role of wordplay in Mark Twain's prose.

Margaret Noodin holds a master of fine arts degree in creative writing and a doctorate in English and linguistics from the University of Minnesota. She is currently an associate professor at the University of Wisconsin–Milwaukee, where she also serves at the director of the Electa Quinney Institute for American Indian Education. She is the author of *Bawaajimo: A Dialect of Dreams in Anishinaabe Language and Literature* (Michigan State University Press, 2014) and *Weweni: Poems in Anishinaabemowin and English* (Wayne State University Press, 2015). Her current projects are available at www.ojibwe.net, where she and other speakers of Ojibwe have created a space for language to be shared by academics and the Native community.

Anne K. Phillips is a professor of English at Kansas State University, where she specializes in American children's literature. She is a regular reviewer of books about Laura Ingalls Wilder, and she and Gregory Eiselein have coedited the Norton Critical Edition of *Little Women* and three other Alcott-related volumes. She is the current president of the Louisa May Alcott Society.

Dawn Sardella-Ayres recently completed her dissertation on gender, race, and class in the Little Colonel series and its film adaptation at the University of Cambridge. She is developing a book-length exploration of girlhood as performance and commodity in pre–World War II North American girls' texts.

Katharine Slater is an assistant professor of English at Rowan University, where she teaches courses on children's and young adult literature. Her previous publications include an article on the regionalism of *Little House on the Prairie* as well as essays for the *Children's Literature Association Quarterly*, *The Lion and the Unicorn*, and a collection on early readers. She is currently working on a book project that considers how spatial constructs contribute to the ideologies of visual narratives for young people.

Lindsay Stephens is a doctoral candidate in English at the University of South Dakota. She writes about settler colonialism and South Dakota tourism as well as petroleum cultures and ecocatastrophe in the twentieth and twenty-first centuries. A fourth-generation South Dakotan, she is fascinated by the lasting effects of Laura Ingalls Wilder's and Rose Wilder Lane's work on South Dakota cultural imaginary. She is the author of a historical guidebook, *The Adventure Climbs of Herb and Jan Conn* (Sharp End, 2008).

Jericho Williams is a professor of English at Spartanburg Methodist College. His current research interests include American literature, rural cultures, and education in literature. His essays have appeared in the *Thoreau Society Bulletin*, *Ecogothic in Nineteenth-Century American Literature* (Routledge, 2017), and *Critical Insights: Edith Wharton* (Salem Press, 2017).

INDEX

Abe, Keiko, 202
Abe, Masahiko, 207n3
adaptations, xix, xxv–xxvi, 6, 14, 99, 197–98, 204–6. *See also* Japanese reception; *Little House on the Prairie* (television series)
Adomat, Donna, 43
Agee, James, 148, 154
Albert, Susan Wittig, xxviiin6
Allexan, Sarah S., 32
American Country (aesthetic), 202–4, 206
American Foundation for the Blind, 36, 40
American Girl, xix, 78
Amish, 176
Anderson, Emily, xxi, 4, 7, 12–16. See also *Little: Novels*
Anderson, Gertrude, 194n2
Anderson, William, xx, 6, 18–19, 30n2, 91–93, 178n1, 197
Anishinaabe, 183, 186. *See also* Ojibwe
Anne of Green Gables, 201
Arai, Yoko, 202
Arngrim, Alison, 196
Association for Library Service to Children (ALSC), xvi–xvii
Atkins, Jeannine, xix
Ayala, Emiliano C., 36

Baldwin, James, 120
Baudrillard, Jean, 173

Baum, L. Frank, 192
Beauchamp, Miles, 36
Beck, Ken, xxviiin2
"Benders of Kansas, The," 9–10, 16n4
Berkhofer, Robert F., Jr., 75n6
Berg, Scott W., 185
Bergson, Alexandra, 119–24, 126, 129–30. *See also* Cather, Willa; *O Pioneers!*
Bernstein, Robin, xxiii, 66–68, 75nn4–5
Beto, Rhea Rheinhardt, 183
Black Hawk War, 83
Black Hills, 188, 191
Blackford, Holly, 71, 79–80, 129
Bohlke, L. Brent, 130
Bosmajian, Hamida, 117n1
Brandt Revised version, 9, 16n4
Brock, Timothy C., 183
Bruner, Edward M., 168
Bullock, Christopher, 189
Burnett, Ann, 183
Burns, Louis F., 161n2
Burr Oak, 136, 165, 171. *See also* Iowa
Butler, Dean, 99
Butler, Judith, 5, 12

Callahan, S. Alice, 61n4
Campbell, Donna M., 51, 127–28
Carnegie, Andrew, 42
Caroline series, xviii, 77–88, 89n3. *See also* Wilkes, Maria D.; Wilkins, Celia

Carpenter, Martha, 79
Case, John F., 99
Cather, Willa, xxiv–xxv, 107, 119–24, 126, 129–30, 130n2, 134–35, 140–45. *See also* Bergson, Alexandra; Kronborg, Thea; *My Ántonia*; *O Pioneers!*; Shimerda, Ántonia; *Song of the Lark, The*
cayuse, 56–57, 60
Charlotte series, 77–78, 80–82, 88, 89n2. *See also* Wiley, Melissa
Cheney, Connie, 177
Cheney, Larry, 176
Children's Literature Legacy Award, xvii, xix
Chopin, Kate, 120–21
Chung, Wendy, 36
Civil War, 119, 135, 185, 187
Clark, Beverly Lyon, 43
Coats, Karen, 7, 15–16
Cockerell, Dale, xxviiin2
Collins, Wilkie, 111
Cooper, Katherine, 91, 94
Country Gentleman, 98
Cramer, Marian, 177
Cressman, Jodi, 44n2
Crèvecoeur, J. Hector St. John de, xxv, 148, 150–51, 155–56, 160
Crow, Liz, 41
Cummins, Maria, xvi
Custer, George Armstrong, 188

Daily Missourian, 36
Daisogen no Chiisana Ie no Kiruto no aru Kurashi [*Life with Quilts in "Little House on the Prairie"*], 205
Dakota: government, 42; Ingalls residence, 110–12, 173; landscape, 54, 108–12, 115, 189; novels, xxiv, 105–9, 111–14, 117; Territory, xxiv, 22, 92, 105–8, 111–15, 123, 128, 188, 190–91. *See also* Black Hills; De Smet; South Dakota
Dakota (people), xxvi, 67, 75n8, 181–83, 185–93
Dakota War, 67, 185–86, 194n1
Dawes Act, 52, 61n4, 190
Dear America, xix

Delano family, 184
Deloria, Ella, 192
Derrida, Jacques, 5
De Smet: boom, 108, 112, 166, 169; citizens, 58, 116, 172, 174; civic activity, xxiv, 26, 112–17, 176; Ingalls residence, 30n2, 92, 106, 112, 115, 131n5, 136–37, 168, 189, 191; tourist sites, xxv–xxvi, 165, 168–72, 175–78, 178n2, 202; violence in, 75n9; Wilder residence, 51, 93. *See also* Dakota; *De Smet News*; Laura Ingalls Wilder Society; South Dakota
De Smet Historical Society, 178
De Smet News, 171
Dickinson, Emily, xvi
Dōru Hausu: Laura no Chiisana Ie [*Doll House: Laura's Little House*], 204–5
Dowker, Ann, 36, 44n1
du Chêne, Soldat, 49, 51, 59–61, 61n1, 187
Dutcher, Rose, 134–35, 137–40, 145n4. *See also* Garland, Hamlin; *Rose of Dutcher's Coolly*

Eastman, Charles Alexander, xviii, 50, 53
Eastman, Seth, 194n2
Eco, Umberto, 173
Education for All Handicapped Children Act, 36
Erdrich, Louise, 183
Erisman, Fred, 154
Evans, Walker, 148, 154

Farley, Walter, 61
Fellman, Anita Clair: Ingalls's attitudes toward Native Americans, 83, 86; Ingalls family dynamics, 42, 79; Little House in classrooms, xix–xx, 6, 135, 196; Wilder and Lane's collaboration, 178n1; Wilder and Lane's ideology, 10, 33, 35, 149–50, 167; Little House reception, 121, 130n2, 166–67, 182
feminism, xxi, 94
Ferguson, Kelly Kathleen, xix, 99
Floyd, Janet, 82
Formanek-Brunell, Miriam, 72

Foucault, Michel, 130n1
Fraser, Caroline, xx, xxi, 6, 30n2, 194n1
Frey, Charles, 64, 68
Fryer, Judith, 126
Furusawa, Emiko, 205, 207n7

Garland, Cap (person), 93
Garland, Hamlin, xxiv–xxv, 134–40, 145, 145n4. *See also* Dutcher, Rose; *Rose of Dutcher's Coolly*
Garry, Lavonne, 176
Giants in the Earth, 105, 108–9, 111, 114–15
Glasgow, Ellen, 121
Goodreads, 11, 12
Gordon, Della, Harold, and Stan, 174
Gormley, Myra Vanderpool, 184
Graham, Ruth, xxviiin7
Great Seal of Minnesota Territory, 194n2
Great Seal of the Territory of Wisconsin, 194n2
Greeley, Horace, 148, 153–56
Green, Melanie C., 183
Grey, Zane, 131n4
Griswold, Jerry, 117, 117n1
Gutschke, Anna, 93

Hagio, Moto, 207n4
HarperCollins, xxviiin1, 78
Harper's, 111
Harris, Daniel, 204
Hastings, A. Waller, 16n2, 17
Heidi, 35
Heldrich, Philip, 51, 83, 88, 158, 182
Hello Kitty, 198, 207n4
Herbert, David, 174
Herbert Hoover Presidential Library, xx
Hermann, Dorothy, 36, 38, 42
Hill, Pamela Smith: *Laura Ingalls Wilder*, 18, 24, 34–36, 42, 92–94, 130n2, 131n5, 152, 156–57; mooc, 170; *Pioneer Girl*, xv, xxvii, 4, 7–13, 16, 16nn3–4, 51–52, 61n5, 83, 89n3, 114. *See also* Wilder, Laura Ingalls: *Pioneer Girl*
Ho-Chunk, 187
Hoelscher, Steven, 176

Holtz, William, xx, 18, 24, 27, 35, 130n2, 178n1
Homestead Act, 52, 186
hooks, bell, 95, 125, 130n1
Hughes, Chloe, 44n1
Hussein, Saddam, 196

Independence, 9, 165, 170. *See also* Kansas
"Indian Territory," 51–52, 57, 61n3, 65–66, 160, 167, 184, 187–89, 192
Indians. *See* Native Americans
Ingalls, Caroline Lake Quiner (person), 78–79, 88, 131n5
Ingalls, Charles Phillip (person), 9, 114, 131n5, 161n2, 172–74
Ingalls, Edmund, 184
Ingalls, Mary (person), 32, 42–43, 136, 139, 173
Iowa, 136, 172, 187; College of the Blind, 34, 42; Ingalls residence, 32, 187; Wilder travel, 93. *See also* Burr Oak; Herbert Hoover Presidential Library
Iowa (people), 187
Ishihara, Hideki, 200–201

Jameson, Elizabeth, xx, xxii, 79, 88–89
Japanese reception of *Little House*, xix, xxv–xxvi, xxviiin5, 197–207
Jefferson, Thomas, xxv, 148–50, 156, 160

Kaguya-hime, 198
Kammen, Michael, 168
Kaneko, Nobuhisa, 207n3
Kansas, 53, 78; Ingalls residence, 9–10, 51, 54, 61n3, 75n9, 82, 108, 110, 112, 118n1, 158–60, 187; landscape, xxv, 110, 117, 187; Native residence, 49–50, 52, 54–58, 61n1, 83, 159; Territory, 49–51. *See also* Independence; Kaye, Frances W.; Native Americans; Osage; Osage Diminished Reserve; Wilder, Laura Ingalls: *Little House on the Prairie*
Kaplan, Amy, 161n3
kawaii, xxvi, 196–206, 207nn3–4
Kaye, Frances W., xvii, 50, 52, 61n2, 64, 73, 75n7, 83, 159, 166, 182, 186–87

Keith, Lois, 35, 44n1
Keller, Helen, xxii, 33–43, 44n2
Ketcham, Sallie, 130n2
Kickapoo, 187
Kindell, Alexandra, 152
King Philip's War, 158
Kinsella, Sharon, 206
Kirshenblatt-Gimblett, Barbara, 172–73
Kleege, Georgina, 41–42, 44n2
Konjaku Monogatarishū, 198
Koupal, Nancy Tystad, xx, 42, 197
Kronborg, Thea, 134–35, 140–44
Kudlick, Catherine J., 41

Ladies' Home Journal, 39
Lakota, 189
L'Amour, Louis, 131n4
Lancaster Raid, 158
Lane, Rose Wilder: authorship question, xvi, xx, xxviiin6, 130n2, 178n1; biography of, 3; collaboration with Laura Ingalls Wilder, xviii, xxi, xxvii, 5–6, 9–11, 15, 16n4, 18, 21, 26–29, 30n4, 34, 42, 58, 61n7, 77, 89n3, 95, 105–11, 114, 116–17, 133, 140, 145n2, 167, 171, 178n1, 192; ideology, xxi–xxii, 10, 15, 19–20, 22–29, 33, 43, 140, 167; interviews of Almanzo Wilder, 93–94, 100n1; journalism, xx; relationship with Roger Lea MacBride, 78, 89n1, 171, 178n2; writings, xxii, 23–24, 91, 140
Lantz, Charles, Doris, and Everett, 171
Larkin, Susan, 149
Lash, Joseph P., 36
Laura, the Prairie Girl. See *Sougen no Shojo Laura*
Laura Ingalls Wilder Award, xvii
Laura Ingalls Wilder Legacy and Research Association, 182
Laura Ingalls Wilder Museum, 178
Laura Ingalls Wilder Pilgrimage Trail, 170
Laura Ingalls Wilder Society, 169, 171–73, 176
Laura no Oryouri Nouto [*Laura's Cookbook*], 204

Laurapalooza, xix, 182
Lawson, Robert, 87
Leckey, Vona, 169, 172–73
Lee, Hermione, 130n2
Lefebvre, Benjamin, xxxviiin4
Lefebvre, Henri, 130n1
Levitt, Aimee, 173n2
Libertarianism, 10, 18–20, 23–27, 29, 33, 42–43, 167. See also Lane, Rose Wilder
Lichty, Irene V., 193
Life Shop Many, 201–3
Limerick, Patricia Nelson, 166–67
Lincoln, Abraham, 168, 185
Lindsay, Nina, xvi–xvii
Little House on the Prairie (television series), 99, 150, 168–69, 174–75, 193, 196, 201, 202, 204, 207n7
Little: Novels, xxi, 4, 12–14, 15. See also Anderson, Emily
Little Town at the Crossroads, 80, 84–86, 89n5. See also Caroline series; Wilkes, Maria D.
LittleHouseonthePrairie.com, 182
Louw, Pat, 118n1, 182. See also Caroline series; Wilkes, Maria D.
Ludlow Amendment, 20

MacArthur, Douglas, 199
MacBride, Roger Lea, 77–78, 81, 83, 87, 89n1, 89n6, 171–72, 178n2. See also Lane, Rose Wilder; Rose series
MacDonald, Bonney, 106, 115–16
Macy, Anne Sullivan, 36, 39, 44n2
Macy, John Albert, 39
Maher, Susan Naramore, 50, 54, 60
Makura no Soushi, 199, 207n3
Malone, 91–92, 152–53, 155, 171. See also New York
Mancino, Nicole, 94
Mansfield, xx, 36, 138, 145, 165, 170–71, 173, 178n2, 193. See also Missouri; Rocky Ridge Farm
Mansfield Farm Loan Association, 138

Mansfield Mirror, 36
Martha series, 77–82, 89n2, 89n4. *See also* Wiley, Melissa
Massachusetts (people), 182
Massachusetts Bay Colony, 184
Massey, Doreen, 124, 126
Matthews, Jean V., 135
Matthews, Maureen, 186
May, Jon, 171
McCabe, Nancy, xix
McCall's, 92
McClure, Rhonda R., 184
McClure, Wendy, xix, 170
McGill, Meredith L., 8
McGillis, Roderick, 43
Mdewakanton, 188
Miller, Bethany, 169–70
Miller, John E.: *Becoming Laura Ingalls Wilder*, xx, 18, 19, 21, 24, 26, 30n4, 36, 75n9, 93, 98, 130n2, 138, 196; *Laura Ingalls Wilder and Rose Wilder Lane*, 3–4, 35, 137, 145n2, 192; "something solid," 3–4, 15; Wilder's attitude toward Native Americans, 51–52
Miller, Sarah, xix
Minnesota, 136, 177, 188; Ingalls residence, xxi, 55, 82, 92, 107–8, 112, 123, 187–88; Native residence, 188; statehood, 194n2; tourist sites, xxv, 165, 171. *See also* Dakota (people); Dakota War; Spring Valley; University of Minnesota; Walnut Grove; Wilder, Laura Ingalls: *On the Banks of Plum Creek*
Missouri, 22, 36, 78, 82, 87, 170, 187. *See also* Mansfield
Missouri Ruralist, 92, 98, 133, 138, 143
Missouri State University, 170
Mito, Nobue, 207n3
Miyadai, Shinji, 200–201
Mogilner, Alijandra, 36
Moore, Rosa Ann, 18, 131n2
Mourning Dove, xviii, 50, 56–57, 59–60
Mowder, Louise, 60, 64, 69, 71

Munro, Eleanor, 126
Murray, Gail Schmunk, 43
My Ántonia, xxiv, 119, 122–23, 129, 140. *See also* Cather, Willa; Shimerda, Ántonia

Narragansett, 158
Native Americans: appropriation, 13–14, 51, 53, 65, 150; authors, xviii, 61n4 (*see also* Callahan, S. Alice; Eastman, Charles Alexander; Erdrich, Louise; Mourning Dove; Zitkála-Šá); conflation of, 75n8; erasure of, xxi, xxiv, 14, 75n7, 86–87, 89n1, 120, 182–83, 185; iconography, 50, 57, 60–61, 116, 190; identification with, xviii, 64, 67, 74, 88, 127; literary/thematic elements, xviii, 50, 53, 55–56; perspectives, xviii, xxv, 49; prejudice against, xvi–xvii, 61n2, 161n3; representation of, xvii–xviii, xxiii, 52, 63–64, 66, 75n6, 78, 83–88, 115, 127, 158–60, 166, 170, 190, 194n2; rights/sovereignty, 183, 191; scholarship, xvii–xviii, xxvii, 61n2; violence against, 14, 67, 75n9, 83, 158, 160, 191–92. *See also* Anishinaabe; Dakota (people); Ho-Chunk; Iowa (people); Kickapoo; Lakota; Massachusetts (people); Mdewakanton; Narragansett; Naumkeag; Nipmuc; Odawa; Ojibwe; Omaha; Osage; Pawnee; Ponca; Potawatomi; Sauk and Fox; Sioux; Sisseton; Wahpekute; Wahpeton; Wampanoag
Naumkeag, 184
Nebraska, 93, 121, 123, 140
New Deal, 19, 167
New Orleans Exhibition, 93
New Salem, Illinois, xxvi, 168, 173
Nguyen, Bich Minh, xix
Nielsen, Kim, 36, 41, 43
Nikolajeva, Maria, 29
Nipmuc, 158
Noodin, Margaret, xviii
Nostalgic na Zakka no Mise yori, 201, 203
Novotny, Ellen Simpson, 69, 74

O Pioneers!, xxiv, 107, 119, 121–23, 126, 129, 140, 144. See also Bergson, Alexandra; Cather, Willa
Odawa, 186
O'Dell, Scott, 61
O'Donnell, Alice and Terry, 193
Ojibwe, xxvi, 182, 185–87, 190, 193–94. See also Anishinaabe
Omaha, 187
Orr, Margaret, 193
Ortberg, Daniel Mallory, 15
Osage, xxvi, 49–61, 63–66, 74, 75n8, 83, 157–60, 161n2, 182–83, 187, 190, 193
Osage Diminished Reserve, xxi, 49, 149, 157–58, 161n2, 186
Oshima, Yumiko, 207n4
Ōtsuka, Akiko, 200–201
Ōtsuka, Eiji, 200–201, 207n4

Palmud, Cheryl, 169
Parlevliet, Sanne, xxiii, 77
Pawnee, 187
Pechan, Beverly, 171
Pepin, 149, 152, 157, 165, 169–70, 202. See also Wisconsin
Perry, Ernest, 57
Phillips, Anne, 116–17
Pilgrims, 172, 188
Pioneer Girl Perspectives, xx
Pioneer Girl Project, xx, xxvii
Plimoth Plantation, xxvi, 172–73
Plymouth Colony, 184
Plymouth Rock, 172
Pokagon, Simon, 193
Ponca, 187
Potawatomi, 89n5, 186–87
Prairie du Chien, Treaties of, 83

Quantic, Diane, xxiv, 105, 108–11, 116, 117n1
Quicke, John, 36

Reagan, Ronald, 167
Reese, Debbie, xvii, 61n2, 66, 166
Rehabilitation Act, 36

Reimer, Mavis, 5, 15, 17
Rhuel, Oscar, 97
Rice, Edmund, 184
Robinson, Laura, 6, 17
Rocky Ridge Farm, 78, 93, 171, 173–74. See also Mansfield; Missouri
Rølvaag, Ole, xxiv, 105, 108–9, 111, 114–15
Romines, Ann: *Constructing the Little House*, xix, 4–6, 11, 51, 53–54, 60, 61n3, 64, 68–69, 73–74, 78–79, 89n3, 94, 106, 117n1, 121, 125, 128, 130n2, 149, 188; *The Home Plot*, 129; *Pioneer Girl Perspectives*, xx
Roosevelt, Franklin D., 19, 167, 184
Rose of Dutcher's Coolly, xxiv, 134–37, 141. See also Dutcher, Rose; Garland, Hamlin
Rose series, 77–81, 87. See also MacBride, Roger Lea
Rowlandson, Mary, xxv, 148, 150, 157–58
Rubin, Ellen, 44n1
Ruiz de Burton, Maria, xvi
Russell, David, 151
Russo, Maria, 178n2

Sandoz, Mari, 107, 114
Sandy Lake Tragedy, 185
Sauk and Fox, 84, 187
Saunders, Kathy, 33
Schneider, Bethany, xviii, 50, 53, 74n1, 75n2, 75nn8–9
Secret Garden, The, 35
Sedgwick, Catharine Maria, 121
Segel, Elizabeth, 64, 71
Seven Council Fires, 182
Shanley, Kathryn, 86
Sherwood, Aubrey, 171
Shimerda, Ántonia, 119–24, 126, 129–30. See also Cather, Willa; *My Ántonia*
shojo, 197–98, 200, 202–5, 207n4, 207n6
Shojo Minzokugaku, 200–201
Shōnagon, Sei, 199
Short, Emma, 91, 94
Sioux, 188
Sisseton, 188

Slater, Katharine, 106, 112, 114, 117n1, 149, 151, 197–98
Smith, Henry Nash, xxv, 148–50, 155
Smulders, Sharon, 14, 17, 50–51, 53–54, 61n2, 63, 65, 75n6, 166
snugness, 6, 105, 107, 110–15, 117, 117n1, 118n2, 151, 157
Soja, Edward, xxiv, 120, 122, 124–29, 130n1
Soldat du Chêne, 49, 51, 59–61, 61n1, 187
Song of the Lark, The, xxv, 134–35, 140–42, 144. See also Cather, Willa; Kronborg, Thea
Sougen no Shojo Laura [*Laura, the Prairie Girl*], xix, xxviiin5, 207n6
South Dakota: government, 42, 191; Ingalls residence, 82, 131n5, 136, 165; landscape, 54, 173; tourist sites, xix, xxv, 177, 202. See also Black Hills; Dakota; Dakota (people); De Smet; Wounded Knee
South Dakota Historical Society Press, xv, xx, 177, 197. See also Koupal, Nancy Tystad
Spaeth, Janet, 70–71, 74
Spring Valley, 92–93, 99, 171. See also Minnesota
Springen, Karen, xxviiin1
St. Louis, Treaty of, 84
Stegner, Wallace, xxiv, 105–9, 115–16
Stephens, John, 43
Sturges Treaty, 161n2
Sullivan, Tim and Joan, 172–73
surveyors' house, 171, 173. See also Dakota; De Smet; Wilder, Laura Ingalls: *By the Shores of Silver Lake*
Suzuki, Noriko, 196–97, 199, 200
Sweet Home, 203

Takemiya, Keiko, 207n4
Taketori Monogatari, 198
Thomas, Alfred, 57
Thompson, Dorothy, 26
Three Fires Confederacy, 182, 186
Thurman, Judith, 177
Tompkins, Jane, 127–28, 131n4

Trachsel, Mary, 50, 55, 59
Tschopp, Marie, xix
Turner, Frederick Jackson, 148, 155, 157, 160, 167

University of Minnesota, 170

Wahpekute, 188
Wahpeton, 188
Walnut Grove, xxv–xxvi, 34, 165, 168–69, 171, 174–78, 187, 202, 205. See also Minnesota
Walnut Grove Tribune, 171
Wampanoag, 158
Watashi no Kantorii [*My Country*], 202–4
Watson, Emily Strauss, 44n1
Wayne, John, 127, 131n4
Westerman, Gwen, 181, 189, 191
What Katy Did, 35
White, Bruce, 189, 191
Whiting, Ella, 97
Whiting, Lee, 97
Wilder Home and Museum, xx
Wilder, Almanzo James (person), xxiii, 21, 91–94, 98–99, 136, 138, 143, 145, 170, 183
Wilder, Eliza Jane, 92
Wilder, Laura Ingalls
  "All in the Day's Work," 143
  Barnum, 57–60, 97
  Brewsters, 94, 143, 191
  By the Shores of Silver Lake: coming of age, 40, 92, 96, 106–8, 137, 188; correspondence about, 106–7, 110; horses, 50, 54, 55, 56, 57; Ingalls residence, 172; landscape, xxiv, 107–9, 111–12, 123, 181, 189; perspectives on farming, 30, 55; and *Pioneer Girl*, 38, 56–57; place-making, 107, 109–12, 117; representations of Native Americans, 55–57, 181, 189; sisterhood, 68; surveyors' house, 109, 110. See also Dakota; De Smet; *Giants in the Earth*; Rølvaag, Ole
  Charlotte (doll), xviii–xxiii, 63–69, 71–73, 75n4, 75n9

Dear Laura, 170
Detroit Book Fair Speech, 77, 91, 184, 207n1
"Farm Dining Room, The," 98
Farmer Boy: agrarian ideal, 149, 153–56, 159–61; in classrooms, 150; composition process, xxii, 16n1, 19, 23–24, 26, 28–29, 91, 161n1; consumption, 13–14, 150; fictionalization, xxiii, 91–92, 183; ideology, 24–29; scholarship about, 156–57. *See also* Lane, Rose Wilder; Wilder, Almanzo James (person); Wilder, Laura Ingalls: Wilder, Almanzo (character)
"Favors a Small Farm Home," 138
First Four Years, The: composition process, 20, 140, 145n3; economics, 20–22, 26, 30n2, 95, 144; horses, 21, 59–61, 95, 128; ideology, xxii, 19; independence, 21, 30n1; marriage, xxiv, 21–22, 26, 57, 59–62, 95, 128, 133, 143, 183; omission from *Pioneer Girl*, 16n1; posthumous publication, 6, 20, 57, 92, 128; scholarship about, 60
Garland, Cap (character), 30n4, 94, 97–98. *See also* Garland, Cap (person)
Ingalls, Caroline "Ma" (character): adaptations, xviii–xix, 77–87; alignment with Mary, 70–73, 124, 126, 130; attitude toward Native Americans, 54–55, 73–74, 83, 88, 127, 161n3, 188–91; community, 28; domesticity, 37, 55, 59–60, 71–72, 109, 112–13, 124, 151, 157, 160, 200, 204; femininity, 27, 50, 55, 59, 68, 71, 79–80, 107, 129, 157–58, 188–89; opposition to Laura, 50, 52, 54–55, 59, 63, 65, 70, 72–74, 79–80, 89n3, 124, 127; parenting, xxiii, 14, 27, 34–35, 55, 59, 64–65, 68–70, 72, 137, 185, 188; and *Pioneer Girl*, 89n3; racialization, 61n6, 71–72, 151; relationship with Charles, 9, 60, 92, 107–8, 113, 129, 157, 160, 189–91; scholarship about, 50, 68, 71, 79, 88, 89n3, 129, 131n5, 191; stoicism, 6, 40, 55, 79–80, 139, 160. *See also* Caroline series; Ingalls, Caroline Lake Quiner (person); Wilkes, Maria D.; Wilkins, Celia
Ingalls, Carrie (character), 27–28, 68–70, 73, 96, 109–10, 157–58
Ingalls, Charles "Pa" (character): alignment with Laura, 69–70, 73, 83, 94–96, 127–30; attitudes toward Native Americans, 49, 66, 74, 83, 184, 186–91; civic engagement, 27, 113–17, 137, 139; entitlement, 112; failures, 23, 108, 114, 157–60, 192; ideology, 30n4, 58, 140, 149, 157; making do, xxi, xxiv, 42, 60, 105–9, 111–12, 115–17, 151–53, 156–57, 160, 189, 192; music, xix, 109–10, 113–16, 151; parenting, 65, 68–70, 74, 158, 185; and *Pioneer Girl*, 89n3; relationship with Caroline, 60, 80, 107–8, 157; reception, 79; scholarship about, 79, 106, 114, 117n1, 131n5. *See also* "Benders of Kansas, The"; Ingalls, Charles (person)
Ingalls, Grace (character), 14, 27, 34, 61n6, 112
Ingalls, Laura (character): alignment with Native Americans, xviii, xxii, xxvi, 49–57, 60–61, 61nn2–3, 63–68, 70, 72–74, 83, 88, 89n3, 127–28, 181, 183, 193; childhood, xviii, xxiii, 54, 64, 66–67, 69, 183, 185; coming of age, 50, 54–55, 57, 59, 82, 88, 89n3, 106–7, 133 139, 141, 188, 190–91; community, 26–28, 134, 140–41, 144; connection to landscape, xviii, xxiv, 21, 53–54, 109, 112, 119–30, 139, 181, 183, 185, 191; emotion, 9, 65, 67–68, 73–74, 113, 127, 157–60, 185, 187, 189; family dynamics, xxiii, 6, 21–22, 28, 34–41, 63–74, 79–80, 109–13, 124, 129–30, 150–51, 184, 192; fandom, 166–77; 182, 196, 206; femininity, xxiv, 26–27, 50, 53–58, 60–61, 61n6, 69–72, 79–80, 89n3, 94–95, 122–26, 129; horses, 50–51, 54–60, 129; ideology, 20–23, 26–29, 30n1, 94–95, 129, 144; and *Pioneer Girl*, 52, 56–57, 89n3, 96–98; relationship with

Index

Almanzo, 20–22, 26, 57–61, 92–100, 129, 133, 144, 191; racialization, 14, 61n6, 70, 72, 88; resilience, 55, 134, 140–41, 144; scholarship about, 60, 61n2, 63–64, 69–70, 74, 79, 127–29, 166; vocation, xxiv, 30n2, 127, 133–41, 144, 191. *See also* adaptations; *Little House on the Prairie* (television series)

Ingalls, Mary (character): agency, 28, 32–38, 40; adaptations of, xix, 14; alignment with Ma, 27–28, 69–74, 124, 126, 129–30, 157–58, 160; disability, xxii, 14–15, 32–44, 55, 127, 188; education, 35, 42–43, 127, 139; and *Pioneer Girl*, xxii, 32–35, 38; relationship with sisters, 6, 28, 34, 38–39, 41, 66, 69–74, 110, 124–27, 129–30, 136, 150, 157–58, 160, 187. *See also* Ingalls, Mary (person)

Jack, xxi, xxviiin7

Laura Ingalls Wilder's Fairy Poems, 145n1

Lena (character), 30n1, 54–56, 58, 61n5

Little House in the Big Woods: agrarian ideal, 149–50, 155, 157, 159; Christmas scene, 64–65; colonization, 184–86; counternarrative to, 183–84; cover, 69; coziness, 96, 112, 151, 156, 204; extended family, 68, 69, 71; fandom, 170; fictionalization, 61, 79, 80; music of, 110; scholarship about, 61n3, 70, 79, 118n1; structure, 70, 107, 156, 185; westward expansion, 149, 161

Little House on the Prairie: as captivity narrative, xxv, 157, 159, 174, 182; disruption of agrarian ideal, 108, 115, 149, 156–57, 160, 167; domesticity, 69–70, 112, 114, 117, 205; fandom, xix, 202, 205; fictionalization, 51, 61n3; liberty, 50, 61; and *Pioneer Girl*, 52, 89n3; representations of Native Americans, 49, 51–53, 60–61, 63–65, 72, 75, 83, 85, 87, 159, 161nn2–3, 186–87; scholarship about, xviii, xxii, 51, 53, 68, 83, 106, 117n1, 118n1; and truth, 3. *See also* "Benders of Kansas, The"; Independence; Kansas; *Little House on the Prairie* (television series); Native Americans; Osage; Osage Diminished Reserve

Little Town on the Prairie: coming of age, xxiv, 40, 94, 96, 117, 133–34, 137–39, 143, 191; community, 58, 114–15, 137, 143; composition of, 19, 21, 26–28, 30n4, 42, 58, 61n7; family dynamics, 27, 41, 114, 137; Independence Day, xxii, 19, 26–28; and *Pioneer Girl*, 30n3; scholarship about, 30n4, 42, 137; structure, 21, 118n2. *See also* Lane, Rose Wilder

Long Winter, The: adaptations of, 14; agency, 37, 40, 57, 92, 94, 113–17, 191, 200; coming of age, 57, 190; community, 113–17; composition of, 30n4, 110; hardship, 21, 57, 92, 112–13, 116, 137, 190; music, 110, 114–17; and *Pioneer Girl*, 35; point of view, 94, 96; reception, 197, 199–200; representations of Native Americans, 115–16, 190–91; scholarship about, 89n3, 117n1. *See also* De Smet; *Giants in the Earth*; Japanese reception; Rølvaag, Ole

"My Ozark Kitchen," 98

Oleson, Nellie, 58, 97

On the Banks of Plum Creek: family dynamics, 69–72, 108, 110, 117n1, 124–27; fandom, 176; landscape, xxiv, 123–27, 187–88; loss, 65, 68; representations of Native Americans, 65–67, 71–72, 187–88; scholarship about, 71, 188; settler violence, xviii, 66–67, 71; structure, 21, 65–66. *See also* Dakota War; *Little House on the Prairie* (television series); Minnesota; Walnut Grove

On the Way Home, 51–52

Pioneer Girl, 133, 136, 142, 193; analysis of, 4, 7–13, 15–16, 16n1, 16nn3–4, 52, 61n5, 83, 89n3; comparison with fiction, xxii, xxvii, 19, 30n3, 32–35, 37–38, 52, 56 57, 83, 89n3, 92, 95–97, 114; reception, xv–xvi, xx–xxi, xxvii, xxviiin7, 4 7, 11–12, 170, 177, 197. *See also* Hill, Pamela Smith

Selected Letters, xx, 6, 19, 92, 95, 98, 106, 110, 138. *See also* Anderson, William
"Shorter Hours for Farm Women," 138
Skip, 57–60, 97
These Happy Golden Years: coming of age, 35, 57–61, 72, 94, 97, 128, 129, 137, 143, 191; education, xxiv, 133–34, 137, 143–44, 191; fandom, 99; horses, 57–59, 97; landscape, 128–30, 191; music, 110; and *Pioneer Girl*, 30n3, 97–98; racial identity, 61n6, 191. *See also* Barnum; Brewsters; Dakota; De Smet; Skip; Wilder, Laura Ingalls: Wilder, Almanzo (character)
"To Buy or Not to Buy," 137
Wilder, Almanzo (character): childhood, 13–14, 24–26, 28, 91, 150, 152–56; as farmer, 20–22, 30n2, 144, 191–92; fictionalization of, 91–93, 95–98; heroism, 30n4, 57, 94; horses, 21, 28, 34, 50–51, 54, 57–61, 97, 129; naming, 20, 92, 96; philosophy, 20–22, 26, 28–29, 140, 144, 156; reception, 99, 155; relationship with Laura, xxiii, 20–21, 29, 30nn2–3, 54, 57–61, 72, 78, 91–92, 94–99, 107, 128–29, 133, 144–45, 191; scholarship about, 94. *See also* Farmer Boy; Wilder, Almanzo James (person)
Wilder, Father (character), 24–26, 149, 152–56, 159
Wilder, Mother (character), 13–14
Wilder, Royal (character), 25, 94, 96
"Woman's Place, The," 98
See also Lane, Rose Wilder
Wilder, Royal (person), 92–93
Wiley, Melissa, 77–78, 80, 83, 88, 89n2. *See also* Charlotte series; Martha series
Wilkes, Maria D., 77–78, 80–83, 85–86, 89n5. *See also* Caroline series
Wilkins, Celia, 77, 83. *See also* Caroline series
Williams, Garth, xix, 69, 78, 96, 171. *See also* Wilder, Laura Ingalls: *Little House in the Big Woods*

Williams, Heather (Tui Sutherland), 99, 100n2
Williamson, Chilton, Jr., 165
Wilson, G. A., 172
Wilson, Waziyatawin Angela Cavender, xvii, 63, 67, 166
Winnemucca, Sarah, xvi
Wisconsin: ethnic/cultural heritage, 187; frontier, 152, 160; Ingalls residence, 9, 107, 110, 112, 136, 149, 151–52, 157, 159–60, 167; Native residence, 83, 87, 183, 185, 194n2; Quiner residence, 78, 82–84; tourist sites, xix, 165, 169–70, 202. *See also* Great Seal of the Territory of Wisconsin; Pepin; Wilder, Laura Ingalls: *Little House in the Big Woods*
Wister, Owen, 131n4
Wolf, Virginia L., 70
Wong, Teresa Duryea, 207n7
Woodard, Maureen, 159
Woodress, James, 130n2
Woodside, Christine, xx, xxvii, 18, 20, 30n4, 35, 61n7, 140, 161n1, 178n1
Woolf, Virginia, 131n3
World's Fair, 1893, 193
Worthy, Tatanisha, xxviiin3
Wounded Knee, 191–92. *See also* Dakota; Dakota (people); Native Americans; South Dakota
Wyckoff, Eliza, 53

Yamane, Kazuma, 207n4
Yomota, Inuhiko, 199, 207n3

Zitkála-Šá (Gertrude Bonnin), xviii, 50, 53
Zochert, Donald, 30n2, 53

CPSIA information can be obtained
at www.ICGtesting.com
Printed in the USA
BVHW072259210519
548975BV00001B/4/P